Writing Voices

The perspectives of children, teachers and professional writers are often absent in the pedagogy of writing. *Writing Voices: creating communities of writers* responds to such silent voices and offers a text which not only stretches across primary and secondary practice, but also gives expression to these voices, making a new and significant contribution to understanding what it means to be a writer.

Drawing on recent research projects undertaken by the authors and others in the international research community, this fascinating text considers the nature of composing and the experience of being a writer. In the process it:

- explores the role of talk, creativity, autonomy, metacognition, writing as design and the shaping influence of literature and other texts;
- examines young people's composing processes and attitudes to writing;
- considers teachers' identities as writers and what can be learnt when teachers engage reflectively in writing;
- shares a range of professional writers' practices, processes and perspectives;
- gives prominence to examples of writing from children, teachers, student teachers and professional writers alongside their reflective commentaries.

This thought-provoking text offers theoretical insights and practical directions for developing the teaching and learning of writing. It is an invaluable read for all teachers and trainees, as well as teacher educators, researchers and anyone with an interest in the pedagogy of writing.

Teresa Cremin (Grainger) is Professor of Education at the Open University, UK.

Debra Myhill is Professor of Education at the University of Exeter, UK.

Writing Voices

Creating communities of writers

Teresa Cremin
and Debra Myhill

Routledge
Taylor & Francis Group

LONDON AND NEW YORK

First published 2012
by Routledge
2 Park Square, Milton Park, Abingdon, Oxon OX14 4RN

Simultaneously published in the USA and Canada
by Routledge
711 Third Avenue, New York, NY 10017

Routledge is an imprint of the Taylor & Francis Group, an informa business

British Library Cataloguing in Publication Data
A catalogue record for this book is available from the British Library.

Library of Congress Cataloging in Publication Data
Cremin, Teresa.
Writing voices: creating communities of writers/Teresa Cremin and Debra Myhill.
    p. cm.
    Includes bibliographical references and index.
 1. Language arts–United States. 2. Reading comprehension–United States.
 3. Literacy–United States. I. Myhill, Debra. II. Title
 LB1576.C7785 2012
 372.6–dc22   2011012109

ISBN: 978–0–415–57980–3 (hbk)
ISBN: 978–0–415–57981–0 (pbk)
ISBN: 978–0–203–80333–2 (ebk)

Typeset in Galliard
by Swales & Willis Ltd, Exeter, Devon

Printed and bound in Great Britain by
TJ International Ltd, Padstow, Cornwall

Contents

Figures

Acknowledgments

We would like to acknowledge not only the many writers who have contributed their reflective insights to the book, but also Gabrielle Cliff-Hodges and Eve Bearne who, some years back, conceived the idea of a series on 'Thinking Critically about English'. We were invited to co-author the writing one, and whilst, due to other priorities, the series never reached a publisher, the idea has been simmering on the back burner ever since, awaiting its time to come to the boil. We also wish to acknowledge the many teachers and co-researchers who have worked with us over the years; their voices, views and understandings have enriched our own. Finally, we would like to thank the various funders who have supported our work, including: the Economic and Social Research Council (ESRC), the Esmée Fairbairn Foundation, the Arts Council, the Qualifications and Curriculum Development Agency (QCDA), the United Kingdom Literacy Association (UKLA), Creative Partnerships, Canterbury Christ Church University, the University of Exeter, and the Open University.

With kind permission from Springer Science and Business Media for the figure taken from 'The impact of prior knowledge on the socio-cultural (re)production of written genres' (2005), in T. Kostouli (ed.), *Writing in Context: Research Perspectives and Pedagogical Applications*, pp. 117–36.

With kind permission from English Teaching Practice and Critique for the figure taken from Cremin, T. and Baker, S. (2010), 'Exploring Teacher–Writer Identities in the Classroom: Conceptualising the Struggle', *English Teaching: Practice and Critique*, 9(3): 8–25.

Introduction

Multiple voices

In the last decade, whilst literacy has remained very high profile, arguably insufficient attention has been given to the teaching and learning of writing. Internationally, there has been significantly more research examining the nature and development of reading than writing, and in England, despite numerous national and local initiatives, writing performance scores remain significantly behind those in reading in both the primary and secondary years. During this period, writing has been conceptualised by some governments as little more than an unproblematic set of technical skills and has tended to become increasingly focused on written outcomes, genre knowledge and skill mastery. This has impacted on professional understanding and practice and has prompted pressured teachers to prioritise tests, targets and written products, arguably sidelining reflections on the processes of writing and the experience of being a writer (Grainger et al., 2005; Turvey, 2007; Yeo, 2007).

In contrast, this book explores the nature and process of writing and what it means to be a writer in contemporary times. It does so through attending to numerous voices: the voices of young writers, teachers, and professional writers, whose views and insights are offered as provocations and prompts for consideration by you as readers and by us as authors. Acknowledging their perspectives, we seek to explore the complex recursive nature of composition and the challenges involved in teaching writing and in developing young writers. Most of the writers you will encounter in these pages are highly reflective about their writing; they demonstrate considerable 'insider knowledge' and show how they draw on social, cultural and literacy experiences in order to design their texts.

Whilst surveys of young writers have been undertaken, relatively few studies or practising teachers seek out students' views and build on their perspectives in the writing classroom. In *Writing Voices: creating communities of writers* we seek to respond to these sometimes silenced voices and to attend to young people's conceptions of writing, their views of themselves as writers, of their teachers as writers and of the experiences of writing within and beyond school. In a not dissimilar manner, we also seek to explore the conceptions, practices, habits and experiences of teachers and student teachers as writers, and of professional writers, writing at home, at work and alongside younger writers in the classroom.

The book stretches across primary and secondary practice, arguing that in order to develop an in-depth understanding of writing, teachers deserve to be offered opportunities for supported engagement in and reflection on writing and on themselves as writers. Recently perhaps routines and recipes have been offered rather than time and space to consider different ways of thinking about writing and of teaching writing. Through listening to multiple voices, drawing on research evidence and a number of our own studies, we hope to prompt renewed consideration of writing and writers in the twenty-first century.

Our own studies

We have been involved in a number of research studies examining aspects of writing and the teaching of writing, including: studies of young people's composing processes; surveys of their attitudes to writing; boys and writing; teachers as writers (both writer-teachers and teacher-writers); the role of creativity in teaching writing; the relationship between talk and writing; and how meaningful attention to grammar supports writing development. These projects are not detailed within the main text, but are drawn on to advance our argument and to prompt reflection, so we offer a brief résumé of them here to contextualise these studies and to make evident part of the research trajectory on which we are drawing. They are situated within a wider community of researchers in disciplines beyond education on whose work we also draw.

Project JUDE (1998–99)

This project involved a pyramid of schools in South West England, including first schools, middle schools, and a high school. Funded by the schools themselves and the University of Exeter, the project sought to investigate boys' underachievement, with a particular focus on literacy. An important part of the project was eliciting the perspectives of boys and girls, not just about literacy but more broadly about gender. The research was undertaken through interviewing teachers about their views on gender and boys' underachievement, and through conducting lesson observations with follow-up interviews with a sample of boys and girls. The project indicated that often stereotypical views of boys and girls were shaping how teachers viewed their work in the classroom and were also shaping boys' and girls' views of themselves and each other (Myhill, 2002; Jones and Myhill, 2004a; Jones and Myhill, 2004b)

We're Writers (2001–03)

This project, undertaken in southern England, was funded by a consortium of nine primary schools. It examined both teachers' and children's perceptions about writing and current practice and the critical influences on these. It sought to develop children's written voices by empowering teachers to use and develop their own and the children's creative potential. The 18 Project Focus Group (PFG) teachers (2 from each school) were involved as action researchers and carried out case studies on 3 disaffected writers in their classes. The project involved surveys, interviews, observations and analyses of children's work. In the final year, it also involved documenting teachers' involvement as writers. The work argued that to help children find their voices, a fine balance between knowledge about language and creative language use needs to be wrought, and that openness and 'not knowing' need to be encompassed alongside generative improvisational play in order to allow writing and thought to work together creatively (Grainger et al., 2003a, b, 2005; Grainger, 2005b).

Patterns and Process (2003–05)

This project, funded by the Economic and Social Research Council (ESRC), investigated linguistic development in writing in teenage writers, and their composing processes. The first phase of the project involved a linguistic analysis of 718 pieces of writing, half narrative, half argument, to determine patterns of linguistic development. The second phase involved working with four secondary schools, observing young people writing in writing lessons, and interviewing them subsequently about their composing process and their linguistic choices. The study provided an outline of linguistic development at this age (Myhill, 2008, 2009a, 2009c) and of composing and revising processes (Myhill and Jones, 2007; Myhill, 2009b).

Raising Boys' Achievements in Writing (2004)

This United Kingdom Literacy Association (UKLA) project, funded by the Primary National Strategy (PNS), involved 30 leading teachers from Birmingham, Essex and Medway. They took part in action research in order to raise boys' engagement, motivation and achievements in writing through employing film and drama as motivating tools in an extended unit of work. Teachers selected a focus group of underachieving boys and kept writing samples and assessments, as well as observations and their own reflections. The project made a marked impact on the disaffected boys' attitudes and attainment and increased their commitment, motivation, persistence and independence as writers. This work led to the reconceptualisation of the teaching process as described by the Strategy, which came to recognise a more extended and integrated process of teaching writing (Bearne and Grainger, 2004; UKLA/PNS, 2004).

Drama and Writing (2004–05)

This study, funded by the UKLA, sought to understand the nature of the support that drama offers children as writers and to identify features of writing which regularly surfaced in drama-related writing. Working as participant researchers, the three teachers trialled two approaches connecting drama and writing: the first, labelled 'genre specific', involved working towards a particular text type during improvisational drama; the second, labelled 'seize the moment', offered spontaneity and choice during an imagined experience. The study revealed that the main features of drama which influenced the children's engagement and facilitated the production of effective writing were: the presence of tension; full, affective engagement; time for incubation; and a strong sense of stance and purpose gained in part through role adoption. When all these connecting threads were evident in drama and a moment for writing was seized, the case study showed children's writing became consistently higher quality. The children's concentration and ability to focus and follow through their written work was also positively affected by their involvement in improvisational drama (Cremin et al., 2006).

From Talk to Text (2004–06)

This project, funded by the Esmée Fairbairn Foundation, and undertaken by six- and seven-year-olds, worked with teachers to explore the relationship between talk and writing, and particularly the movement from ideas in the head to words on the page. The study involved teachers working with the university research team to create teaching strategies which supported the generation of ideas for writing, the oral rehearsal of text for writing, and reflection on writing. The study showed that using talk to generate ideas was the most common use of talk, but that both oral rehearsal and reflection helped young writers to become more aware of their written text and how to talk about it (Fisher et al., 2010; Myhill and Jones, 2009).

Creativity and Writing (2004–05)

This research and development project emerged from concerns expressed by head teachers in a South-East England consortium about a perceived lack of child involvement in writing. Funded by the consortium, the project sought to enable teachers to develop their own and their pupils' creativity in writing. It also sought to track the relationship between the teachers' development as writers and their efficacy as professionals, teaching for creativity in writing. The 16 PFG members worked as collaborative researchers, undertaking case studies in school and researching their own compositional processes through composing logs. The team also used reflective interviews, field notes and writing histories as well as observations to explore the research questions. The study indicated that conceptions of teachers as expert writers fail to recognise their potential role as fellow writers, engaged in creating, crafting and coping with the emotional and cognitive demands of writing (Cremin, 2006; Grainger et al., 2006).

Writing at Home (2006–08)

This small-scale case study of four child writers in one primary school built on the project Creativity and Writing, and revisited an earlier and unexpected finding which revealed rich practice around writing at home. Funded by Canterbury Christ Church University, the research sought to examine the children's reasons for writing, their identities as writers and the myriad of influences on their writing, some pieces of which travelled between home and school. It involved tracking writing at home, analysing writing composed at home and at school, and extended interviews with the case study learners, their parents and teachers across the two years.

Writing is Primary: Redrafting the Teaching of Writing (2007–08)

This Esmée Fairbairn-funded project was undertaken in three areas of England: Bury, Worcester and Medway. The southern site afforded a central role to the experience and practice of the teacher as composer, both within and beyond the classroom. This was one of four interrelated strands of the southern project in which the teachers were engaged as writers, as pedagogues, as researchers and as change agents. The research sought to investigate the new knowledge about writing which developed when the 17 teachers engaged in supported writing workshops and came to share their compositional journeys, both with one another and with professional writers. Data collection methods included interviews, observations, field notes in project sessions, teachers' writing histories, compositions, logs and collages. The team also sought to examine the pedagogical consequences of the teachers' reflective engagement and repositioning as writers in the classroom. The work indicated there are benefits in terms of subject knowledge and classroom practice when teachers come to review the writing process from an insider's perspective (Goouch et al., 2009; Ing, 2009).

Grammar for Writing? (2008–11)

This large study involved a quantitative and qualitative exploration of whether drawing attention to linguistic structures relevant to the genre being studied would support improvement in writing. The study involved 32 schools and more than 800 children in the Midlands and the South West. Thirty-two classes of 13-year-olds formed the sample, and teachers taught fictional narrative, argument and poetry writing schemes of work: half the sample used schemes which embedded grammar meaningfully, whilst the other half were free to develop their own lessons within the overall frame. The results show a strongly significant positive effect for the embedded grammar, although especially for more able writers. The lesson observations and interviews also highlight the important of explicitness, of generating dialogic talk about writing, and the role that linguistic subject knowledge of teachers plays in mediating learning (Myhill, 2011).

Writing Identities: Modelling Writing (2009–10)

This investigation, funded by the Centre for Research in Education and Education Technology (CREET) at the Open University, drew on new data from case studies of two of the 'Writing is Primary' practitioners. Both of these teachers seek to model their engagement as writers in order to support young writers; they undertake this through demonstrating writing in whole class contexts and composing individually alongside children. The work sought to examine the nature of their identity work and how they position themselves and are positioned as teacher-writers in the literacy classroom. Data collection methods included classroom observation, interviews, video-stimulated review and examination of written texts. The data shows that the writing classroom, in which the practitioners performed and enacted their identities as teacher-writers and as writer-teachers, appeared to be a site of struggle and tension. It revealed that whilst institutional and interpersonal factors influence their identity positioning, intrapersonal factors are also highly significant (Cremin and Baker, 2010).

Emerging voices

Through connecting to our own and others' research and co-authoring this text, we have tried to make the familiar strange, re-examining the process of composition both in the light of past perspectives and different theoretical lenses and by attending to the experiences and understanding of writers. In the chapters which follow, we explore the key issues in teaching and learning writing, including: the role of talk, the shaping influence of literature and other texts, the role of agency, autonomy and choice, and the value and role of developing one's metacognitive and metalingusitic understanding as a writer. We also explore writing as design; a highly active process of creating and crafting text and making choices in order to realise one's authorial intentions and we seek to show how these different elements of being a writer weave and interweave across contexts and according to purpose. We also reflect on teachers as writers, and turn to the insights developed by practitioners as they consider their identities as writers, document their own compositional journeys, and reflect on the consequences for their pedagogic practice and the positioning of younger writers. Finally, we highlight the voices of professional writers, enabling the education profession to tune into and learn from their insights and practices.

Throughout the text, interspersed between the chapters, we offer reflective vignettes and examples of writing from children, teachers, student teachers, professional writers and ourselves; alongside their reflective commentaries on the compositional process, some also include considerations of individual's writing histories and current practices. We hope these too will trigger conversations, prompting each of as professionals to reflectively examine the act of writing and the experience of being a writer.

Drawing on notes from my writing log, I created this compositional collage in a workshop with teachers in which we sought to explore the influences on a single piece of our writing, in my case a short story, *Here Today – Gone Tomorrow*, about the life and times of our family's hamsters, long since buried. Several events in the month preceding the act of composition had triggered memories of Crème Brûlée and Cream Tea (known as Creamy), whose lives I enjoyed reworking, reshuffling and relating to their new fictional owners, although I still felt the presence of my own children beneath the surface. In writing the tale for young readers, I struggled to find the 'right voice' – I'm not sure I ever did. It doesn't have the immediacy I was aiming for and may yet be reworked if I write their further adventures in the future. This extract is from early in the tale.

She was perfect. Her wiry white whiskers seemed to have a life of their own, twisting this way and that as she investigated every corner of the three tiered cage. To Callum's relief, she fairly quickly found the food he'd left and sucked urgently on the water bottle. Mum didn't come in that first day, she'd never wanted 'vermin' in the house and had taken some persuading, but dad, also fascinated by her antics, watched alongside Callum and helped him name her . . . 'Creamy' after dad's favourite dessert – cream caramel! Once, she pouched so many fragments of toilet roll in her mouth that her cheeks bulged and her tiny eyes momentarily disappeared. Callum had nearly cried out, but almost immediately she'd spewed it all out, mixing the scraps with sawdust to make a miniature nest. At bedtime that night as he studied her toffee coloured fur gently rising and falling, he willed her to wake up and look at him. He dreamt of her on his pillow beside him. She was incredible.

Over the days that followed Callum saw life though the bars of her cage; he watched intently as she skittered up and down the plastic tubes, collected pumpkin seeds to store or ran endlessly on the wheel as if her young life depended on it. Sometimes, when his sister was safely attached to her headphones, he talked to Creamy, telling her about his new friend Jo, his rows with mum and his worries about the maths test. The little creature became his friend and confidante. One weekend gran came and insisted he took Creamy out, that was when he held her for the first time. He hadn't dared to before in case she was frightened or escaped, but it was fine; her soft warm body settled into the quivering cup of his hands and when she nibbled on the pine nut kernels, he felt her tiny teeth on his skin. She was extraordinary.

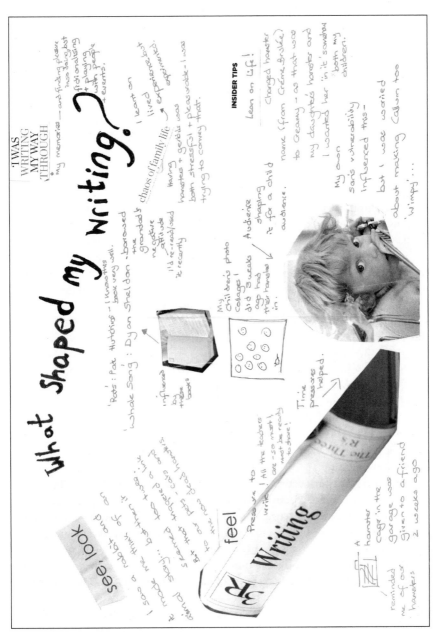

Teresa – author

Chapter 1

Laying the foundations for teaching writing

Introduction

Being able to write is a gateway to empowerment. Not only does academic success in most countries still depend on writing as the dominant mode for assessing learning, but being able to write gives access to social and cultural power. Think of the very real consequences of a well-written letter of complaint, or an incisive report on an important issue, or an emotionally persuasive campaign leaflet. And there is little doubt that the power of the message is shaped by the medium: it is not just the persuasiveness or authority of what is communicated but the way in which it is written. A PGCE student who had worked in a well-known high-street store once reported that scruffy, badly expressed letters of complaint were simply thrown in the bin on the basis that their authors were unlikely to put up much of a fight! But writing is also about how we express and understand ourselves and how we communicate with those closest to us, be that a verse composed for a Valentine's card or a chatter on MSN. Writing can hold records of the past and shape visions of the future; it can bring down politicians and build up personal relationships; it can make us laugh, weep or scream. Yet writing is not a natural activity.

Unlike learning to talk, which almost all of us learn naturally through our social interactions, writing is a more deliberative activity which has to be learned. Critically, from the perspective of this book, it is an activity which has to be taught. And it is a highly complex activity, requiring us to shape our thoughts into words, frame those words into sentences and texts which are appropriate for our intended audience and purpose, and pay attention to shaping letters, spelling words, punctuating sentences, and organising the whole text. Kellogg (2008) suggests that engaging in a writing task is as mentally demanding as playing chess. And unlike many other activities which are initially hard to learn but become easier with practice, writing remains a highly demanding activity even as we become more experienced. Even though many of the aspects of writing which are highly effortful for very young writers, such as shaping letters, understanding word boundaries, spelling and punctuation, do become automatised in older writers, the effort involved in these activities transfers to higher-order activities related to increased expectations of what texts can or should do. Writing your first academic assignment at university can suddenly make you feel like a novice all over again!

This chapter sets out to offer you an overview of research and theoretical thinking about the writing process and the teaching of writing. We hope it will demonstrate that there are multiple perspectives of the writing process, drawing on different ways of thinking about writing, and that it will challenge you to reflect on your own practice as a teacher of writing.

Writing as a social act

The dominant theoretical view of writing at present is that writing is a social act; in other words, when we write, we are participating in a social practice which is shaped by social and historical understandings of what writing is and what texts should do. When we teach children to write, we teach them what is valued by our culture. For example, English culture tends to place a high premium on accuracy in spelling, and in academia or the workplace, spelling errors are frowned on. But there is no reason why spelling should be so significant – Shakespeare managed very well without standardised spelling, and it would be a quite reasonable position to argue that spelling only matters when errors impede the communication of meaning. The importance of spelling is a culturally validated stance. In the same way, social views of writing distinguish between Standard English and non-Standard English and privilege the Standard version. These examples of what is socially valued in writing are, of course, the views of the powerful and the privileged in our society, and may not be shared by other social groups. A Yorkshire writer may value a text written in Yorkshire dialect much more highly. The way that writing as a social practice is influenced by views on Standard English is highly contested. It was at the heart of national debates about the first National Curriculum for English in 1988, and Brian Cox, the architect of the first version, argued that learning how to write in Standard English was an entitlement: 'in our democracy Standard English confers power on its users to explain political issues and to persuade on a national and international stage. This right should not be denied to any child' (Cox, 1991: 29). There is a robust body of argument on this issue (Pound, 1996; Crowley, 2003; Myhill, 2011) but, in essence, they all counterpoint the notion of access to Standard English as an entitlement with the notion of dominance and power of the privileged being exerted over those with less social power. The very public debates about spelling, grammar and Standard English are vivid examples of the way that writing is a social practice.

But writing as social practice is far more than the ways in which conventions of accuracy and language use are played out in writing. The way we use language in speech or in writing is fundamentally expressive of who we are and how we create meanings for ourselves. Richardson (1991: 171) argues that language

> . . . begins with everyday experience, with perception, and yet it controls the very way in which we experience, understand and manage our lives. It is a

window on to our innermost thoughts, the most intimate part of ourselves as individuals, and yet its words, and the grammatical patterns which shape and hold them together, come entirely from outside ourselves. Our social context teaches us our language, and language makes us ourselves.

Texts themselves are socially constructed and culturally validated artefacts: for example, what is acceptable in a formal letter varies from culture to culture, and expectations about the structure of argument writing are very different in western cultures when compared with Chinese culture. Written genres are sociological constructions, representing particular views and values, and shaped by the communities who use them. Swales (1990: 42) defined genres as 'goal-directed communicative events', or as Martin (1985: 250) expressed it, 'Genres are how things get done, when language is used to accomplish them'. Genres in school are often taught rather formulaically as a fixed set of conventions, whereas theoretical views of genre are more diverse, recognising that genres have an essential stability, but that they are also flexible and negotiable. Genres represent 'preferred ways of creating and communicating knowledge within particular communities' (Swales, 1990: 4) but they shift, transform and evolve through the communities who use them.

Young writers do not simply reproduce the genres they encounter or are taught; they actively use them to make sense of their life experiences and their literacy experiences. In this way, writing is an act of social meaning-making: learning to make meaning in texts is about learning to make meaning in contexts. Dyson (2009) illustrates how Marcel, an enthusiastic footballer, appropriated and adapted social practices in writing, drawing on both his own experience and understanding of football commentaries and of written conventions. His report on a football match is set out like a television sports report 'borrowing the symbolic and graphic arrangement of score-reporting practice' (ibid.: 237). He does not observe left-to-right conventionality but sets out his text with vertical directionality, inviting the reader to read downwards, not across. This mirrors the visual text presentation he has seen on television. But he inserts the words 'in Texas' between his column of team names: Dyson suggests that this represents the voice of the commentator reading the score, which the writer has transformed into written text. Marcel draws on his own social experiences to adapt and shape his writing. Marsh (2009) and Merchant (2007) have both illustrated how young writers draw on their out-of-school experiences of popular culture and of digital technology to shape their writing in school. And although writing in school is dominated by linear verbal text, many researchers (Kress, 1994; QCA/UKLA, 2004; Walsh, 2007; Kress and Bezemer, 2009) have shown how writers in both the primary and secondary age phases use their understandings of multimodal constructions of text to inform the way they compose texts and shape meanings. Walsh (2007) describes young writers as multimodal designers who develop 'repertoires of practice' (ibid.: 79) in which they creatively and imaginatively transform their knowledge of writing in the world to recreate their own meanings in text.

We can see this exemplified in Figure 1.1 below. It was written in school by Tasha, an eight-year-old, following lessons on how to write instructional genres. She has been taught about how instructional texts include lists and diagrams to help the reader, and how instructions are often given through the use of imperative verbs. You can see clear evidence of these features in her text. But she moves beyond what has been taught to design a text which combines the visual and the verbal, with the catching apple shape enclosing the recipe, and with elements of the persuasive genre blended with the instructional genre. She tries to encourage her readers to have a go at this recipe by enticing them with 'This mouthwatering crumble is excellent with a spot of custard' and she signals the usefulness of this recipe in making other fruit crumbles which 'you can make by this recipe too!'

Tasha is writing within a community of practice framed principally by the expectations of school writing; but she also uses wider community knowledge, perhaps her own experience of recipe books at home in the family, to support the creation of her text. As a writer, she brings to the classroom a unique set of social, cultural and literacy experiences which remind us that 'every child's pathway to

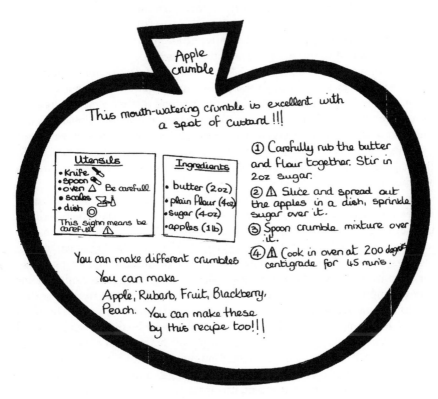

Figure 1.1 Instructional text incorporating both multimodal and persuasive features

Source: Springer Science and Business Media (2005). Used with permission.

literacy is a distinctive journey shaped by personal, social and cultural factors' (Bradford and Wyse, 2010: 140) and that every act of writing is an act of social meaning-making.

Language development in writing

Children begin to build their knowledge and understanding of writing well before they are formally taught to write. Their social and environmental experiences of print teaches them how print makes meaning and by the time children begin school they have already developed a significant repertoire of understandings about writing. Of course, the nature of this repertoire is very varied, depending on the individual child's social and cultural experiences. Rather than thinking of early years children as non-writers, we should think of them as *emerging* writers. The notion of emergent writing owes much to the breakthrough work of Teale and Sulzby (1986) who first showed how children 'emerge' as fully fledged writers through a series of developmental steps. Writing development begins with the earliest marks children make on paper and their growing awareness of symbolic representation, that the marks carry meaning. Early mark-making may be as simple as lines or squiggles on paper, but Lancaster (2007) demonstrated that children under two could distinguish between writing, drawing and numbers, showing a high level of symbolic understanding. These early marks develop into more deliberative writing practice, although still pre-writing rather than writing. Children begin to scribble, drawing straight and wavy lines, and they may include drawings or scribbles which look like letters, even if they are not from our alphabet. Then they start to use random letters and increasingly letter strings, some of which may look like words. All of these pre-writing activities are important developmentally: they support both the refinement of fine motor skills and understanding of writing as a meaning-making enterprise.

The first steps of more formal writing develop alongside the development of handwriting skills. Young writers have to learn about the orthography of writing, the way language represent spoken words in written form. Initially, this involves learning about the left-to-right directionality of print, the shaping of letters, and discriminating words as separate linguistic units. In speech, although we use words, the boundaries between them are not visible in the way they are in writing. Some very common words in English are the outcome of a historical word-boundary confusion at a time when most of the population were not literate. The word 'apron', for example, was originally 'a napron' and word-boundary confusions led to its current usage. Young writers often write in what is called *scriptio continua* (Ferreiro and Teberosky, 1982), a continuous stream of text with no spaces between words. Once young writers have a fair grasp of phonics and grapheme-phoneme correspondences, they can attempt new words for the first time using invented spellings. Invented spelling 'plays an important role in helping children learn how to write. When children use invented spelling, they are in fact exercising their growing knowledge of phonemes, the letters of the alphabet, and their confidence in the alphabetic principle' (Burns, et al., 1999: 102). It also indicates that the child is thinking on their own about the relationship between letters, sounds and words.

Once young writers have mastered these crucial basic processes in writing, there is a well-documented trajectory of linguistic development which can be traced through the primary age range. In particular, young writers have to learn about the sentence as a unit unique to writing (Kress, 1994) and the many options and varieties for different syntactical structures. In the UK, the two studies by Perera (1984) and Harpin (1976) are the most significant. Both found that clauses and sentences increased in length with age, and that whereas young writers use simple active verbs, they become increasingly adept at using more complex constructions, such as the passive and modal verbs. They found that writers move from using coordination as the means of joining two sentences to an increasing use of subordination (a finding confirmed more recently by Allison et al., 2002). Perera's research also indicated that noun phrases lengthen and become more complex with age, but that primary writers sometimes have difficulty mastering appropriate use of pronouns and causal and adversarial connectives. Many of these linguistic trajectories continue in the secondary phase, but there are some subtle differences. More able writers in their teenage years develop greater variety in sentence structure and length, so a developmental feature is not increasing sentence length and increasing subordination, but achieving greater variation in sentence length and greater use of the simple sentence alongside sentences with subordination (Myhill, 2008). They also vary how their sentences start, not relying on repeated use of the subject in the start position. Indeed, the key characteristic of linguistic development in the secondary age range is variety, both lexical and syntactical. Older writers are better able to compose texts with readers in mind, making word and image choices and varying syntactical structures for rhetorical effect.

A further characteristic of language development in writing is learning the difference between talking and writing. Writing is not speech written down: indeed, if we did write as we speak it would look extremely odd and be very difficult to follow, as speech is typically full of long, often unfinished utterances, with hesitations, rephrasings and repetitions. Speech is also very dependent on the context in which it takes place and many words in speech refer to a shared understanding of the context; for example, the utterance 'this one' will almost certainly be accompanied by pointing to something which both speaker and listener can see. In writing, young writers have to develop what Kress call 'the habit of explicitness' (Kress, 1994: 37), providing the right level of detail and information to help an unseen reader understand the text. Wells and Chang (1986) note the difficulty young writers have in transferring from speech to writing, particularly because the absence of response and feedback from the reader puts all the responsibility on the writer to sustain the writing. In effect, they have to imagine their reader and their reader's responses.

Evidence from Loban's (1976) study suggests that although writing and talk appear to develop in tandem, language constructions found in speech did not appear in writing until about a year later. Perera (1986) found that by age eight, most children are able to distinguish between speech and writing and use few specifically oral constructions in their writing: in other words, 'children are differentiating the written from the spoken language and are not simply writing down what they would say' (Perera, 1986: 96). At the secondary stage, whilst no writers write literally as they speak, the influence of oral linguistic patterns on writing is a feature of less able writers who have not yet acquired confidence with more writerly forms (Myhill, 2009a).

Cognitive models of writing

Research into psychological models of writing have focused on the cognitive processes and sub-processes which are involved in the act of writing. Perhaps surprisingly, given the rich reservoir of research on cognitive processes in reading, the first cognitive model of writing (Hayes and Flower) was not published until 1980. It is therefore still a relatively young field of research. The model proposed by Hayes and Flower was generated through investigating how writers described their composing process: they asked them to 'think aloud' – that is, to say what they were thinking as they wrote. From this information they devised their model, which suggested that there were three core processes involved in writing:

- Planning: this describes the process of organising oneself to write and generating the ideas for writing. It includes thinking about the nature and purpose of the writing task and how the writing might fulfil that. It is about far more than preparing a written outline of the writing.
- Translating: this describes the process of moving from ideas to text. It is essentially about the process of text generation.
- Reviewing: this describes the evaluation aspects of writing, where the writer rereads his/her text and revises and edits it.

The Hayes and Flower model also acknowledges the role of prior knowledge in the writing process, noting that the writer's knowledge of the topic of the writing, his/her knowledge of the genre on the writing, and his/her knowledge of the audience for the writing are all stored in long-term memory but inform the planning, translating and revising. For teachers, the principles of planning, drafting and revising are very familiar and advocated in the National Curriculum for English. However, Hayes and Flower emphasise that their model is not linear or chronological, but recursive. In other words, planning, translating and reviewing interact with other each during composition and are not sequential activities. They suggest that a mental 'monitor' switches the writer's attention from one process to another as appropriate. Most mature writers will be familiar with this in their own writing. As we begin a writing task, we have various ideas about what we might write and we evaluate and reject some of these: this is planning and review-ing interacting. As we are writing, we pause to reread our text to evaluate how things are going and where to go next: this is translating and reviewing interacting. When we have completed a draft, we reread our text to judge how effective it is and may decide that a section needs development and elaboration: this is reviewing and planning interacting. From the perspective of the writing classroom, this recursive and interactive aspect of composition is very important, as if we impose too sequential and linear a model on young writers, we may restrict and constrain their development as writers.

Since this first model of writing, there have been many refinements of it, with each new version developing more detailed understanding of the process. For example, Hayes's model (1996) pays more attention to the social nature of writing, whilst Berninger, Fuller and Whittaker's model (1996) focuses on the writing process in novice writers. Significantly, Berninger et al. highlight a difference between young writers and the expert writers who informed the Hayes and Flower model. They observe that 'in skilled writers, planning, translating and revising are mature processes that interact with one another. In beginning and developing writers, each of these processes is still developing and each process is on its own trajectory, developing at its own rate' (Berninger et al., 1996: 198).

This recognition that the processes may be different for novice writers is an important one and links to the role that working memory plays in writing. Working memory, or short-term memory as it is sometimes called, refers to the part of the brain which holds and uses information temporarily in order to allow us to undertake activities (Baddeley and Hitch, 1974). If someone gives you spoken instructions on how to fix a problem with your computer, you have to hold those instructions in your head and put them into operation. This is your working memory in use. But working memory has only limited capacity – as most of us will have experienced in our everyday lives. I can comfortably add up 12 and 26 in my head, but ask me to add up 137 and 459 and I am reaching for a piece of paper! Working memory grows in capacity through childhood and adolescence, so very young writers have even more limitations on what they can hold in their working memory. This is why emergent writers who are focusing all their working memory on how to shape letters and form words cannot also think about the creation of images or the direction of the whole text. Once young writers have reached a stage where their handwriting is reasonably fluent and when spelling and punctuation are more or less automatised, they can devote attention in working memory to higher-level aspects of the writing task. In the writing classroom, strategies which encourage writers to pay attention to different aspects of the writing process at different times can help alleviate the working memory problem. So, for example, encouraging young writers to orally rehearse their sentences before writing them (Myhill and Jones, 2009) or encouraging teenage writers to articulate their rhetorical intentions for a task in the planning stage may reduce the pressure on working memory.

There are two important critiques of cognitive models. Firstly, by definition, a model is a generalisation of data and although it might show the overall trends and tendencies, it may not actually mirror the way any individual writes. Think of the statistical generalisation that the average family in Britain has 2.2 children – it reflects an overall pattern but no one, to my knowledge, has 0.2 of a child! Secondly, cognitive models emphasise the lone writer, struggling with ideas and mental processes, and pay much less attention to the social process in writing, described earlier. Nonetheless, cognitive models are useful tools for understanding and thinking about compositional processes in the classroom because they give us ways to think very specifically about different elements in the writing process.

Writing as process

We have just been considering cognitive models of writing which attempt to describe the writing process. Perhaps rather confusingly, the process approach to writing has relatively little to do with cognitive models and represents a strong pedagogical movement, which was very popular and influential in the 1970s and 1980s. This movement argued that the teaching of writing should pay particular attention to the writing *process*, rather than focusing solely on the writing *product*. In this way, the process movement is a clear counter-movement to the rather limited view of writing pedagogy which preceded it, and which was principally concerned with accuracy in the writing product. Two seminal pieces of work, from the United States and England, created the impetus for the process approach to writing. In the US, Emig (1971) undertook a detailed study of the composing processes of 12th graders, and she argued that they composed in two modes, reflexive and extensive. Extensive writing is formal and concerned with communicating information, whereas reflexive writing is more concerned with personal experiences and emotions. Emig argued that children had insufficient opportunities to write in a reflexive mode in school. In England, Britton et al. (1975) conducted a large-scale study of the kind of writing children were asked to undertake in school, and they categorised the writing as either *transactional* (conveying information); *poetic* (creating aesthetically pleasing texts); and *expressive* (personal writing exploring ideas and feelings). They found that the vast majority of writing undertaken in school was transactional, giving students limited opportunities for poetic or expressive writing. Both Emig and Britton, therefore, were arguing for more personal writing and less transactional or extensive writing. Britton's team maintained that transactional writing could only develop effectively if writers were allowed to write expressively as part of the learning process.

It's worth noting here, however, that both these pieces of research were critiqued. Emig's conclusions were based on working with just eight children, which is an extremely small sample from which to generalise, and Hillocks (1979) pointed out the poor agreement there had been between the researchers in allocating writing categories in Britton's study. More importantly, he demonstrated how the categories had been too rigid, ignoring the way writing constructs meaning in real-life contexts. So, for example, a report on famine in Africa which would have been classified as transactional might well have elements of poetic or expressive writing within it.

Nonetheless, Emig and Britton's work was highly influential in the blossoming of the process approach to writing in England, the United States, Australia and New Zealand. The process approach, most coherently advocated by Graves (1983), generated a move away from writing exercises and drills and gave primacy to personal writing – the expressive writing of Britton. At its heart was a teaching pedagogy which foregrounded the planning-drafting-revising cycle of composition, encouraging young writers to produce several drafts before arriving at a completed version. The writing conference, a detailed conversation between the teacher and the writer, was designed to give ownership to the writer and to help writers understand their own composing processes and see themselves as writers. The role of the teacher in these conferences and in the writing classroom was to facilitate talk and understanding about the composing, not to provide direct instruction. The teacher's role was recast not as an authoritative arbiter of knowledge about writing but as an enabler, working with what children already knew. In particular, the process approach advocated the creation of classrooms as writing communities where composing, and its joys and tribulations were made visible. In facilitating writing, the teacher was expected to share his/her own thinking about writing with the children. Graves argued passionately for children to have the opportunity to see how writing occurs:

> Students can go a lifetime and never see another person write, much less show them how to write. Yet it would be unheard of for an artist not to show her students how to use oils by painting on her own canvas, or for a ceramist not to demonstrate how to throw clay on a wheel and shape the material himself. Writing is a craft.
>
> (Graves, 1994: 104)

However, the process approach as advocated by Graves and his peers has been subject to strident criticism. Firstly, there has been very little robust research into the efficacy of the approach: Smith and Elley (1998) note that only success stories are reported, Beard (2000a: 41) argues that much of the writing is 'evangelical reportage', and Smagorinsky (1987) suggests Graves's work is not research, but classroom observation. He condemns Graves's emphasis on helping children to write like professional writers, because the professional writers used are always writers of fictional narrative, ignoring the raft of professional writing of other kinds. He also points out that there is no clear justification for why the approaches of professional writers should provide valid models for novice, developing writers.

The process approach has also attracted critics on the basis of equality and diversity. With its emphasis on personal voice and ownership, it gives licence to the validating of voices which may be offensive or privileged. Lensmire's (1994) powerful interrogation of his own process workshops shows how the children are not innocent creative beings, but are shaped by the social world around them and its ideologies. He found that some children can be 'calculating, untruthful, and adept in exploiting the newfound freedom to use texts to hurt, to dominate, to assert social status and boundaries, to represent the world to their own advantage, and to gain and maintain social power and control over other children' (Lin, 1997: 503). Others have highlighted how giving primacy to personal voice allows the privileged to remain privileged: Schreiner (1997), for example, suggests that process pedagogy ignores how educational and cultural differences play out in the classroom, and Smagorinsky (1987) argues that only certain voices are valued and encouraged. The Australian genre theorists have been particularly vocal in contesting the cultural bias inherent in a process approach:

> With its stress on ownership and voice, its preoccupation with children select-ing their own topics, its reluctance to intervene positively and constructively during conferencing, and its complete mystification of what has to be learned for children to produce effective written products, it is currently promoting a situation in which only the brightest middle class children can possibly learn what is needed. Conferencing is used not to teach but to obscure. This kind of refusal to teach helps reinforce the success of ruling-class children in edu-cation; through an insidious benevolence other children are supportively encouraged to fail.
>
> (Martin, 1985: 61)

In light of this, it is possibly more helpful to think about writing as process, rather than process approaches to writing. Few teachers in practice believe that there is no role for direct instruction in the teaching of writing, and teaching strategies such as modelling, shared writing and guided writing are all strategic interventions in writing which can sit comfortably with a view of writing as process. Teachers who create communities of writers in their classrooms, with opportunities for writing for authentic purposes, for writing for self as well as writing for others, and where dialogue about writing and the writing process is seen as central are establishing a healthy environment in which writers can flourish.

One other aspect of writing as process deserves attention here. We have already noted that the elements in the writing process – planning, generating text, reviewing – are not strictly sequential, but in the classroom and in the National Curriculum, plan-draft-revise-edit have tended to be taught as a chronological sequence. But if this is followed too rigidly it may limit writers by insufficient acknowledgment of the way they write. A key distinction to be made here is between those who devote a lot of time to the planning stage and those who need to write first in order to generate ideas. Hayes and Flower (1980) characterised writers as Mozartians and Beethovians: Mozartians undertook extensive planning, then framed and improved their writing sentence by sentence, with text production and revision undertaken simultaneously. In contrast, Beethovians planned and generated a first draft quickly, then engaged in a lengthy revision process. Sharples (1999) argued that these two composing profiles contrast *Discovery Writers*, who write to find out what they want to say, with *Planner Writers*, who reflect a lot throughout the composing process. They allocate time to planning pre-writing, and their composing rhythm is equally thoughtful, with a 'rapid alternation between engagement and reflection' (ibid.: 113). Professional writers vary in how they approach the task of writing: J. K. Rowling began writing each Harry Potter story by 'constructing the RULES: I have to lay down all my parameters. The most important thing to decide when you're creating a fantasy world is what the characters CAN'T do' (South West News Service interview, 8 July 2000), whereas children's novelist Tim Bowler approaches the writing process in a different way:

> Some writers plan in detail before they start writing, but many do not, and some do no planning at all. I do very, very little. Every story I have ever written has changed so many times during the course of the writing and ended up so unlike my original conception of it, that a predetermined plot would have been pointless. What I have learned instead is to trust my imagination to guide me, to accept that it will occasionally lead me down wrong avenues but also that – given time and patience – it will help me find the true north of the story.
>
> (Bowler, 2002)

If you are a Discovery Writer, then being obliged to plan may be a wholly redundant activity; instead you need to devote much more time and energy to revising and reshaping your text once you have worked out what you want to say. Alternatively, if you are a Planner Writer, time invested in planning early in the process is likely to mean that the nature of revision is different for you, probably focusing much more on word or image choice or sentence shaping, rather than wholesale reshaping of the text.

We know that teenage writers are aware of these differences in their own composing processes. They are able to reflect on how they write and understand how they approach writing and can articulate the thinking that accompanies writing. Our research (Myhill, 2009b) suggests that teenage writers, like Hayes and Flower's adult writers, exhibit tendencies towards being Planner Writers or Discovery Writers – you can hear some of their own voices below:

Discovery Writers:

- Well, I didn't know what I was going to write about and then I just decided that, start and see if I got any ideas when I started writing.
- It just flows really; I just start writing . . . as I write it just comes to me and new words, new sentences, just different things, different ideas . . .
- Some people presumably find it easier to plan something before they write it, but I find it easier just to sit down and write it.

Planner Writers:

- This one I found quite easy because I'd made quite a easy plan, like what I was doing for each of the paragraphs so all I really needed to do was think up the sentences but I already knew what they were going to be about . . .

- I think about it in my head first. I think before I write.
- I'll probably just think about it in my head, how I'm going to set it out and then do it after I've thought about it.
- I think about how I'm going to start the story and how I'm going to continue it.

We do also know that some discovery writers do not revise – once that final full stop is reached, the pen is put down and the job is done! Understanding that these writers need considerable help with revision is one important way of thinking of writing as process and adapting the writing classroom to suit writers' needs.

Of course, being a teacher who is attentive to writing as process and can accommodate different ways of approaching writing is much easier if you are a teacher who writes and reflects on your own writing process and can share this with young learners. We look specifically at teachers as writers in chapters 7 and 8.

Creativity and writing

If we are to address creativity in writing, the first thing we need to do is untangle the tangled knot of creative writing and creativity in writing. The term 'creative writing' is one largely restricted to the school writing curriculum and to university or arts-based creative writing programmes. You can, for example, undertake an MA in Creative Writing at several universities. In general, when used in this way, creative writing refers to the writing of specific genres, such as fiction, poetry or play scripts. Indeed, the University of Oxford Masters in Creative Writing refers to teaching writing skills in the novel, short fiction, radio drama, TV drama, screenwriting, stage drama, and poetry. These are all written genres that most people would agree involve creativity and imagination, and are all key to the flourishing creative industries in this country. Yet the term 'creative writing' does not occur anywhere in the National Curriculum for English. At GCSE, one component of the assessment of writing is creative writing, described as Imaginative Writing by Oxford Cambridge and RSA Examinations (OCR), and as a personal and imaginative written response by Edexcel. One reason for this apparent avoidance of the term 'creative writing' might be due to its association with a tendency some years ago to generate a rather contrived and artificial kind of writing which was called creative writing. Bullock (DES, 1975) critiqued this because:

> It usually means in actuality, colourful, or fanciful language, not 'ordinary', using 'vivid imagery'. It is often false, artificially stimulated and pumped up by the teacher or written to an unconscious model which he has given to the children. It is very often divorced from real feeling.
>
> (DES, 1975: 11.3)

One feature of the creative written genres commonly addressed in MA courses is that they tend to be strongly oriented to public audiences and publishing opportunities. In the contemporary writing classroom, many teachers create contexts where authentic audiences are identified and where there are opportunities for publication. But creative teachers also give young writers the chance to write for themselves, to find their own writing voices, and to write in order to find out what they want to say.

However, we would argue that creativity in writing goes beyond the boundaries of the creative written genres. Just about all writing is creative. Perhaps highly functional types of writing such as a shopping list might be exceptions, but writing literary critical essays, instructional texts, journalistic pieces, arguments, campaign material, and so on, all require a creative way of thinking about language, texts and audiences. It is a mistake to see this kind of writing as uncreative. Creative writers push language to its limits, and are inventive and playful in how they create texts. Consider, for example, the creative language play in tabloid newspapers. Many would argue that *The Sun's* headline, following the 3–1 defeat of Celtic by Caledonian, ranks as one of the best headlines ever: *Supercaleygoballisticcelticareatrocious* (*The Sun*, 8 February 2000)! And creative writers creatively subvert: they do not stick compliantly to genre conventions but bend and break them, perhaps adding an emotive personal narrative to an argument text to engage the reader emotionally, writing an instructional text in poetry, or reframing a science report as a narrative. Creativity in writing is about recognising and using the infinite possibilities of language.

In many ways, this more inclusive approach to the idea of creativity in writing sits well with creativity theory. Research in creativity has radically altered in the last ten years, and has transformed from a largely psychological analysis of traits of creativity and a desire to design tests which could measure creativity to one which thinks about creativity much more in social and cultural terms. Defining what creativity is remains contested, however, particularly concerning whether creativity is a quality restricted to a few, and whether creativity is about a creative process or a creative product. Historically, the idea of creative genius has been a powerful shaper of thinking about creativity, confining creative productivity to an exceptional few. For teachers of writing, this would mean that we would expect most of our young writers to be unable to achieve creative outputs, and we would be hoping for the chance to teach a future Dickens or Duffy! Contemporary thinking is much more democratic and argues that everyone has the capacity to be creative, and that creativity is possible in all areas of human activity (Robinson, 2001). This is a much more helpful way to approach creativity in the writing classroom.

Sternberg (1988) drew a distinction between *process* and *product* creativity, arguing that whilst producing a creative product which is original, innovative and important may be limited to a smaller group of people, process creativity is a way of thinking and tackling problems inventively, which is common, to differing degrees, to all people. Csikszentmihalyi (1999) suggests there is a distinction between what is good for an individual, which he sees as 'little-c' creativity, and what is good for society, 'big-C' creativity. Interestingly, from the perspective of writing, he also maintains that self-expression is rarely creative, even though it may well be personally important and therapeutic. At the core of little c creativity is 'possibility thinking'. Possibility thinking means being able to pose questions in multiple ways, asking 'what if' questions, and engaging fully with the problem at hand. This work has been extended and elaborated in the work of Craft (2005), Craft, Cremin and Burnard (2007), and Jeffrey and Woods (2003) in the context of primary classrooms and creative partnerships.

It is probably worth giving some explicit consideration at this point to Romantic notions of creativity and inspiration, as they remain pervasive, especially with reference to poetry. These are views of creativity which place a high premium on the role of the unconscious and on the role of inspiration in writing, believing that inspired writing cannot be taught. Hayes and Flower (1980) called this the *inspiration paradigm* and dismissed it as 'pure bunk' (1980: 32), and Banaji and Burn (2007) see this rhetoric of creativity as essentially elitist. Yet such views of writing persist, particularly in relationship to poetry. Wilson (2007, 2009) has shown how teachers often think differently about the writing of poetry when compared with writing elsewhere in the curriculum, frequently seeing it as an inspired form of writing, which resists either teaching or assessment. The metaphors teachers use to describe poetry (Wilson, forthcoming) are revealing of this way of thinking about poetry as inspiration. Yet few of us would deny that the writing process is surprising and unpredictable, with some words, phrases and sentences agonised over with surgical precision, whilst other phrases arise, unexpected, unbidden and effortlessly. Koestler (1964: 36) argues that we can create when we let go of familiar routines and habits, which restrict the imagination and our generative powers – the moment of discovery 'often means the uncovering of something which has always been there but was hidden from the eyes by the blinkers of habit'.

So what might this mean for creativity in writing? If we accept that almost all writing can be approached creatively, then we should be establishing classroom environments which explore the possibilities of ideas and the possibilities of language to express those ideas. At the heart of creativity in writing is seeing things differently, what Bruner described as 'a placing of things in new perspective' (Bruner, 1979: 20): the insight of a different voice, the aptness of a metaphor, the freshness of a new idea. Writing classrooms should be playful, risk-taking and experimental, allowing young writers to have 'failed' attempts because through those attempts they have been pushing the boundaries of their own use of language. Testing and assessment regimes can unfortunately encourage children, and their teachers, to play safe, to reproduce genres formulaically and to accept the teacher as arbiter of quality. A creatively constructed writing classroom recognises the authority and expertise of the teacher and will include explicit teaching of writing, but this occurs within an environment of democratic participation, where children's voices are heard, where they have ownership of their texts and their decision-making, and where they can articulate with confidence their reasons for their writing choices.

Curiously, given how much our thinking about creativity has changed, one of the earliest psychologists investigating creativity, Guilford, outlined a set of characteristics of a creative person which actually relate very well to writing creatively. He argued (1950) that a creative person would have:

- a sensitivity to problems;
- fluency – the ability to produce a large number of ideas quickly;
- an ability to produce novel ideas;
- a flexibility of mind;
- a synthesising and adapting ability;
- an adeptness at reorganising of ideas;
- competence at evaluating results.

All of these characteristics are ones that we would want to encourage in young writers as they approach writing tasks; all of these characteristics are ones we would argue can be fostered by teachers who allow for playful risk-taking and experimentation.

One final aspect of creativity in writing which is worth discussing is the relationship between creativity and mastery, or between the creative and the critical. Sometimes there is a reluctance to subject 'creative' work in the classroom to criticism or judgement: Wilson (2009), for example, found that many teachers were reluctant to assess or to comment critically on children's poetry writing. But judgement is important in both creative processes and creative outcomes, and all creative endeavours require mastery of the tools of the trade, the necessary skills to enable creative activity to flourish. As the National Advisory Committee on Creative and Cultural Education argues (NACCCE, 1999: 6), 'creativity is not simply a matter of letting go': rather genuine creative work 'relies on knowledge, control of materials and command of ideas' and involves not just innovation, but also knowledge and skills. Children's author Tim Bowler, reflecting on his own writing process, expresses the relationship between the creative and the critical very clearly:

> Why is writing so tricky? Because it requires mastery of two conflicting skills: a creative skill and a critical skill. The former is of the imagination, the latter of the intellect, and they come from different brain hemispheres. To write well, we have to employ both to maximum effect.
>
> For me, the best way to do this is to give each its turn but not to try to do the two together. If we try to be creative and critical at the same time, we run the risk of stemming the flow of inspiration or having one skill dominate the other, leading either to stories that are well-structured but lacking in invention, or stories that are rich in invention yet lack shape. By giving the imagination free rein first, as in brainstorming, then bringing in the critical hammer afterwards, both skills operate without constraint.
>
> (Bowler, 2002)

This recognition that writing creatively demands both creative energy and flow, and critical engagement is important for the writing classroom. It means that we need to generate writing environments which create space for the imagination, for serendipitous moments, for playfulness, but also environments which support critical thinking about writing processes and texts produced. Tim Bowler (2002) also draws attention to different composing processes, noting that although he finds it useful to separate the creative periods from the critical periods, this 'is not the only way to write, of course, and many writers do indeed manage to create freely and yet edit themselves critically as they go along'. Just as we have noted earlier that we should be flexible about how we use the 'plan-draft-write-edit' model in the classroom, so too should we be flexible about how we manage creative and critical moments in our writing classrooms.

Conclusion

This chapter has offered a synthesis of multiple ways of thinking about writing, the writing process and the teaching of writing, and has illustrated how writing combines linguistic proficiency, with cognitive process, within a framework of social context. It sets the scene for more detailed exploration of writing in the chapters which follow. And it has highlighted just how complex and challenging the act of writing is! In a book which celebrates letting writing voices be heard, it seems appropriate to give the last words in this chapter to a writer, reminding us of the very real ordeals of writing:

> Don't panic. Midway through writing a novel, I have regularly experienced moments of bowel-curdling terror, as I contemplate the drivel on the screen before me and see beyond it, in quick succession, the derisive reviews, the friends' embarrassment, the failing career, the dwindling income, the repossessed house, the divorce . . . Working doggedly on through crises like these, however, has always got me there in the end. Leaving the desk for a while can help. Talking the problem through can help me recall what I was trying to achieve before I got stuck. Going for a long walk almost always gets me thinking about my manuscript in a slightly new way. And if all else fails, there's prayer. St Francis de Sales, the patron saint of writers, has often helped me out in a crisis. If you want to spread your net more widely, you could try appealing to Calliope, the muse of epic poetry, too.
>
> Sarah Waters in *The Guardian* (2010)

This vignette from nearly three-year-old Summer shows how very young writers begin to make meaning from marks on the page.

Here, Summer is scribble-writing. She picked up a pen and said, 'I'm writing Summer' and wrote the top line. Then she wrote the next line and said, 'That's Mia – she's smaller than me.' Mia is her baby sister, and Summer does what many emerging writers do – she links the size of the writing with size in real life. Underneath this she explained that she had written Mummy and John (her stepdad). Throughout she uses left-to-right directionality and lines, and her conversation as she writes indicates that this is writing, not drawing.

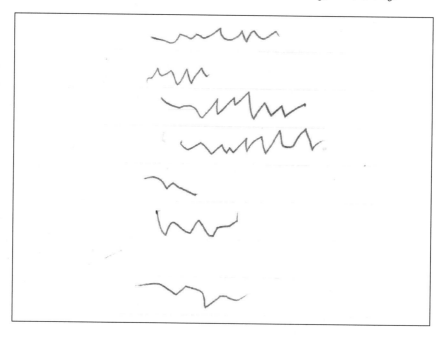

In this image, Summer has drawn a giant. You can see a very large head, eyes, nose and mouth, and stick arms and legs. To the middle-left of the image there is some scribble-writing, which Summer explained says 'giant'. She is distinguishing between pictures and texts, and understands the concept of labelling.

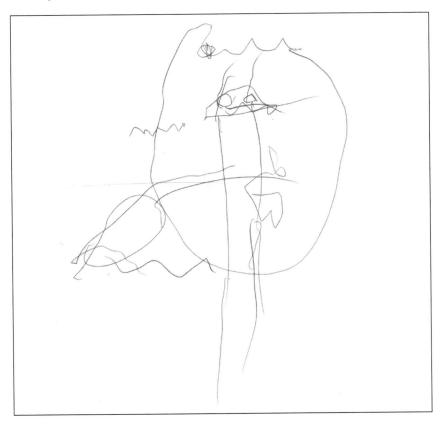

Part I

Children as writers

Chapter 2

The role of talk

Introduction

James Britton famously described reading and writing as 'floating on a sea of talk' (1970: 29), an image which aptly emphasises the fundamental significance of talk in becoming a reader and a writer. Early language development is principally about becoming a speaker, an oral communicator, and learning what words can do. It is a social learning experience, dependent on meaningful interactions with others to shape language into resources for making meaning. Learning about written language involves far more than learning a new multimodal code for representing meaning, it involves entering new social dialogues with oneself and others; exploring the dynamic between talk and writing. Whilst there is a vast body of research on oral language development in the early years (e.g. Halliday, 1975; Bruner, 1983; Tomasello and Bates, 2001), there is comparatively little research on the talk-writing interface. However, professional experience and research does suggest that in a rich interactive community of writers, when ideas are explored, inhabited, discussed and represented in a myriad of ways prior to writing, this offers strong support to young writers. Such productive talk, whilst it can support ideational fluency, does not always translate directly into writing, so further time for thinking and talking through options as well as reviewing the writer's choices are needed. Writing is not merely an act of scribalism, as author Celia Rees notes:

> It took me a very long time to realise that writing is not just about sitting at the word processor or a pad of paper and getting things down. Writing is everything: reading, going to the library, visiting places, researching, taking photos, talking and even thinking – thinking is an inherent and very important part of the writing process
>
> (Celia Rees, 1999: 201–2)

Playful exploration and frequent ongoing conversations about writing can help involve and engage young writers, enabling them to focus on what they might want to say, to whom and for what purpose. Stepping in and out of texts to play with ideas, create connections, inhabit role positions, and voice their views involves seriously creative play and the spoken word has a central role in this endeavour, as it does in translating such ideas onto page or screen and in reviewing and evaluating one's writing. Through talking about their own and others' texts young people can widen their understanding about writing, as thought is not simply expressed in words but comes into existence through them (Vygotsky, 1978). This chapter explores the subtle inter-relationship between talk and writing; how talking, writing and thinking support each other and foster the development of voice; the differences between talking and writing; the ways in which talk can help writers of every age to generate and shape their ideas and rehearse their written texts, as well as the opportunities talk provides for reflection teacher–writer and peer–peer review.

Talking, writing, thinking and voice

All young children talk to themselves, often in the form of a running commentary on what they are doing. Piaget (2002) called this egocentric speech and argued the existence of a developmental pathway from this kind of individualistic, self-centred language to more social language which is communicative and oriented towards others. In contrast, Vygotsky (1978) called this private speech, and maintained it was important in developing thinking (or inner speech) and that social interaction with others is critical to this process. More recent research (Flavell and Wong, 2009) suggests that young preschoolers are aware of the difference between private and social speech, and realise 'that they and other people are conscious cognitive beings' (149). Talk, in other words, develops thought: private speech is, in effect, thinking aloud. Vygotsky suggests that the process of thinking aloud (private speech) becomes silent thought in one's head (inner speech) and illustrates why, as children get older, the amount of private speech diminishes. But most of us, even as adults, sometimes still think aloud. For example, in moments of frustration or when a task is particularly challenging, private speech re-emerges, as Berk (1994: 78) notes: 'it is a tool that helps us overcome obstacles and acquire new skills'.

As writing is demanding, it is therefore natural that young people talk aloud during the process. You can often observe primary children vocalising their words as they write, although this tends to disappear in secondary school; yet adult writers, ourselves included, often read their texts aloud to hear its voice. When composing collaboratively too, young writers frequently read aloud, and we find when working with MA and PhD students, we read aloud extracts from their drafted texts on screen to help hear what is happening in the writing. Sometimes we model how to alter the writing style, articulating our thinking about why a particular change may be advantageous.

Parallel to the idea that talk develops thought is the idea that we think through writing. Writing is not a simple process of 'translating' fully formed verbal messages in our heads into text on the page or screen. Instead, we think as we write, and the very act of writing generates new ideas – frequently we do not know exactly how a piece of writing will unfold and even when we are engaged in writing it, new possibilities emerge. With explicitly creative written forms, such as poetry, narrative or play scripts, often the seed of an idea prompts an impetus to write, but it is only through writing that the seed grows and develops (or withers!). In more transactional or academic writing, we also use writing to think through our ideas and arguments; most writers find that they discover ideas and things to say as they write. This sense of discovery is highlighted by David Almond in his book *My Name is Mina*, when through his protagonist's perspective he considers this aspect of writing:

> When I was at school – at St Bede's Middle – I was told by my teacher Mrs Scullery that I should not write anything until I had planned what I would write. What nonsense!
>
> Do I plan a sentence before I speak it?
>
> OF COURSE I DO NOT!
>
> Does a bird plan its song before it sings?
>
> OF COURSE IT DOES NOT!
>
> It opens its beak and it
>
> SINGS so I will SING!
>
> (David Almond, 2010: 13)

However, Mina wishes to be a 'good girl' and so she does as her teacher requires and makes a plan, but as she notes: 'when I started to write, the story wouldn't keep still, wouldn't obey. The words danced like flies. They flew off in strange and beautiful directions and took my story on a very unexpected course' (Almond, 2010: 14). The emergent nature of writing and the role of thinking one's way forwards through writing are arguably under-recognised in schooling, yet writing, thinking and talking are intimately intertwined and mutually supportive. Writing can help students think through their ideas and find out what they want to say; it can provide the context for effective talk about text; and it can allow them to follow and develop a creative impulse. Talking can help writers test out their initial ideas or share in evaluating their writing; it can help them think about how they approach writing tasks; and it can help them hear the voice of their text. A vibrant writing classroom creates a learning environment which gives space not just for writing, but also for talking and thinking about writing.

Differences between talk and writing as communicative modes

Although linguistically talk and writing are language systems which have much in common, as communicative modes they operate in different ways. For the emerging writer, as we noted in Chapter 1, learning that writing is not talk written down is an important developmental marker. For all writers, managing the different ways that talk and writing work is important. On one level, this is about linguistic differences, but on another level, it is about the different ways that talk and writing achieve their communicative goals.

From a linguistic perspective, the differences between talk and writing are well rehearsed (O'Donnell, 1974; Perera, 1986; Crystal, 1995). Talk is characterised by incomplete utterances, by utterances which repeat themselves or stop and start again, by hesitations and fillers (such as 'mm' or 'uh'), and by very long chained sequences of talk, linked by 'and'. In writing, this would look ungrammatical and incoherent, and would be hard to understand, whereas this causes listeners no problems in understanding talk. Talk is also full of social tags which oil the conversation and sustain the relationship between speakers and listeners. For example, we hedge a lot in talk, with phrases such as 'perhaps', 'or something' and 'sort of', and we end utterances with tag questions such as 'Isn't it?', or 'Do you see?' These markers of social interaction would look strange if replicated in writing. We also help our listeners by structuring the information in an utterance to help them remember key information: often this involves foregrounding certain information and providing more explanatory detail before moving on to the point of the sentence, as in the two examples below:

That girl, Jill, her sister, she works in our office.
The white house on the corner, is *that* where she lives?

(Carter, 2004:17)

Seeing these utterances transcribed as sentences helpfully illustrates how patterns which are perfectly acceptable and effective in spoken discourse cease to be appropriate when written down.

Another significant difference between talking and writing is in vocabulary. A high proportion of words are commonly used in both talking and writing, but there are important differences. There are words we use in talk which we rarely use in writing, such as 'thingummyjig' or 'whatsit' (and we don't really know quite how to spell them!). There are also many words which are far more common in writing, typically vocabulary which is literary, academic or formal. The effect of using too much of this kind of vocabulary in speech is that you risk sounding pretentious or pompous. Moreover, we have more choices to make in writing because for most writers 'one's "writing vocabulary" vastly exceeds one's "speaking vocabulary"' (Olson, 2006: 140). These linguistic differences reflect the very different ways that talk and writing work as communicative modes. The range of possibilities for shaping and reinforcing meaning is different in talk and writing. Talk is lubricated by non-verbal features, such as hand gestures or eye contact, which help reinforce the communicative message. We can also vary the pitch, tone, modulation, pace, and emphasis of something we say, using sound as a key component in making meaning. In writing, these things can only be achieved by skilful use of punctuation, by varying sentence structure and by graphic choices, such as the use of bold, italic or different font sizes, for example. Equally, of course, we can't 'say' a table or diagram, but we can read one. So one aspect of developing as a writer is being able to make 'writerly' choices and being able to achieve effects possible in talk through writerly means.

Another important distinction (as noted in Chapter 1) in the way talk and writing work is in terms of the audience – the listener or the reader. When we talk, we receive instant feedback from our listeners, both in terms of non-verbal gestures, such as nodding or frowning, and verbally in terms of comments on what we say, rephrasing of what we say to clarify it, and active completions of our unfinished utterances. In essence, a dialogue is a co-constructed text, composed by two or more speakers who share an intention to understand each other. In contrast, in writing there is none of this feedback or co-construction (unless we are writing collaboratively) and one reason writing can be so difficult for young writers is that it can be a very lonely experience. In speech we can see or hear our listeners, but in writing we have to imagine our readers and anticipate how they will be reading our writing.

Writing through talking and talking through writing

In strong writing communities, teachers and students engage in a variety of interactions before, during and after the act of literally writing on page or screen. The knowledge and skills needed for independent writing are taught through social interaction in the classroom – interaction with the teacher and peers. Through engaging in a range of open-ended exploratory activities, teachers and young writers spend time researching themes, inhabiting roles, responding to texts, representing possibilities and generating ideas together. Establishing students as expert 'others' and encouraging informal talk can enable knowledge about writing to be socially shared and distributed in the classroom (Geekie et al., 1999; Dyson, 2003). Through modelling writing and offering explicit teaching, teachers not only talk about writing, but also talk through their writing, voicing their own thinking as they compose, sharing their responses to blank spots or other problems, as we discuss further in Chapter 8. Teachers also offer opportunities for students to reflect on their own compositional process in order to extend their meta-cognitive understanding of the process, as we discuss in Chapter 4. So shared and guided contexts are full of talk. Descriptions of independent writing, however, tend to focus on individual students and, as Davidson (2007) notes, give limited attention to the social interaction that occurs between young people in such contexts. Her analysis highlights the social and collaborative nature of all writing, even when the activity is called 'independent', and reveals how young writers negotiate their independence. She invites us to rethink what we mean by independent writing, and suggests we 'need to acknowledge peer interaction and the social activities that constitute independent writing' (ibid.: 21).

In one of our recent projects, From Talk to Text (Fisher et al., 2010), worked with teachers of six- to seven-year-olds on the role of talk in supporting writing, looking at three ways in which talk helps the writing process: how talk supports the generation of ideas, the formulation of written text, and how it can foster metacognitive reflection on writing. These are not particular to early writing instruction, however, and are useful frames to prompt further discussion about the role of talk in writing.

Oral exploration to generate and shape ideas

Through talk at the initial stages of the process, young writers generate and share ideas, playfully experiment with options, listen to one another's contributions and consider what it is they might want to say. This period of oral exploration, whether undertaken through debate, discussion, drama, storytelling or the performance of poetry, for example, can offer a rich resource when students come to commit their ideas to paper or screen. Improvisation and playful engagement with issues, ideas and concerns play a significant role in the compositional process from the earliest age. Barrs (1988: 114) acknowledges this when she notes that 'the roots of writing lie in the other forms of symbolising', such as drawing, dramatic enactment, play and model-making, that young children take part in before they experience the abstract system of writing. In this way, early playful interactions prepare young people for the development of written language; later, their knowledge about writing and the development of ideas for writing continue to be actively constructed through interaction with others. A writer's private speech/inner speech (Vygotsky, 1978) develops through play and social interaction. Through creating and crafting physically, visually and verbally, young people move through the process of composition and this multimodal journey influences the development of their voices as writers.

So as part of the extended process of composition, young writers need opportunities to respond imaginatively and personally to texts, to share ideas, understand others' perspectives, alter and develop their opinions and try out new possibilities. On this conversational journey towards writing, thoughts and feelings, attitudes and information will be shared and the substantive content for the written communication may be generated. In school, pressured by time and the expectation of written outcomes, we tend to rush too soon and too fast into requiring writers to commit to paper or screen. In focusing on the textual elements of language at the expense of the ideational and interpersonal components (Halliday, 1978), we may also inadvertently downgrade the role of writers' ideas and their individuality, agency and desire to make meaning. As professionals our attention may have been diverted away from the playful exploration of possibilities which shape each author's emergent intentions and meaning-making. Our work suggests that if young people are engaged in the serious play of composition, they come to develop their ideational fluency and enhance their ability to make connections and unusual associations in their writing through verbal, visual and mental play with ideas and options (Grainger et al., 2005; Cremin et al., 2006).

In process drama, for example, our work, alongside that of others, has shown that improvisation is a generative ideational tool, one which contributes not only to writing attainment (Fleming et al., 2004) but also to more positive attitudes to writing and to the depth, detail, stance and quality of the writing produced (Crumpler and Schneider, 2002; McNaughton, 1997; Cremin et al., 2006). As we found, if drama teachers, responding to their own informed intuition, 'seize the moment to write', young people often appear to write with relative ease; the tension of the imagined experience, their emotional engagement in the scenario and their inhabited role perspectives appear to combine and offer significant ideational support resulting in enriched writing. At the heart of this process is the power of improvisational play.

> Children at play, Vygotsky argued, often travel further and in such contexts act as if they are 'a head taller than themselves' (1978: 103); in drama, motivated and engaged young thinkers move almost seamlessly into writing, and in so doing capitalise on the source and substance of their improvised work. Their imaginative engagement in the tense scenarios of drama appear to help them form and transform experience and create, cultivate and effectively communicate their own and each others' ideas in written text.
>
> (Cremin et al., 2006: 289)

In such world-making play contexts, young people will be generating ideas and options and engaging critically with one another's suggestions for the construction of an imagined scene; many of these possibilities will be challenged and alternatives created and debated. This process of selection and refinement of ideas and meanings parallels the processes of the generation and evaluation of ideas, enabling, as Bearne (2002: 25) observes, 'the outer experience of discussion, justification, role play and drama [to] feed into the inner voices of a critically reflective writer'.

Time to stretch one's voice and rehearse, converse, percolate and revisit options is central to an extended notion of composition which involves the generation, incubation and evaluation of ideas and possibilities, prior to and during writing. For example, as oral tellers of tales, young writers will imitate and lean on known narratives (both personal and traditional), and will over time come to innovate and invent new ones, drawing on their repertoires built through reading and retelling. Many children's writers who have emerged from the world of teaching attest to the valuable experience of orally telling tales to young writers. Philip Pullman (1999: 183), for example, notes that as a writer, teaching offered him the chance to refine his skills through repeatedly retelling tales such as the *Iliad* and the *Odyssey*, and embellishing and polishing his writer's voice in the process. As he notes, visual artists often draw the same figure repeatedly to gain perspective, and musicians and dancers also practise their technique through exercise. Writers, he believes, especially fiction writers, can do this through oral storytelling. As tellers of tales they can expand their repertoires, learn about pace and timing, widen their vocabulary and internalise different narrative structures, thus stretching and tuning their voices as storytellers and story writers.

The formulation of written text and oral rehearsal: writing aloud

Whilst open-ended oral activities offer opportunities for generating rich ideas and possibilities, teachers know that young writers, both emergent and adolescent, often produce better oral than written work. It is easy to underestimate the difficulty of moving from ideas in the head to spoken words, to actual text on a page or screen. The frustration of 'writer's block' is not just about the flow of ideas, but is also about the flow of text in ways that satisfy the writer. There are two key reasons why this interface between talking and writing can be hard to bridge: firstly, the cognitive load that writing demands, and secondly, the specific challenges of formulating text. Giving young writers the opportunity to orally rehearse their actual writing can ease these challenges and there are different ways of so doing.

Writing demands that we multitask between thinking of ideas, evaluating their quality, creating phrases and images, managing the requirements of spelling, grammar and punctuation, reviewing what we are writing, and, if we are very novice writers, coping with shaping letters and writing in lines. This makes high demands on working memory, which psychologists describe as 'cognitive load' (Sweller, 1988): the amount of stress a particular task exerts on our working memory. One way to reduce this load is to break a task into sub-tasks, so that we can pay attention to one thing and do not have to think about the others. In writing, when teachers advise children to plan, then draft, then revise, they are in effect helping reduce the cognitive load; likewise, the guidance to use invented spellings or just put a line and return to check the spelling later helps reduce cognitive load during writing. By orally rehearsing a phrase or sentence out loud before writing it, the tasks of generation of written text and transcription of written text are separated, thus reducing the demand. In the extract below, two seven-year-olds are both drafting a piece of writing and the process of oral rehearsal is visible. Rosie orally rehearses one of her sentences to her partner, Jack, then begins to write it. She forgets how her sentence developed and asks Jack if he can remember. Jack supplies the connecting 'because' at the same time as Rosie but cannot recall the ending and suggests she thinks of another idea. After a pause, Rosie remembers her original sentence and rehearses it again, with a questioning tone, seeking confirmation from Jack. In such examples of oral rehearsal, the tone of voice is very different from natural dialogue. It is deliberate, slower, with less prosodic variation – this is represented in the text below in bold type.

Rosie: **I am heartbroken because ever . . . ev . . .** (*Looks away*) **I've . . .**
because . . . there is no room around me.
They continue writing.

Rosie: What was the thing I said? (*Taps Jack*) **I am heartbroken . . .**

Rosie: **because}** (*In unison*)

Jack: **because}**
I don't know. Why don't you come up with another idea?

Rosie: (*Long pause*) **I am heartbroken because there is no room around me?**
(*Looks at Jack for approval*)

Another specific way that oral rehearsal may help young writers is with the process of formulation. The translating phase of the writing process is concerned principally with the transformation of ideas in the head to words on the page. Cleland and Pickering (2006) describe this process as twofold, involving conceptualisation, deciding on the communicative idea to be written, and formulation, the shaping of that idea into syntactically coherent text. In other words, translation demands that 'the ideas collected during planning have to be formulated into words, and these words need to be ordered into grammatically and syntactically correct sentences to form a cohesive text' (Negro and Chanquoy, 2005:106).

As writers we know that this is not a straightforward process. Moving from ideas to a satisfying expression of them frequently involves false starts, word revisions, altering where information is placed as well as deletion. Alamargot and Chanquoy (2001) have broken the stage of translation into four sub-processes: elaboration, linearization, formulation and execution. Elaboration is the first step, when we decide what idea we are going to write about: this may be as embryonic as a feeling, or an image, or a sense of where a narrative is going next. During linearisation, we move from this half-formed idea to a clearer sense of the message to be conveyed, although it is still pre-verbal and not articulated words. The formulation process shapes this pre-verbal message into words and a syntactical structure, and during execution the words are written down. Oral rehearsal supports the formulation stage. For very young writers in particular, it helps the creation of a written sentence; and for all writers, oral rehearsal allows for the testing out of different possibilities for the sentence. In the extract below, Libby and Robert are working together, writing a set of instructions on how to write a text about instructions. Initially, Libby uses oral rehearsal to formulate a sentence – the false starts, hesitations and reformulations are very evident before she finally speaks a fully formed sentence, which she then writes down.

Libby: (*Grabs Robert and directs him to task*) Come on, Robert . . . Don't say please, don't say . . . in . . . in . . . don't put please in instructions in . . . at . . . in . . . the . . . um . . . the . . . um . . . at the . . . of . . . a . . . a . . . instruction . . . start of a sentence.
Don't put 'please' at the start of an instruction.
(*Begins writing*)

In order to support the oral rehearsal of written text, in our From Talk to Text project (Fisher et al., 2010), we encouraged children to Say it, Write it, and with the teachers developed classroom activities related to this. Two of these, invisible writing and the magic pencil, were particularly successful. Invisible writing activities involved children being given a blank piece of paper – in the form of a letter in an envelope from the class teddy bear, for example – and being told that the paper had invisible writing which only they could read. The children read the contents of their letter to their partner before 'writing over' the invisible ink so that everyone could read the writing. Observing this activity, it was noticeable how many children pointed to the invisible words on the page, moving their finger along the lines, fully engaged with the imaginative act of 'reading' the invisible writing. The magic pencil activity was similar. Children were given a magic pencil, an imaginary pencil (although one teacher gave out physical magical pencils which had no leads), and children were told that only they could make this pencil write and only they could read it. As with the invisible writing activities, the children then wrote texts that they read aloud to their partners before using a real pencil to write the text visibly. What seemed to be successful about these activities was the nature of the imaginative engagement with the task, and the evident opportunities it provided for rehearsing written text. As the project progressed we decided that the best way to talk about oral rehearsal with young children was to call it 'writing aloud', which makes clear both the oral and written elements of the activity. It is important to stress, however, that this particular kind of oral rehearsal, with its very explicit focus on sentence construction, is part of a wider repertoire of strategies for oral rehearsal in the writing classroom. It was embedded in vibrant writing classrooms, which gave young writers rich experiences of books and stories, and preceded various activities such as the above with interactive and constructive chances to generate and play with ideas.

Another form of oral rehearsal involves the teacher in the careful manipulation of different drama conventions in order to enable young writers to voice their thoughts orally in roles immediately prior to writing in a form closely aligned to the written genre. Whilst several conventions may be used to percolate ideas and involve the learners, the final convention employed needs to link closely to the chosen genre. In this way, the last improvised scenario acts a kind of dress rehearsal for their writing and can help young people bridge the talk–to–writing interface, the movement from talk to text. For example, in working towards diary writing a teacher, basing her work on a chosen text, might invite the class in threes to inhabit the row that a daughter has with her parents (voicing argumentative talk). Later, she might prompt the daughter to ring a friend on her mobile to tell her about this altercation (voicing a dialogue, powered by the daughter's retelling, which may include reported speech), before finally positioning the protagonist in her bedroom that night through using the 'interior monologue' convention (the class may each voice the reflective views and thoughts of the daughter at the close of this difficult day). This inner-voice, first-person narration will be most closely aligned with the diary writing to follow and will act as a final oral rehearsal – 'a dress rehearsal' – which, whilst influenced by the previous dramatic scenarios, will be scaffolded into existence and eased onto the page through the role perspective adopted and voiced. In such cases, writing may not be perceived as a separate task to be undertaken but as an extension of the imagined experience.

Additionally, collaborative writing, when two or more writers compose one piece between them, can offer opportunities for oral rehearsal. Writing with a partner involves young people in sharing possible ideas together and working to commit these to paper. It often involves oral rehearsal as they offer one another possible phrases and sentences for inclusion and through discussion agree these or formulate others which may be more suitable. It may also involve them in voicing out loud their internal dialogue and help them appreciate the dialectical processes of composition – that ever-present debate between form and meaning (Bereiter and Scardamalia, 1987). As both author and audience, collaborative writers read and hear their work, evaluating the tenor and tune of their emerging composition and discussing 'possible solutions with each other, rather than having to wrestle with them alone' (Cliff-Hodges, 2002: 9). As teachers, whilst we appreciate that learning is often a mutual accomplishment and that collaboration is a valuable tool, we may still frame writing as a solitary activity, perhaps in response to the system of individualised assessment. Yet collaborative writing is a valuable activity which can help foster creativity and commitment whilst easing the process of translation from talk to text (Vass, 2002, 2007). As three nine-year-olds observed:

- It's more fun when we write together, we share ideas and it makes it easier. Casey is good at spelling and I'm good at punctuation and checking.
- I like writing with Nathan, but we don't always agree on what we want to happen and we swap things round a lot.
- My favourite writing partners is Liam, we're doing a really long story, the longest we've ever written.

Reflecting on their written texts

Talk is an invaluable tool for reflecting on writing and being a writer and involves considering *oneself as a writer*, reflecting *during* the compositional process and reflecting on the text *after* it has been completed. This will include teacher–student as well as student–student conversations. As we foreground in Chapter 6, young writers need to develop a reflective metalanguage (the terminology of grammar) to talk about writing and themselves as writers, enabling them to voice their views, listen to others, and develop new knowledge and understanding. Through this they may come to clarify their original intentions and evaluate the extent to which they have achieved these. Such conversations can help them become more conscious of the choices they are making and the options available to them.

In reflecting on one's emergent text during the process, in small-group guided writing or in conversation with teachers, students can refine their thinking and clarify one another's ideas. Discussing her relationship with her editor, Berlie Doherty notes: 'I feel she knows my writing better than anyone else does, and so

I can talk an idea through in a way that I wouldn't with anyone else' (1999: 151). (Although intriguingly she observes that her editor tried to block *Children of Winter*, one of her most popular novels, as at that time historical fiction was hard to sell.) It is often useful for informal response partnerships to be established, although young writers will need support to critically evaluate the writing of their peers and to be flexible and responsive to their partner's comments. Often as writers we demonstrate considerable allegiance to our first drafts and need to be convinced that alternatives will be more effective. Working with professional writers can help highlight the everyday nature of revisiting, reviewing and reworking one's writing, as comedy scriptwriter Dave Smith (2010) indicates:

> This is something I'm keen to point out to them – I'm not a trained writer. I've only got to the point where I can earn a decent living as a writer through practice. I find it heartening to look at something I wrote two years ago and spot ways that I'd have done it differently now. I'm definitely not the finished article myself and I know I'm improving and that's normal, you always can as a writer and children need to know that.

When young writers engage in dialogue around their evolving writing, the nature of this conversation will be quite different from a teacher–student discussion, but through these conversations, students can be helped to recognise the strengths of their unfolding texts and areas for development or which deserve attention (Vass, 2007; Corden, 2001). Such evaluative conversations may benefit from the use of prompt questions to encourage active reflection, which Sharples (1999) describes as the key to breaking through to the 'what next?' stage. It is important, however, that authors retain ownership and control of their evolving texts and emergent meanings in and through these partnerships.

Working with response partners provides another opportunity for oral rehearsal, when writers hear the voice of their text through reading it aloud to their partner. Oral rehearsal can be thought of as a kind of private speech for writing. Feigenbaum (2010) argues that private speech allows the young child to practise the communicative, interpersonal language skills needed for communicative competence, providing an arena in which the speaker can adopt multiple positions and rehearse the perspectives of others. The same can be argued for oral rehearsal, especially when reading aloud. This helps all writers become the readers of their text and adopt an alternative position, hearing the text from the perspective of another. It also helps the writer hear the voice, the cadences and the rhythm of the text, which is an important element of writing. This practice is advocated by many professional writers, as revealed in an article on tips for writing fiction:

> Read it aloud to yourself because that's the only way to be sure the rhythms of the sentences are OK (prose rhythms are too complex and subtle to be thought out – they can be got right only by ear).
>
> Diana Athill

Listen to what you have written. A dud rhythm in a passage of dialogue may show that you don't yet understand the characters well enough to write in their voices.

Helen Dunmore

A story needs rhythm. Read it aloud to yourself. If it doesn't spin a bit of magic, it's missing something.

Esther Freud

Once the book is finished in its first draft, I read it out loud to myself. How it sounds is hugely important.

Michael Morpurgo (*The Guardian*, 2011)

Research by Barrs and Cork (2001) found that students' writing can be improved if their teacher reads it aloud at an early stage, giving it life and breath and helping the author hear the tunes and patterns they have created. Such oral rehearsal through reading aloud can also be modelled by the teacher when demonstrating writing. This is discussed further in Chapter 8.

Once completed, the opportunity to make writing public and share it orally or through written publications is valuable. Students benefit from hearing their more polished voices and gaining feedback and responses from their intended audience. In seeking to develop students' ability to reflect independently and critically on their writing (during or after composing), teachers can use their own and the students' writing as a resource for communal reflection. They can also model responding to writing with EASE:

Engagement: internalising the message

What thoughts, feelings, visual impressions come into your mind as you read?

Appreciation: considering the writers' achievements

How did the writer make you engage in this way?

Suggestion: considering specific ways to develop the writing

What can you suggest to improve the writing as present?

Extension: considering possible strategies and ideas to extend the writing

What can you suggest to extend the writing, what more is needed or would enrich?

(Goouch et al., 2009)

This involves readers/response partners:

- revisiting the author's intention – asking what they were trying to achieve;
- listening to the author read it aloud or reading it to them;
- responding – orally or in writing with EASE.

Developed from the work of D'Arcy (1999), this response framework seeks to foreground the engagement of the reader, his/her thoughts, feelings and personal response to the text, and to recognise and identify the author's skills which created this level of engagement. Additionally, the reader is invited to suggest possible strategies for shaping the text. Teachers can model the use of this framework in order to help students reflect on and critique their authorial choices and the impact of their composition on the reader. It was developed in one of our projects, in response to teachers' concerns that they were not responding to the meaning of the student's compositions, but were tending to profile targets and lesson objectives which were predominantly focused on language features. In guided writing, using their own unfolding drafts, the teachers sought to explain their authorial intentions, read their draft aloud to the group and invited them to respond with EASE, often initially on Post-it notes which were then read, considered and discussed. In such contexts, teachers sought to help children articulate their engagement (or lack of it) in their teachers' writing and then consider their craft, as well as suggest ideas for improving and developing the work. As one teacher commented:

> Initially the children were reluctant to criticise my personally written drafts, but when they found I wanted their advice and sometimes acted on it if I agreed with them and I needed to, they were more forthcoming. We share and borrow each others' ideas much more now and talk about our intentions – what am I trying to say here, what effect am I trying to achieve- that sort of thing. Before it was just writing – without an author – if you know what I mean, now I profile the author's purpose more and we talk more about our readers too.

However, the framework, like any set of prompts, requires extensive modelling and regular use as well as a supportive ethos to foster reflective and focused conversation.

Conclusion

Although there are differences between talk and writing as communicative codes and young writers face real challenges in making the transition from talking to writing, talk can support them in learning about writing and in developing and shaping their writing. It is a useful generative tool and a means for developing content for writing, and it plays a crucial role in the formulation of written texts through reading their work aloud. It operates as an oral rehearsal for the linguistic and structural demands of writing. Furthermore, reflecting on writing through talking about one's text as it unfolds and reviewing one's work in partnership with other writers can be valuable.

Talking, thinking and writing are woven together in a number of ways: talking can help us as writers try out our ideas on others, share our emerging text, and review and evaluate what we have written; through 'writing out loud' we can also hear our own voices and tune in to the patterns, harmony or discord created, making changes as a consequence of this. As writers we also think through ideas and discover what it is we want to say, and may make new connections through talking about our texts. In an energising community of writers we are also likely to be discussing our attitudes and identities as writers. Developing external and internal conversations about writing has the potential to make a significant contribution to the development of writers.

In this vignette six-year-old Ellie has chosen a favourite piece of writing and commented on her choice. She selected her visual and verbal description of the character, Mrs Twit from Roald Dahl's book *The Twits*. The vignette reveals the impact that this text has had on her and the positive influence of her friends' and teacher's response.

She has disgusting double chin.
She has mouldy old stick-out-teeth.
She has a doble messy and smelly thick-hair
She is smelly and she ainoying.
She extremely ugly and crooked.
She has sticking out thick hair.
She is ful of ugliness.
She is very slimy and messy.
She has mouly old teeth.
She is very agey.
and she has mouldy old cake.

You have used some fantastic adjectives Ellie!

My writing is about a character in the twis.
I felt famous Because I Laughed.
I felt good. I want People to think it
is fanny. I enjoy it Because my teachers
and my frens think it is good to.
    I found it easy to write. I get
my ideas from other People and my
imagination.

Ellie – student

Chapter 3

The role of texts

Introduction

As we seek to express ourselves as writers and stretch for new meanings, we draw on a wealth of different resources. As Philip Gross and his colleagues (2006: 22) observe, 'no writer, like no artform, is an island'; all writing resonates and reverberates with traces of other texts both spoken and written. Experience too tells us that many of our more able writers are also keen and able readers, and that if young people are taught these language modes separately, it makes them harder to learn. We know too that reading repertoires enrich writing repertoires, although we know rather less about how this relationship operates; how reading enriches writing.

The word in language, Bakhtin (1981: 293) argues, is always 'half someone else's', so writers come to lean on the 'voice strewn landscape' – a constantly changing landscape of texts – making use of all the cultural resources available to them, and borrowing from and adapting the voices of others. Through appropriating, imitating and inhabiting the voices of others, young writers both shape their own voices and have them shaped by the texts of school, home and community. As authors they move across textual boundaries, imitating, designing and transforming texts, and variously accepting and resisting the ways they are positioned, as well as finding new ways to position themselves (Dyson, 1997, 2001).

This chapter explores the shaping power of texts and the influence of the texts of life, of literature and of popular culture on writing. The role that texts play in the generation of ideas and in developing knowledge about text structure and an ear for language is also considered, as well as the importance of developing approaches in the classroom that explore the interplay between reading and writing and being a reader of one's own and others' writing.

Voices that echo and resonate

Other people's speech makes it possible, Bakhtin (1986) argues, for us to generate our own and thus it becomes an indispensable factor in the creative power of language. Young people's writing is influenced by the texts that they have heard, read, watched and experienced; the stories, rhymes, songs, television shows, films, dramas, video games, websites, books, magazines, newspapers and other texts that make up their multimodal textual experiences. We can discern echoes of these in the texts they produce, in the verbal, visual and sound devices they employ; their repertoires of experience.

Many years ago, as a new teacher, I had the privilege of listening to Philippa Pearce, author of classic texts such as *Tom's Midnight Garden* and *A Dog so Small*, at a conference in Cambridge. She read from some of her work and then the chair invited questions. At one point, in responding to a query about the way in which aspects of her book *The Way to Satin Shore* resonated with *Great Expectations*, she explained with a degree of irritation that she was no different from any other author; she listened and looked, borrowed, stored and stole ideas from different texts and contexts for later development and use. But, pursued her questioner, where do you get *your* ideas from? In an impassioned tirade, Phillipa spoke at length about life and literature, and about news and others' views being the rich substrate for her writing, a resource she mined, transformed and polished as she built her own fictional worlds. She was clear that without a rich reading life, an 'interior life' I believe she called it, and a rich daily life she would be bereft as a writer. As she drew her extended response to a close, she turned back to the teacher. 'Whatever do you think I do, my dear?' she asked. 'Make it all up?!' The frisson in the room was palpable. There was a long and potent pause. I sat there wondering whether this is exactly what I/we regularly asked young writers to do. To invent, imagine and construct their texts, to make it all up without offering significant support and opportunities to lean on texts, both life texts and other printed and oral forms for ideas, for thinking and for writing. 'Trying other people's voices', as Britton (1970: 57) observed, 'may be a natural and necessary part of the process of finding one's own.' This assertion is borne out by the views of a number of professional writers, who, in recognising the sea of voices on which they draw, highlight that young writers too need rich text experiences and the opportunity to hear, inhabit and give voice to many texts on their journeys as writers.

Echoes of narrative texts

Writers often comment on the impact of reading on writing, and our book offers many examples of more and less experienced writers reflecting on such connections. In particular, fiction writers appear to stress the reciprocity involved. Terry Deary, for example, recognises his debt as a writer to Roald Dahl, who he perceives made both horror and black comedy in children's books acceptable; and also to Rosemary Sutcliffe and Henry Treece, who in Terry's teenage years were publishing historical fiction which he devoured and in many ways sought to reproduce. He observes he began by imitating their work, later transforming and combining styles to develop his own 'populist' voice in the form of the 'Horrible Histories' series, which offered a new and accessible take on the past.

Writers learn to write in the same way they learn to speak. They imitate. And in the same way you develop your own way of speaking and conversing, you develop your own way of writing. But initially, if you want to be a writer, you imitate, like a parrot . . . I'm very conscious of my author's voice. Some writers are consciously literate in their style. I'm consciously populist or accessible, but some people look down their noses at these qualities.

(Terry Deary, 1999: 96)

Jacqueline Wilson's trajectory as a writer was also shaped by her early literacy experiences and pleasure in reading and creating texts. In recalling Enid Blyton, Noel Streatfield and Catherine Cookson as powerful childhood favourites, she also notes that she read voraciously and wrote avidly too. Aged nine, she recalls writing a story called *The Maggots* about a working-class family that was directly influenced by Eve Garnett's *The Family from One End Street*. As she comments, 'most of the stories I wrote then were like juvenile versions of what I do now – stories about families with problems', later adding, 'I feel there is a direct line – unaffected by my journalism – stretching from the Maggots through to my work now' (Wilson, 1999: 235).

Berlie Doherty (1999) talks too of the influence of others' writing and discovering through her own childhood reading, that what young people (and she believes adults) want in a book is to find themselves, as she found herself, in L. M. Montgomery's *Emily Climbs*. Through reflecting on her own experiences and her aims in writing, she describes her intention to create 'a kind of emotional landscape where the young reader finds that they dare to go into and can find a way out of it again' (ibid.: 151). Working with this maxim in mind she takes research for her books very seriously – for example, visiting schools to interview and listen to teenagers talk about pregnancy in preparation for her novel *Dear Nobody*.

Research studies also indicate that literature can influence young writers and that more experienced and able readers also tend to be more able writers (e.g. Fox, 1993; Mallet, 1997; Barrs and Cork, 2001). Their enriched repertoires offer a wealth of possibilities for them as authors. The Teaching Reading and Writing Links (TRAWL) project indicated the advantages of wide reading, and the value of close critical reading and investigation of texts (Corden, 2000, 2003). It also showed that young people's growing text knowledge gained through reading and reflection supports their emerging understanding of authorship. Through having their attention drawn to specific literary devices in context, the 9- to 11-year-olds involved in this study, who were simultaneously being read to and exploring texts as well as studying them, came to 'transfer the knowledge and insights gained into their own writing' (Corden, 2000: 153). As they become well acquainted with literary rhythms and patterns, they begin to play with these forms and innovate, borrowing ideas and language features for their own narratives. The work of Barrs and Cork (2001) also demonstrates a clear link between young people's involvement with literary texts and their development as writers, suggesting that their ability to imagine a reader, to lean on literary styles and rhythms, and write from inside a fictional context are all influenced by their engagement. They identify three kinds of literature that impact most on the young: emotionally powerful texts, traditional tales, and texts written in a clearly poetic style – 'poeticised speech', as they call it, which often has a strong oral quality. They argue the orality of some fictional writers, such as the work of Kevin Crossley Holland, Michael Morpurgo and Geraldine McGaughrean, is richly resonant and poetic in nature, potentially increasing its influence on young writers' texts.

Echoes of oral poetic texts

In tune with this research, some professional writers talk less of the written texts which influenced their early journeys as writers, and more of listening to and voicing oral texts. Many reflect on how tales (personal and traditional) and other oral and poetic texts played a significant role in their childhoods and how the habit of listening and attending to the music, rhythm and cadences of such texts tuned their ears and shaped their voices. Benjamin Zephaniah (1999), for example, in considering his own emergence as a writer and performer, notes that whilst fiction was not plentiful in his childhood home, the Bible was read aloud frequently (both his parents were preachers), his mum shared oral poetry from her childhood with him and he listened avidly to the radio. Through this and watching the news, he developed an early and impassioned interest in current affairs which he retains today, alongside his evident sense of rhythm and beat. It seems that Zephaniah, who disliked reading and writing as a child, found his voice though listening and performing, as Seamus Heaney also observes:

> In practice you hear it coming from somebody else, you hear something in another writer's sounds that flows in through your ear and enters the echo-chamber of your head and delights your whole nervous system . . . you recognise [this] instinctively as a true sounding of yourself and your experience. And your first steps as a writer will be to imitate, consciously or unconsciously, those sounds that flowed in, that in-fluence.
>
> (Heaney, 1980: 44)

In school, imitating poems with strong structures at the primary phase is not only common but popular; this begins much earlier, however, well before writing has been introduced formally. Children's first steps into this world of language play and imitation begin with carer conversations and develop through nursery rhythms and rhymes and early playground songs and chants; their speech too is full of word play and exploration. Fed by the media as well as the oral tradition, these interactional practices ensure young people hear and participate in a diverse range of oral and poetic voices from the earliest age in the home (Grainger and Goouch, 1999), in the playground (Grugeon, 2001) and in the community too – through football songs and chants and religious texts, for example. Popular music too offers rich rhythms and potent lyrics, voices which young people unconsciously learn to sing and subvert, both individually and collectively. Their conversations as well are full of anecdotes and idioms, suggesting that, as the Cambridge and Nottingham Corpus of Discourse in English (CANCODE) indicates, oral language play is a creative social practice woven through everyday life (Carter, 2004). In the playground, on their mobile phones and in friendship groups, young people lean on and transform the texts they have met in different oral contexts, physically playing poetry into existence and elaborating on their own and others' life stories in an energised and engaged manner (Maybin, 2005). Yet in the classroom, this energy and oral vitality is not always capitalised on; oral storytelling and performance poetry, for example, are afforded relatively little attention in the primary or secondary years. Both depend on the interaction between text, audience and performer for their efficacy, and both could lead to writing or feed writing, but the predominance of the written text appears to hold sway.

Echoes of oral narrative texts

In relation to oral storytelling, several ex-teachers and now well-known authors, such as Philip Pullman, David Almond and Michael Morpurgo, refer to the scope the role of educator afforded them to tell and retell tales and to develop their confidence as oral storytellers, shaping, honing and polishing their words with an audience of young writers. Michael, for example, whilst acknowledging his literary mentors, Robert Louis Stevenson, Ted Hughes and Sean Rafferty, also reflects on his time as a teacher telling oral stories 'to 35 expectant children' at the end of every day. During this period he believes he was testing himself as a storyteller and taking 'his first tentative steps as a writer' (2006: 75). Mary Medlicott, in Chapter 9, also explores the relationship between oral and written artistry, highlighting the sense of fluency as an author gained through oral storytelling.

If young people are offered the chance to voice and re-voice traditional tales as well as hear them, to rehearse the fluency and flow, feel the emotional temperature and position themselves as tale tellers, this can, over time, make a marked contribution to their writing. Folktales have a particularly important role to play in providing a bridge from oracy to literacy, since they are highly structured, with strong elemental themes and characters. Just like the bards and storytellers of old, students expand their repertories through telling and retelling stories and internalising story structures in the process. They may discuss memorable language, evocative words or lyrical phrases, and make notes of any runs or repetitions which contribute to the effect and shape of the tale. Through experiencing and reflecting on this language and voicing some of it in their own unique retellings, a richer understanding and use of language can develop which will eventually surface in their written work, albeit transformed in a new context (Grainger et al., 2005). There is, however, no direct route between being aware of a story's structure or evocative language and the use of these in writing, although with time to listen and to voice, attend and discuss, represent and explore, young writers do come to play with these elements, borrowing from and connecting to the voices of storytellers before them, as the following opening sentences indicate:

> When I was your age sonny, my granny told me a story, it was a long time ago so I ain't sure about everything, but let me try, this is the tale of how a jellyfish got the better of my ol' grandma.

> Many years ago when the earth was new and humans were but a twinkle in the eyes of God, there lived an animal, an animal with the longest neck you could ever imagine.

> In the world before our world began, when beasts could sing, crickets could dance and birds could talk, there lived a cheeky kookaburra and a very cheeky kookaburra he was to be sure.

> From the very second that William felt the stone, he knew it was no ordinary stone that the tramp had given him.

> I was almost eleven before I discovered I had a particular magic power, a very inconvenient power at that.

These openings, collected in the weeks after an extended storytelling focus, variously introduce traditional and more modern narratives. They indicate that these nine-year-olds are echoing the tunes and patterns of tales they have heard, told or read. None are direct imitation however, all have been made new by their authors, played into existence on the back of other openings; transformed in their new narrative contexts.

Echoes of life texts

Writers also lean on the texts of their lives as a rich source of inspiration and possibility, not only mining incidents and involving people they know, albeit often fictionalised, but also connecting to places of significance. As Murphy (2002: 87) asserts, to ask people to read or write, in whatever form, is in some ways 'to ask them to engage in an act of self-identification that echoes biography, history and a sense of place'. Many writers alter elements of their lives, as Jackie Kay (2008) reveals in discussing her poem 'The Stincher'. She observes that whilst the real incident she describes – about telling her parents that her brother had drowned in the river – actually happened by the river Erskine, she liked the name Stincher better (it is a river near Ballantrae) 'because it sounded like an onomatopoeic word for lie. I could imagine someone saying, "she told a right stincher", meaning she told a whopper!' (ibid.: 21). In his personal reflection on writing, *Singing for Mrs Pettigrew: A story-maker's Journey*, Michael Morpurgo also considers this issue of leaning on life as he intersperses short stories with reflections on their genesis, teasing out their tangled traces in an engaging conversational commentary. He stresses that, for him, narrative writing, whether in the form of a script, a short story or a novel, is always highly personal, and draws on his reservoir of life experiences, his sense of place, and commitment to and interest in particular issues and causes. He offers this advice: 'Don't pretend. Tell your tale. Speak with your own voice. We are what we write, I think even more than we are what we read' (Morpurgo, 2006: 78). He draws on his knowledge and experience of holidaying on Bryher in the Scilly Isles, for example, and refers to the transformation that moving to Devon wrought on his writing, suggesting that living there in a small community:

> I inadvertently enriched myself hugely as a person, and so as a writer. I grew up. When I wrote now, I really had something I knew about, something I wanted to say indeed needed to say, I came to know a place and its people, became fascinated with their history and their lives, Now I was beginning to write about what I cared about, not imply to entertain children or anyone else for that matter, I was exploring my own stories, my own hopes and doubts and fears engaging with my own past and present. I was finding my voice.
>
> Michael Morpurgo (2006: 77)

Ted Hughes, in a not dissimilar manner, suggests in *Poetry in the Making* (1967: 123) that in order to 'truly possess' one's experience, authors need to immerse themselves in the world around them and in the 'inner universe of experience'. Such indwelling and leaning on life is a feature common to writers, who, as we explored in Chapter 1, use writing to make sense of life and re-create their own meanings. In interviewing Derek Walcott, the prize-winning poet, Payne (2011) shows how he is heavily influenced by writers of the colonial past, but also by his commitment to St Lucia, its scenery, history and people, and how Derek draws on all of this in his writing. Derek explains that whilst the deep source of his inspiration remains the same, he no longer feels beholden to writers from the past; although acknowledging his debt to them, he observes, 'When you're young influences count', but as you develop 'you want to hear your own voice at an honest pitch'. The concept of voice, which as 'a fingerprint reveals identity' (Andrews, 1989: 21), reflects the uniqueness of individual writers, who, like Derek, Ted, Michael and Jackie, lean on their lives, the people they have met and the places they have visited, as well as the voices of others whose work they have read and heard.

Young people too, through their engagement in living, in family stories, anecdotes, reminiscences and gossip, lean on lived experience. Through sharing personal tales, young authors can revisit their lives, learn to distance themselves, and may choose to re-sculpt their experiences as authors, voicing their observations on living through fictional accounts (Armstrong, 2006). In the process they will be participating in 'the continual process of re-inventing [and] rewriting' their worlds (Dyson, 1997: 185). In one of our projects, analysis of the questionnaires completed by the young people revealed that relatively few (under a quarter of the 390 writers between the ages of 5 and 11) were aware of borrowing events from life as a source of ideas. They were conscious of leaning on specific books, on television, on personal interests and on their teachers, but appeared not to consider they could use their life experiences as a resource for writing. Several of the older children expressed the view that this would somehow be cheating and would only be possible if the work was expected to be autobiographical:

> 'You have to make it up or it's not a real story.'

> 'You mustn't mix up autobiography and fictional writing, that's wrong.'

> 'Miss doesn't like it if we bring our own stuff into stories, although we do a unit on autobiography, it's okay then.'
>
> > (Grainger et al., 2005: 123)

Yet as Berlie Doherty (2001) asserts, 'fiction is a combination of I remember and let's pretend' and young writers need to know they can draw on their memories, their lives and lived experience, just as professional writers do.

Echoes of multimodal texts

Writer and illustrator Ian Beck (1999), reflecting on the development of his own style initially as an illustrator and later as a writer, notes that he was heavily influenced by the artwork and writing of Raymond Briggs (his tutor at art college) and by his heroes Edward Ardizzone and Anthony Gross, who regularly illustrated for the *Radio Times*, which Ian read avidly as a teenager and where he later worked. He also notes that, more recently, his daughter has offered him a child's-eye view of the world, which he seeks to convey in his illustrations. As a result of the intense diversification of texts, increasing use of the image and development of new technologies, when young people write and design, they draw on a rich repertoire and experience of such texts. We explore this further in Chapter 4. As Bearne (2003) has shown, this means they often think and work differently from us as adults. Echoes of multimodal texts can be found in the work of young writers who often enthusiastically and consciously recognise and use the 'voice' of the image, of word and sound in interesting combinations (Kress and van Leeuwen, 1996). Yet this is not always recognised or built on by their teachers, and some young people encounter difficulties in developing print literacy due, in part, to their arguably unrecognised experience, ease and pleasure in other modes. Whilst the changing landscape of literacy has reconfigured the nature of both reading and text production, the profession seems somewhat slow to recognise this and to extend curriculum boundaries to ensure young writers can build on their everyday literacy practices and expertise.

Teachers need to find ways of profiling and assessing young writers' multimodal texts, and supporting them as they seek to integrate and balance modes according to purpose and audience, using colour, sound, image and perspective, for example, to engage their readers'/viewers' interest (QCA/UKLA, 2004, 2005). Progression in this area also needs to be mapped so that new challenges can be offered to young text producers as they pay increased attention to design and layout, and use a range of visual, verbal and sound cohesive devices in order to structure their texts (for models of progression, see Bearne and Wolstencroft, 2007). Young text designers can also be supported by working with professional writers from the workplace, whose job it is to design and shape multimodal texts. Such work may help them find a vocabulary to describe the process of multimodal text production.

The influence of young writers' knowledge and experience of popular cultural texts on their composing has also been documented (Marsh and Millard, 2005; Dowdall, 2006; Bearne, 2009). The engaging and energising 'voices' in such texts are mediated through television, the Internet and cinema, as well as through advertising, comics, magazines, films and much related merchandise; whilst many are transitory in nature, they represent a rich resource for adaptation and manipulation due to their motivational nature. When teachers recognise the potential of these texts, they may involve the young in making their own animated films – for example, creating Wallace and Gromit narratives or scripting Simpsons shows – and moving transformatively from one mode to another as they lean on popular cultural texts to create their own meanings.

From reading to writing – finding a balance

Whilst young people's journeys as writers are enriched by the company they keep – that of talented authors, poets, illustrators and designers, for example – they will also need opportunities to develop the craft of writing through increased awareness of the models that surround them. Fine-grained opportunities to study texts in context, to discuss their forms and features and to imitate them can help writers come to understand more about text construction and develop a language to discuss this.

Teaching about written genres, both fiction and non fiction, as we have discussed in Chapter 1, is important in this regard, although too often these have been taught rigidly, with teachers leaning heavily on formulas and frames for writing. This has led to a rather 'static conception of the potential of language' and the 'reluctance on the part of teachers (and thus pupils) to experiment with hybrid forms' (Andrews, 2008a: 13). The features of many genres have been detailed, assessed and assiduously taught to young writers, but 'under the guise of developing writer's linguistic awareness', as Myhill (2001) observes, 'it is all too easy to reduce writing to a set of formulae taught through a series of exercises'. A finely tuned balance in the teaching of writing is needed, and awareness that young writers do not merely reproduce the models they encounter or are explicitly taught; they use them to make sense of their lives and rework and transform them in the process.

Using text exemplars and models for writing and demonstrating the features of different forms is valuable, but, as noted, there has been a tendency to overuse these, with teachers selecting poems or non-fiction text types to imitate. Success in such tightly framed writing may be defined as the inclusion of all the language features of procedural texts, for example– imperative verbs, clear layout, sequential order, list of resources, and so on – at the expense of considering the meaning of the writers' instructions, their communicative purpose in context. Making that ubiquitous cup of tea or jam sandwich has little relevance for many students, yet most will have undertaken such instructional writing at least once in their primary years – demonstrating perhaps that the model has taken precedence over the purpose of the communication. If offered the chance to personalise their own instructions, young writers could no doubt identify a wealth of real world reasons for writing instructions: caring for pets, playing computer games, downloading music, or applying make-up, for example.

The following extract from a collaboratively produced poem emerged from work around two poems, 'Ten Little School Children' by Trevor Millum and 'Eight Brand New Angels' by Brian Patten. Both are counting rhymes which act reductively, starting with ten participants and ending with none. After some time reading, discussing the rhyming couplets, the structure and the differences between the two, groups chose one poem and performed extracts of this before they came to create their own. When they did so, they could be observed clapping, banging the table edge, and improvising on their feet as they choreographed their compositions into existence.

Ten Little Pop Stars

Ten little pop stars dancing in a line
One fell off the stage and then there were nine

None little pop stars opening a fete
One joined a blues band and then there were eight

Eight little pop stars singing with dry lips
One completely cracked up and then there were six

Six little starlets performing on stage live
One lost her confidence and then there were five

Five little Spice Girls posing on the floor
One got a nasty splinter then there were four

Nathan, Dionne, Depa and Damon

In this example the form was set, but the content was open and the group made connections to their own interests and found ways to express themselves within the discipline of the form. Later lines included four little clubbers, three little ravers and 'two little music fans having lots of fun', but 'one got drunk on alcopops, leaving only one'. The model offered a clear shape, structure and rhythm, and ensured some degree of success as well as support for their collaborative composition. Yet if all poetry opportunities were tied to models, there would be little scope for free verse or the autonomy of young writers; their own meanings might again be seen as subordinate to the form, rather than the other way round. So seeking a judicious balance between form and freedom is critical.

Developing an ear for language

Developing an ear for language is an invaluable attribute for writers and readers, and whilst this can be gained by extensive reading, there are a number of other activities which can also nurture close attention to the different voices, tunes and texts evoked by authors. The rhythms and cadences of words read aloud – as, particularly from well-chosen literature –resonate and reverberate, helping young writers internalise some of their language and shapes. Furthermore, if they engage fully in text explorations, focusing on the language, structure, interpretation and meaning of texts through drama and storytelling, or poetry readings and performances, for example this can nurture and refine their 'inner ear'. Such sensitivity to form and language fostered through playful exploration can help students experience language more aesthetically. It can also support them as readers of their own writing when engaged in self-monitoring of the tunes and patterns in their own work. Adopting a receptive stance towards their own compositions, and increasing their attentiveness to listening to their own and others' voices, helps young writers engage in critical self-evaluation. This resonates with Ted Hughes' recommendation to writers to 'keep the audial faculty open . . . listening as widely, deeply and keenly as possible' (1976: 79).

Extending young people's ear for language through personal reading and other text activities can also widen students' vocabularies. In German the word for vocabulary, *wortschatz*, literally means 'word treasure'; inner treasure chests packed with words on which writers can draw, albeit not always accurately at first. But words in themselves are insufficient. Packing sentences with endless adjectives or 'wow' words does nothing to enrich writing, although it has become common practice, particularly in those classrooms that make extensive use of the popular techniques recommended by Ros Wilson (2002). She claims that specific skill practice using 'writing strategies', such as Vocabulary, Connectives, Openers and Punctuation (VCOP), leads to sustained skill use and improved standards. However, there is no evidence to substantiate this assertion or support such 'scientific teaching of the skills of writing' (ibid.: 4) and this widespread approach ignores the influence of reading on writing. Furthermore, it is a highly reductive interpretation of writing, seeing it as little more than an incremental process of skill acquisition, which fails to recognise the role of reading, of texts and of literature in particular as a rich source of imaginative possibilities for writing.

In the final written extract in this chapter, written by Lucy, aged 12, we can see evidence of the shaping influence of reading on writing and this writer's knowledge about fictional text, language and vocabulary applied in context. We can hear echoes of the lyrical writing of Michael Morpurgo, a long-time favourite of this young writer, in particular his short story 'Dear Carlos', which was the partial source of inspiration for this piece, which was also enriched by his collection *War Stories*, that she had recently read. The set homework was to write a letter within a longer tale, the letter was expected to play a significant role in the overall narrative as a structuring device. Her tale begins with the narrator Michael on the quayside at Dover, comforting his mother and his twin sisters as he sets off to the trenches in the footsteps of his dead brother. He carries this last letter from Patrick in his pocket, of which, elsewhere in the text, he says, 'I have read countless times, in fact I know it off by heart'.

Dearest brother,

May 19th – Happy Birthday! How I wish I could be with you today. Has ma and the twins sung happy birthday yet? Or baked a cake with your name in icing? We could have gone to the White Horse and drunk our weight in bitter, at least that's what I did with pa for my 16th! Anyway, whatever you're doing I hope you're having fun. Right now I sit in the trenches waiting for a signal to attack. Although the officers say that *if* we can hold out until the reinforcements arrive we will eliminate the enemy, the atmosphere is one of a defeated force, we are all aware that many men will be lost in this last stand. I wish I was home. At night if I can sleep, for it is a rare indulgence, I dream of our house, the twins running, ma's cooking and us joking around together. I'm tired Mickey, tired of all this, bombs, death, loneliness. I feel more alone than ever, everyone I have cared for here is lost, either in spirit or is dead. I no longer try to talk to other people; we all prefer to be alone in our quiet fantasies of normal life. When I'm alone, at least then I can hear my thoughts more clearly. I'm alone right alone, it's cold here, or so they say, I no longer feel it, it's almost as if the cold has become a part of me. A slowly destroying parasite. I'm sorry brother, I do not want to dampen your mood, but sometimes I just can't escape my own mind. When I get home, for I surely will, I'll buy you a pint and we can laugh and look back together. I think the sergeant's brewed some tea, I must go. But enjoy your birthday, look after ma and the twins for me. I promise, I will see you again. Pray for me, for us.

Love your brother

Patrick

This extract from the longer tale indicates a growing grasp of language, of pattern and rhythm as well as historical knowledge, and reflects Lucy's preparedness to adopt another stance and write in role. The short sentences keep up the pace and offer an immediacy subtly prefiguring Patrick's death by hypothermia in days to come. Enabling young people to recognise the significant influence of others' texts, and to recognise the complex process of imitating, emulating, innovating and transforming others' voices is part of our professional challenge.

Conclusion

In response to Andrews' (2008a: 82) claim that 'there is too little understanding of, and use of, the reciprocity between reading and writing', this chapter has sought to explore the many Literary voices which resonate and echo through our writing. It has offered the contemplative voices of professional writers who not only acknowledge the debt they owe to the writing of others, but also highlight the role of imitation and transformation in their work. The vibrant reflective voices of young writers are also shared. We argue that through inhabiting others' voices and giving voice to texts other than their own, writers come to understand more about the author's craft from a reader's perspective. Leaning on texts can be made even more explicit through discussing the reader in each one of us as writers. We further suggest that whilst different genres of writing should be introduced, if mirroring techniques and forms is not balanced by other more open-ended opportunities, then young people's knowledge about genres may be profiled at the expense of fostering their emergent meanings and communicative purposes. Reading needs to be recruited to the task of writing, and writing recruited to the task of thinking and meaning-making. This can foster the development of both explicit and implicit knowledge about language. Additionally, as educators we need to recognise that reading aloud and other forms of text representation can develop both an ear for language and an understanding of literary form.

This vignette is from nine-year-old Brandon who, after he wrote his text, created a compositional collage/writing 'journey' as a tool for conversation and reflection. The learning objective identified by his teacher was to draft a newspaper article, a free choice of focus was offered. This is Brandon's first draft.

Michael Holmes was in a sky diving accident yesterday over Lake Taupo, New Zealand.

Michael, a professional skydiver, had jumped 2000 times before the accident without even a scare, but this time he wasn't so lucky. He was taking part in the largest ever skydive with 78 people. He jumped from 12,000 ft, but when he went to open his parachute at 35,000 ft, nothing happened! The lines had snagged inside, the chords seemed to be catching on part of his parachute and the others all floating downwards on the wind saw Michael free falling by.

At the last minute his parachute worked and the chords untangled. "I was petrified" he said "My life flashed before me". I thought I would never see my family and my girlfriend again. Michael is now taking some time off skydiving to be with his girlfriend.

Writing Journey

I wanted to get across the Idea of a drama happening. I was influenced by this book which is very dramatic.

The Well
Gary Crew
Narelle Oliver

Wing walking

I wondered if Michael Should die, but chose not, though he could have been a ghost like this.

I have watched and always been fascinated by planes and would love to go in a hot-air balloon. I wondered what it would be like if lots of people sky dived at the same time?

I read lots of news and knew how a report is set out. I read bits to Nathan to see if it sounded scary.

FirstNews

Brandon – student

Chapter 4

Writing as design

Introduction

Imagine you have some play dough in your hands. You are going to make something, a mouse, perhaps. What do you do? Firstly, you might squeeze and manipulate the piece of dough from a rough, stiff lump into something more malleable and smooth. You might roll it into a ball or a sausage shape, or break it into several pieces. You might start to shape your mouse body, and then craft the head. You might take some tiny balls of dough to create ears, eyes and a tail. You might pinch the head to create a sharp, pointy nose. You might puzzle about how to do whiskers. As you create your mouse, you will almost certainly pause to look at it and see how it is coming along; you might even decide that what you have done is not working and screw your creation back into a malleable ball of play dough, and start again.

Michael Rosen gives a lovely image of 'language as putty' (Rosen, 1989) or like play dough. The image is a reminder that when we write, we are using language to shape and craft, and that in doing this we can push, squeeze, manipulate and stretch language to its limits. And just as when you create an object with play dough, you have materials to use, an idea of what you want to achieve, and possibly several attempts to achieve it, writing draws on the tool of language to meet the goals of the task and frequently demands several revisions. This chapter considers the idea of writing as *design*, as an active process of creating, crafting and shaping text and making design choices to realise the intentions for the piece of writing.

The principle of design

The design metaphor is particularly apt for thinking theoretically and pedagogically about writing. The word 'design', like the word 'writing', can be either a noun or a verb. We may create 'a design' for a garden or a new invention. The noun usage reminds us of design as an outcome or a product. As a verb, it foregrounds the process of designing – we *design* a new garden. Both writing and design encompass processes and products. The design metaphor incorporates conceptual thinking around creative decision-making, about fitness for purpose, about the tools and

materials available. It also includes within its metaphorical boundaries the development of prototypes and evaluation. The idea that creating text is a design process
is, of course, not wholly new: medieval monks creating illuminated manuscripts
were designing texts a thousand years ago. But new thinking about writing as
design has emerged more recently as the affordances of technology have altered
the design possibilities open to all writers. Sharples (1999) argued that writing
was an act of creative design, because writing is almost always a problem-solving
activity, set within the constraints of language and personal resources and governed
by the demands of purpose and audience. This means that a writer has to be 'not
only a creative thinker and problem solver, but also a designer' (ibid.: 10).

In his analysis of his own daughter's development as a writer, Kress (1997)
shows how emergent writers are aware of writing as design. He reveals how
children's first attempts at writing draw on all their social experiences of writing
and making meaning from texts. Social encounters with text nearly always combine
the word with the image, and also with colour and shape and other semiotic
features. Young children mix drawing and written words, understand the layout
of particular texts, such as greetings cards or newspapers, and communicate
meaning through combinations of the verbal and the visual. The vignette of the
emergent writer (see page 28, Chapter 1) also shows this mix of the verbal and
the visual, with the drawing of the giant *and* its 'label'. Kress argues that the page
is a particularly important frame for writing, and that young writers need to be
able to control 'the display of the text on the page' but that 'in most discussions
of writing – the page is not considered as a meaningful or significant element
(Kress, 1997: 86). The significance of the visual in writing is also signalled in *More
than Words*, an exploration of early-years writing by the Qualifications and
Curriculum Authority (QCA) and United Kingdom Literary Association (UKLA).
This booklet acknowledges the many changes that have occurred in recent years
in the ways that texts present information (for adults as well as young readers) and
the way this influences early writing. The authors draw attention to the importance
of supporting design choices: 'children need to be helped to make appropriate
choices to suit their purposes for communication. At times writing (or images)
alone can be the best way to get a message across. A useful question might be:
For this message, what can best be expressed in words and what in images?'
(QCA/UKLA, 2004: 18).

What these young writers are doing is making use of all the communicative
resources available to them to create their texts. Cope and Kalantzis (2000) talk
about the design principle and they argue that every act of creating meaning in a
written text is an act of transformation, where writers take all the resources available
to them and recombine and transform them to create a new meaning. What is new
in a piece of writing is a creative synthesis or re-imagining of 'the available resources
of meaning' (Cope and Kalantzis, 2000: 22). And designing writing always
requires writers to make choices – it is a process of taking ownership and responsibility for the writing. Producing written text is fundamentally about choice; as
Kellogg reminds us, 'all writers must make decisions about their texts' (Kellogg,

2008: 2). A recent article in *The Guardian* (20 February 2010) offered 'ten rules' by authors for writing fiction: the authors' advice frequently emphasises the importance of making choices, and especially revising and refining the writing to ensure it achieves what the writer wants it to do:

> Don't sit down in the middle of the woods. If you're lost in the plot or blocked, retrace your steps to where you went wrong. Then take the other road. And/or change the person. Change the tense. Change the opening page.
>
> Margaret Atwood

> Do change your mind. Good ideas are often murdered by better ones. I was working on a novel about a band called the Partitions. Then I decided to call them the Commitments.
>
> Roddy Doyle

> Description is hard. Remember that all description is an opinion about the world. Find a place to stand.
>
> Anne Enright

> Rewrite and edit until you achieve the most felicitous phrase/sentence/ paragraph/page/story/chapter.
>
> Annie Proulx

> Writing fiction is not 'self-expression' or 'therapy'. Novels are for readers, and writing them means the crafty, patient, selfless construction of effects.
>
> Sarah Waters

So the teaching of writing is about supporting writers in developing a design repertoire, developing writers' awareness of the writing processes they use and the linguistic, literary and layout possibilities open to them. Becoming a designer of writing is at once a creative, a cognitive, a social, and a linguistic process in which writers develop 'a growing command of linguistic resources, a broadening under-standing of the multiple ways in which written texts communicate meaning, and a deepening sense of one's own identity as a writer' (Myhill, 2011).

Writing as a visual and multimodal enterprise

One aspect of writing as design is the use of the visual and the multimodal to communicate in written text. Writing in the twenty-first century frequently involves both the verbal and the visual, skilfully combined to convey meaning. At its simplest level, technology has made it very easy for the writer to make choices about a whole host of elements, such as font choice, font colour, the use of white space, and images. This is far more than mere presentational choice. Writing a letter of application or an academic assignment in Comic Sans conveys different nuances than the same texts written in Times New Roman or Arial. Giving advice to those writing job applications, Howson (*TES*, 2011: 8) recommends 'Stick with traditional fonts such as Ariel and Calibri and point size 11 or 12', with the implication that other less traditional fonts create the wrong impression. Indeed, as I write this chapter, the visual effect of a font choice is being linked with cognitive effects: a new report (Dieman-Yaumann et al., 2011) suggests that using Comic Sans may have a beneficial effect on cognitive processes, such as remembering. Of course, the way fonts carry meanings is wholly socially shaped by patterns of usage, but writers, particularly commercial writers, exploit this potentiality to the full. With email and texting, we use emoticons embedded in the verbal communication, and these more informal modes of communication have engendered creative use of capitalisation or bold print to add to the communicative effect.

These influences are evident in the books young people read. Picture books for young readers have long been highly expert at the integration of word and text so that both are intrinsically part of the way the book makes meaning. Illustrations are not simple additions to the verbal text which could be omitted, but part of the way the book unfolds its story. Increasingly, however, books written for older readers incorporate design features. Consider, for example, Mark Haddon's *The Curious Incident of the Dog in the Night-time*. The book makes liberal use of diagrams and drawings embedded within the verbal text as a way of showing how the main character thinks. In the extract below, Haddon uses bold and italic font as part of the characterisation of his main character:

> Mr Jeavons, the psychologist at the school, once asked me why 4 red cars in a row made it a **Good Day**, and 3 red cars in a row made it a **Quite Good Day**, and 5 red cars in a row made it a **Super Good Day**, and why 4 yellow cars in a row made it **A Black Day**, which is a day when I don't speak to anyone and sit on my own reading books and don't eat my lunch and *Take No Risks*.
>
> (Haddon, 2004: 31)

Modern non-fiction texts make extensive use of a sophisticated interplay of the verbal and the visual, as Kress and van Leeuwen (1996) have outlined. Books for adults, such as the *Eyewitness* travel guides, frequently abandon both the notion of the page as the unit of communication and conventional left-to-right directionality. Information is often presented over a double-page spread, with key features, such as a map or a photograph, bridging the page divide. Verbal information is offered in a variety of ways, with small blocks of texts, labels, or lists around the central element. The reader can enter the reading of the page from any point and is not obliged to start at the top left. Contemporary science textbooks for schools have also fully embraced the affordances of using the page as a design space, and many publishers have 'a strong commitment to visual communication of scientific ideas' (Stylianidou et al., 2002) as well as the more conventional verbal communication.

The design of a web page offers even greater possibilities for transforming writing from unidirectional, black-and-white print with a linear message to a multimodal text, which can combine print with audio text, and make use of still or moving images. The way we read a web page is not the same as the way we read a novel, and hypertext allows us to jump backwards and forwards within a text, to other texts or multimodal features. We can lose our place in a book or a web page, but the way we get lost is very different!

Young writers are often very aware of, and enthusiastic about, incorporating visual design into their writing. Figure 4.1 shows three examples of writers of differing ability appropriating the visual. This class of eight-year-olds were preparing information leaflets for a museum dedicated to the Stone Age. One writer combines verbal patterning in 'See it, Want it, Get it' with a visual callout shape. Another writer combines the invitation to the Stone Age museum with a picture

Figure 4.1 Examples of 8-year-old writers using visual design

of the entrance, and anticipates that the reader will work out that 'S A' over the arch represents 'Stone Age'. The third writer integrates the verbal idea of time travel with the visual representation of time in the clock. These are unfinished pieces and they demonstrate that this kind of visual design can naturally be an organic part of the process of creating the text, not simply a presentational issue once the writing is complete.

Language shapers

Much attention has been paid to the visual and multimodal aspects of writing, and young readers' and writers' familiarity with it (Merchant, 2007; Walsh, 2007), largely because the advances in technology have generated new possibilities for writing in visual and multimodal domains. However, of equal importance is the verbal – the shaping and honing of language, like a piece of art, until it achieves the writer's aspirations for the writing. Philip Pullman describes this process as 'fooling about', and in extending the metaphor, recalls for us Rosen's image of language as putty, language which can be stretched, squashed, reshaped and transformed:

> It goes on to consist of fooling about with the stuff the world is made of: with sounds, and with shapes and colours, and with clay and paper and wood and metal, and with language. Fooling about, playing with it, pushing it this way and that, turning it sideways, painting it different colours, looking at it from the back, putting one thing on top of another, asking silly questions, mixing things up, making absurd comparisons, discovering unexpected similarities, making pretty patterns, and all the time saying 'Supposing . . . I wonder . . . What if . . . '
>
> (Pullman, 2005)

Pullman's description also reminds us of the importance of play and experimentation as a fundamental element of design. We need to ensure that we make writing classrooms safe places to play with language and to try things out: an overemphasis on either accuracy or achieving a quality piece of writing can limit young writers' willingness to experiment. There should be a place for writing that doesn't work, as attempting something new, or risky, is fundamental to learning about how to push the boundaries of language. Some of these attempts will fail. This is an important lesson for all writers, and learning how to critically evaluate an experimental piece of writing is a crucial writing skill. One primary classroom I know had a small raffia waste-paper bin on the desk, and children were allowed to throw away pieces of writing with which they were unhappy or dissatisfied, provided they explained their dissatisfaction. Creating enabling classrooms like this means being very clear about the distinction between writing which is being formally assessed for external purposes, such as the award of grades or levels, and workshop pieces which can be regarded as work-in-progress. Portfolios of half-written pieces, embryonic ideas for writing, or initial drafts help to support writers' conceptualisation of writing as a design activity, and language as something to be played with and shaped.

Playing with words

One design element of writing is developing awareness of the power of a word and word choice. Despite Romeo's insistence that a rose by any other name would smell as sweet, the words we choose to articulate an idea or describe an event are powerful tools for trying to influence the response of readers. Menu writers know this and exploit it to the full: consider the difference between 'fried chicken' and 'pan-fried Leversett chicken breast in a crisp tempura batter'. Menu writers are connoisseurs of the extended noun phrase par excellence! Naming and the use of nouns, for example, offers a myriad of possibilities. Commercially, the choice of name for a product is highly important for marketing purposes; schools changing their names are acutely conscious of the message they want the new name to convey; and naming in narrative is highly associative too. Calling your leading lady in a fairy tale a 'beautiful princess' or 'Chelsea' establishes entirely different expectations of how the story will unfold. In the opening paragraph of *Harry Potter and the Philosopher's Stone*, J. K. Rowling establishes that there is a family, comprising Mr and Mrs Dursley and their son, Dudley Dursley: with apologies to any readers called Dudley, the names do not suggest sympathetic characters we are going to like. This impression is strengthened by the knowledge that they live in Privet Avenue, the epitome of suburban ordinariness. And what image or associations are evoked by the name '*Skellig*' in David Almond's novel? But the power of words is not simply about nouns and narrative; in a persuasive argument, for example, the simple choice about whether to use 'should' or 'must' creates subtly different relationships with the reader.

In one study with 14-year-old students, we found that they were more likely to talk about word choices than any other design aspects of writing, both in responding to other people's writing and in talking about their own. The extract below is typical of these conversations, where the writer is able to identify choices which satisfy her as a writer:

Interviewer: Let's have a look at your fire one . . . tell me what choice, words and descriptions do you like?

Student: I like *heartless* and *acidic smoke* and *viciously burning down everything in its path* . . .

Interviewer: So you've got the fire viciously burning, you've got the atmosphere filled with acidic smoke, and the heartless fire, so why do you like those words?

Student: Because I think they describe, like, a fire really well, because fires do viciously burn down everything, and they are always quite heartless and they're always roaring and the smoke makes you choke . . . so it's quite acidic.

In many of the discussions about word choice, these writers reflected on why they wanted to make improvements to their existing selections. One writer wanted to 'choose a better adjective for the first line to make it clearer what's happening'; whilst another wanted to change 'dripped' to 'glooped' in order to make it 'less boring' and change 'shiny' to 'shining' to 'match the pattern of the other –ing words like clenching and pointing'. They are genuinely thinking about words and their effects.

However, there is a major caveat around this issue of word choice. Choosing words is about associations and connotations, about creating visual images, or establishing moods and tones. But many writers think word choice is exclusively about 'description' and that description is exclusively about adjectives. These are messages which students have learned from teachers. Both in primary and secondary teaching, there is a tendency to invite children to use more adjectives to add more description. I like to call this Rottweiler Syndrome: the habit of using a string of adjectives before the noun ('a large, brown, fierce, drooling dog') rather than making a more effective choice of noun ('a Rottweiler'). It is a tendency which is officially endorsed by materials circulated to schools. One guidance document (DfEE, 2001: 168) recommends encouraging primary writers to build up descriptions of nouns by using a series of adjectives, and offers these two examples:

> The small scrumptious slowly melting tomato pizza.
> My tiny appetising fiercely bubbling ham pizza.

The lesson appears to be that the list of adjectives improves the description, but there is no discussion of why or of what kind of text it is supposed to be. The danger is that it becomes just an exercise of thinking up adjectives which could plausibly precede the given noun, rather than anything to do with crafting or design. It is not evident, for example, what nuances are intended from the choice of *small* in one of these examples and *tiny* in the other.

But young writers learn this lesson. The 14-year-olds in our study repeatedly talked of adding more adjectives or adverbs and often gave examples which did not improve the writing but created a rather artificial, overdone style. In responding to a poem about a teacher's red pen where one line was 'I force you to see red', creating a pun through playing with the idea of literally seeing red ink on the page and the metaphorical notion of seeing red in anger, one student suggested that 'I would have put a word in front of red, like a blazing red or something' because 'it's more descriptive, so it's a blazing red it's not just a boring red, because there's so many different reds'. Not only does this ruin the pun but it also disrupts the rhythm of the line. When the interviewer probes this, the student acknowledges that the extra word 'would sort of muck up the way you read it'. This kind of thinking about adding in extra adjectives recurred in other interviews. One student explained that '"the grenades explode with shrapnel" was quite boring, so I put "the grenades exploded with deadly shrapnel"', whilst another argued that 'instead of just plain words like, "I was kicking my legs back and forth", you can say, "I was hastily moving my legs back and forth". The same tendency to encourage young writers to pepper their writing with numerous adjectives or adverbs was also found in primary classrooms, where one writer, for example, came up with the following, in response to a request for more description:

> Within minutes, Tom arrived at an old, knackered, broken bridge. Underneath were billions of deadly, poisonous, big, king cobras.

Sometimes it seems that students are learning the lesson that more adjectives improve writing, in spite of their own instincts as writers. In the interview extract below, the student repeats the notion, as did so many, that adding more adverbs and adjectives is a beneficial thing, and dutifully supplies examples of adjectives which could be added when asked to by the interviewer. But then the student challenges the assumption that this addition is successful and suggests that not using adjectives or adverbs can have a better effect:

Student: I could've used a couple more adverbs and adjectives . . . and made it longer.
Interviewer: Can you see anywhere particularly that you could put in a couple more adverbs and adjectives?
Student: 'Finishing the last of the *delicious* cheese fondue replied my French friend, and by now I should know my way around this, around this *gorgeous* town . . . ' but I think sometimes not having adjectives really works, and not having adverbs . . . sometimes it can make things sound so much better, but sometimes it makes it sound like you've tried too hard almost, a bit complicated.

Word choice as a design choice needs careful and sensitive teaching to avoid these kinds of misunderstandings and to encourage writers to take ownership of the choices they make, rather than following formulaic recommendations. Fostering committed discussions around the associations of words and the images or feelings they evoke, and whether these associations or images are those the writer is trying to achieve, support the development of the ability to make genuine design choices.

Playing with sentences and syntax

Another important aspect of writing as design is being able to exploit the possibilities of language at a syntactical and sentence level. Public and conservative views of grammar often appear to be wholly concerned with the grammatical correctness of a sentence, but fail to realise that whilst grammatical correctness may be necessary, it is not a sufficient condition for lively, engaging writing. Indeed, a grammatically accurate text can simultaneously be very dull and anodyne.

At a syntactical level, where you choose to position a syntactical unit can play a major role in signalling emphasis or creating a particular effect. Look at the opening three sentences of Dickens's *A Christmas Carol*:

> Marley was dead: to begin with. There is no doubt whatever about that. The register of his burial was signed by the clergyman, the clerk, the undertaker, and the chief mourner.

The first sentence begins with a short, simple main clause, which is direct and absolute – 'Marley was dead'. But it is followed by a colon and the non-finite clause 'to begin with', which creates a sense of ambiguity and undermines the certainty of the first statement. The second sentence reaffirms the opening statement. The third sentence evidences this confirmation by listing who has signed the death register. Here, by using the passive voice ('was signed') and thus making the register the subject of the sentence and the signatories the object, Dickens foregrounds the register as the key focus of this sentence, linking back to the 'no doubt' in the previous sentence, and is also able to create a feeling of weighty significance through the listing of signatories at the end of the sentence. Each of these sentences is finely crafted and designed.

Playing with the syntax of a sentence is rather like altering the rhythm of a piece of music; and helping young writers become aware of the rhythm of text is an important aspect of teaching writing as design. We need not just to read and see our writing, but also to listen to it and hear it. The rhythm of a piece of writing is influenced by sentence lengths and patterns, as well as by internal syntactical shaping. Writing which repeatedly uses subject-verb sentences of broadly similar length tends to sound flat and monotonous. Varying the sentence length, or using some form of repetitive pattern, is a strategy used by many writers to create textual rhythm. Sentence patterning is very evident in many books for young children and reflects a playfulness with language and ideas. Think of the repetitive structure of *Dear Zoo*, with its pattern of 'I wrote to the zoo to send me a pet. They sent me an . . . .' and its response of 'He was too . . . . I sent him back'; or *Each Peach, Pear, Plum*, with its combination of rhyme and the repeated line '*I spy . . .* ' introducing a new character and moving the narrative forwards. However, creative use of sentence length and patterning is also evident in writing for older children and adults. Below is the opening section of David Almond's novel *Secret Heart*:

> The tiger padded through the night. Joe Maloney smelt it, the hot, sour breath, the stench of its pelt. The odour crept through the streets, through his open window and into his dreams. He felt the animal wildness on his tongue, in his nostrils. The tiger moved as if it knew him, as if it was drawn to him. Joe heard its footpads on the stairs. He heard its long slow breath, the distant sighing in its lungs, the rattle in its throat. It came inside. It filled the bedroom. The huge head hung over him. The glittering cruel eyes stared into him. The hot tongue, harsh as sandpaper, licked his arm. The mouth was

wide open, the curved teeth were poised to close on him. He prepared to die. Then someone somewhere called:

'Tiger! Tiger! Tiger! Tiger!'

And it was gone.

(Almond, 2007: 1)

This brief extract is full of rich patterning. The short sentence at the beginning introduces readers to the principal focus of the opening, the tiger moving through the night. The very short sentence mid-paragraph ('It came inside') increases the tension of the proximity of the tiger, entering Joe's personal space. The final two lines, with the four repeated one-word sentences and the sudden short final sentence, 'And it was gone', create a sudden release of tension. Between these short sentences, there are more elaborated sentences, the earlier ones building up a sense of the tiger moving closer through space – through the streets, through the open window, into Joe's dreams, on the stairs. The later sentences pick up the physicality of the first few sentences and develop this into a very vivid sense of the tiger's physical threatening presence: its huge head, its glittering eyes, its hot tongue, its wide-open mouth. Four sentences in a row begin with a physical description of the tiger's head, evoking an intensely sensual experience of fear. Like Dickens's *A Christmas Carol*, this is writing which is designed with a writer's feel for language and its potentialities.

Janks argues that control of grammar allows us as writers to 'produce the nuances we need to realise the meaning potential that language affords us. What is selected from the range of lexical and grammatical options determines how this potential is realised' (2009: 130). In our study with 14-year-olds, one of our goals was to support young writers in becoming aware of these lexical and grammatical options and to encourage them to be confident about making their own choices and decisions. Teachers explored sentence patterning and syntactical variety in different types of texts, and also explored other design possibilities, such as whether to use first- or third-person voice, and which tense to use. All of these were introduced as choices at the writer's disposal, with no advocacy of any option as a better option than any other. This approach appears to have been very beneficial, particularly for able writers, as there was a strongly statistically significant improvement in writing attainment for this group when compared with the group who did not receive this kind of encouragement. In the interviews with the students, it is very clear that many of them were beginning to be able to articulate their design choices. One writer suggests that 'a little short sentence is better' if you are writing 'a really frightening story', implying an emerging awareness of how short sentences can be used to establish tension. Another writer has begun to grasp the possibilities of syntactical variation at the start of a sentence, even if she does not yet have the metalanguage to describe this precisely: she notes that she could 'change how some of the sentences start: "my mum", "my dad", "my sister" is a bit boring . . . change the words round.' One writer is clearly grappling with the idea of the omniscient narrator and what that allows the writer to do:

> I think first person and third person depends on what you're writing, but I usually try and write in the third person because it's easier to get in everything and details, and you can sort of show what everyone else is thinking without actually having to say it . . . When you're in third person and you're looking unseen you can say, for instance, someone rolls their eyes, you can think whatever has just happened is really, really stupid and you can kind of understand what they're talking about.'

Below, we can see how one writer reflects on a sentence change he has made in his draft to foreground the idea of panic.

'Help!' Frantic cries were coming from the village, the fire was blazing and blistering through the forest, animals crying, leaping, jumping, doing whatever they could to get away, but there's no escape, one by one they are swallowed back into the rampaging fire of doom. *Starting to panic, the villagers try to get away but there's no escape.*

> This one here I crossed out. It said 'The villagers are really starting to panic' and I changed it around and I put 'Starting to panic, the villagers try to get away'.

The designer's knife

An important element of any design process is evaluation, and in writing, research tells us that many novice writers find revision very hard to do well, largely because they lack confidence in evaluating their writing. Writers at both the primary and secondary ages are more likely to correct spelling or punctuation errors during revision than to make meaning-related changes. Where meaning-related changes are made they are most likely to be word-level changes, rather than any more fundamental revisions of the text. One finding of our studies investigating children's thinking about writing is that young writers tend to conceive of changing text during revision as largely about adding things (Myhill and Jones, 2007). In our recent study, when invited to consider how they would improve the piece they had written, this phenomenon was again very evident. I have already noted the tendency to want to add adjectives and adverbs to improve text, but writers also talked about adding: 'a little more detail'; 'another line'; 'a bit more description'; 'more to the beginning'; 'a few more paragraphs'; and 'more short sentences'. This seems to be predicated on a notion that more is inevitably better. But, of course, this is in stark contrast to the recommendations of professional writers (*The Guardian*, 2010), who are insistent on the need to cut in order to sharpen and hone the text:

> Cut like crazy. Less is more. I've often read manuscripts – including my own – where I've got to the beginning of, say, chapter two and have thought: 'This is where the novel should actually start.' A huge amount of information about character and backstory can be conveyed through small detail. The emotional attachment you feel to a scene or a chapter will fade as you move on to other stories. Be business-like about it.
>
> Sarah Waters

> Cut (perhaps that should be CUT): only by having *no* inessential words can every essential word be made to count.
>
> Diana Athill

> Editing is everything. Cut until you can cut no more. What is left often springs into life.
>
> Esther Freud

> First paragraphs can often be struck out. Are you performing a *haka*, or just shuffling your feet?
>
> Hilary Mantel

> Reread, rewrite, reread, rewrite. If it still doesn't work, throw it away. It's a nice feeling, and you don't want to be cluttered with the corpses of poems and stories which have everything in them except the life they need.
>
> Helen Dunmore

Taking the designer's knife to your writing is a painful process for all writers, but perhaps especially so for young writers for whom the act of generating the text is such an effort, and whose skills of evaluation are still developing. Teaching them to be more confident about cutting and honing writing is an important aspect of a pedagogy of writing as design; but equally important is ensuring that the messages we communicate to students during writing lessons are not overly focused on textual additions.

Implicit and explicit design

This chapter has explored the idea of writing as design and advocates the teaching of writing as a design process. Whilst teaching is always a conscious and explicit process, designing writing is both implicit and explicit. Experienced writers do not explicitly analyse each sentence they write to consider its syntax, or deliberate over every word; often words, images, phrases and structures emerge naturally through immersion and engagement in the process of writing. At other times, just writing a paragraph can be a struggle, and, as Coleridge recalled, 'every line, every phrase, may pass the ordeal of deliberation and deliberate choice' (1817: 485). Revision, however, is always an explicit process and, as noted above, is an aspect of writing which many young writers find difficult. Teaching writing as design needs to take account of the interrelationship between explicit and implicit decision-making. Children who are keen readers and have rich experiences of engaging with books are developing implicit knowledge about design choices which influence their writing and their metalinguistic awareness of the various ways in which a piece of writing can be shaped and structured. Teachers who make the most of reading opportunities to discuss the author's craft and to explore how writers have expressed their ideas are supporting the development of explicit metalinguistic awareness.

Interviewing young writers about their decisions and choices in writing proved an illuminating strategy for capturing their thinking about writing, and at the same time it gave students a chance to be explicit about their design. The teaching had deliberately created many opportunities for peer discussion or whole class discussion of choices and effects, which included some heated debates about choices that some students preferred whilst others disliked them. Few children had difficulty engaging in interview conversations about their writing, but what is evident, including in some of the quotations above, is that these writers are still developing the ability to articulate their choices. Being able to use metalanguage would certainly make some of the reasoning more precise. Much more important, however, would be to develop students' confidence in explaining not just what choices they have made, but also why they have made them.

Conclusion

Teaching writing as design, then, is about developing repertoires of possibility and awareness of choices available. It is first and foremost concerned with learning about writing through play and experimentation, through treating language as putty with infinite potential for creation and re-creation. It combines the explicit development of sensitivity to the potentialities of language with the nurturing of classroom writing communities, which can be the seedbed of implicit learning through engagement and experience. Being a successful writer is about feeing motivated to express an idea and knowing how best to do that. Or, as Orwell reminds us, writing can be reduced to a meaningless exercise:

> Good prose is like a windowpane. I cannot say with certainty which of my motives are the strongest, but I know which of them deserve to be followed. And looking back through my work, I see that it is invariably where I lacked a political purpose that I wrote lifeless books and was betrayed into purple passages, sentences without meaning, decorative adjectives and humbug generally.
> (Orwell, 1946: 11)

Racing through the streets that night
He never meant a lift.
As we sped around the corner, BANG,
He never meant a lift.
Shouting, screaming, lots of noise
He never meant a lift.
I tasted blood and alcohol,
He never meant a lift.
We'd all seen the blue lights flashing,
He never meant a lift.
The worried look upon mark's face,
He never meant a lift.
Flames, I think, but blurred and double,
He never meant a lift.
Too much light, far too bright,
He never meant a lift.
The fire burns, unbearable pain,
He never meant a lift.
I touch my flesh wounds, sore and wet,
He never meant a lift
Tasting smoke and smelling flesh,
He never meant a lift.
I never will forget that thought,
He never meant a lift.

I wrote this poem at school after we had read a play called 'Face'. The main character, Martin, and his best friend, Mark, had been to a night club. On their way home, the boys were offered a lift by two people they knew. They got in but the car turned out to be stolen and the driver had no intention of taking them home. The car was crashed. We had to do a presentation on what Martin would have seen, heard, tasted, smelt, touched and felt.

I thought that repeating the line 'He never meant a lift' gives an idea of how guilty and regretful Martin would have felt.

I like the line 'the fire burns, unbearable pain' because it tells the reader about what is happening and how Martin was affected by that.

I feel that using the word 'flesh' twice in the last few lines didn't work as well as I hoped because it is a bit repetitive. However, I really like the last two lines and the way they affect the pace.

Overall, I am really pleased with this poem.

Annabel – student

Chapter 5

Autonomy and choice

Introduction

As we compose, we make choices and select from among the options available to us in response to our purpose and audience. As you work on an assignment as part of a course, for example, you are no doubt conscious of who is going to read and mark it, what the question requires, what you think you are going to say and how you might most effectively communicate this. Whilst the form and the Harvard referencing are probably non-negotiables, alongside perhaps the font size and pagination, you will still be making decisions about content, tone and style, and will still have to find the words to convey your understanding, critically reviewing others' arguments in order to shape your own. In other less formal situations, when sending a card of congratulations to a friend, for example, you may feel free to be more playful, adding personal notes, drawings or additional exclamation marks to convey your message.

How we exercise our rights as writers varies according to the context and our perceived degree of freedom and independence. As Dyson (1997: 166) observes, 'for children, as for adults, freedom is a verb, a becoming; it is experienced as an expanded sense of agency, of possibility for choice and action'. As teachers we have a critical role to play in nurturing both the autonomy of young writers and their ability to make wise choices, choices which relate to the content, audience, purpose and form of their writing. We need to offer freedom alongside form, and space and time for exploration and innovation, as well as direct teaching and scaffolded activities. If we help the young consider their intentions as writers and designers, encourage them to make choices and to take responsibility for their decisions, we will be fostering increased ownership and authorial agency and will enrich their satisfaction and engagement in the process. This chapter considers these issues and examines strategies for supporting young people's choice, independence, control and ownership in writing

Young people's attitudes to writing

Thirty years ago, research documenting young writers' perceptions of writing revealed that they predominantly viewed it as a product-oriented activity undertaken for the teacher, which encompassed learning about a number of technical skills, such as spelling and punctuation (NWP, 1990; Wray, 1993). This focus on the transcriptional elements has also been noted in later studies, which suggest that young people may be 'playing the game called writing' with little sense of themselves as writers (Grainger et al., 2003b; Cremin et al., 2007). Rather, they may be engaged in performing a schooled version of artificial writing, which has little connection to the real world in which they live. When asked 'What goes through your head when your teacher says "Now we are going to do some writing?", a small but disturbing proportion of the 10–11-year-olds expressed a degree of disaffection and disengagement (Grainger et al., 2002, 2003b). They commented, for example: 'I don't have a view about writing; I just do it when she says so'; 'I don't think about it, I just get on with it'; 'There's nothing I like, nothing I dislike, I just do it'; and 'More writing? Who cares?'. In the follow-up interviews, most reflected little sense of their own volition in the processes of teaching and learning writing, and appeared to view themselves somewhat passively as receivers and producers of written texts for school, not creators and designers of their own.

Some have suggested that the high profile ascribed to writing and the incessant focus on tests and targets has generated such disaffection and lack of interest in writing (Hilton, 2001; Wyse et al., 2007). In a recent survey by the National Literacy Trust (NLT), more than half of the three thousand 8- to 14-year-olds who took part viewed writing with a degree of ambivalence and expressed the view that they could not see the point in it. Negative attitudes to writing were particularly marked in the 11–14 range (Clark and Dugdale, 2009). Boys consistently said they did not enjoy writing and nearly half of those surveyed reported that they were not very good writers, citing their inability to write neatly, spell or punctuate well. Such depressing attitudes, the predominance of skills and low self-esteem should cause us considerable concern, although it may be that the boys were relying on very limited school-based views of what writing is and thus judging themselves too harshly as writers. In the Pew Internet study in the United States (Lenhart et al., 2008), the picture was somewhat different, as 93 per cent of the young people reported writing for pleasure – although this was only if 'electronic' texts were included, and 60 per cent of those same young people did not actually consider electronic texts, such as blogs, social networking sites and instant messaging, as writing. As we explored in Chapter 4, it is important to consider what we perceive as writing and work towards a wider understanding of the multimodal nature of writing in the twenty-first century. Young designers need help with making choices, not only in relation to words and visuals, but also in relation to responding to a writing brief, or creating their own, the purpose, audience and content of which they need the opportunity to choose and shape for themselves.

Young people's views about choice

Writers' choices are always influenced by audience and purpose(interpersonal choices), by content issues (ideational choices) and by their knowledge of texts and their affordances (textual choices), as well as by their identities as writers. Young writers need opportunities to make such choices. Our research shows that they are less keen on writing when tasks are entirely set and framed by their teachers and the curriculum. In particular, they dislike imposed content, always having to follow a set theme or genre, writing to a specific title, timed writing, and completing worksheets in which there is no choice at all. Conversely, both primary and secondary writers in our work indicate that they value and enjoy writing more when they are in a position to exert a sense of their own authorial agency and ownership (Grainger et al., 2005; Myhill, 2005). The older primary writers, in particular, desired more independence and increased imaginative involvement in their writing; many also voiced a marked pleasure in narrative writing:

- I like making stories up as I'm in control and can make anything happen.
- I like it when I can use my own ideas and don't have to imitate other stuff.
- I like writing stories from scratch, then they're really mine.
- Making up my own fantasy worlds and inventing characters who live there is the best kind of writing for me.

As the authors of their own stories, these learners valued the opportunityto shape them in their own way and make their own decision about the events and people within their tales. Their comments suggest they value creating and inventing and the freedom which imaginative-world-making offers, perhaps in a manner similar to many computer games, which allow young players to create their own characters, select their own settings, and create and respond to scenarios as they unfold.

Teenagers, too, share many of these perspectives on writing. When asked what kind of writing they enjoyed, there were a variety of responses, reflecting differing tastes and dispositions. Some enjoyed writing argument, for example, whereas others enjoyed writing stories (Myhill, 2001). However, autonomy and choice were key factors influencing both of these preferences. There was a distinct dislike of writing which was too restricted, particularly writing in curriculum subjects outside English, because the topic of writing was already predetermined:

- I don't like writing history essays, I prefer English essays. History seems more to write about.
- I like stories and poems, but if it's work I don't like it . . . You can use your imagination and write whatever you want. With work you have to write what they say to write.
- If I was writing what I thought then it would be OK, because then I'd be writing about what I think and not what the teacher wanted me to write.

- I find it [writing] relaxing . . . well, it depends what you're writing about, but especially in English, I love writing inEnglish . . . . But if it's, like, an essay on rocks or something boring then my head will just go blank and I don't know what to write.
- There's no, like, freedom. You've got to write, like, facts.

The desire for freedom expressed in these responses also seems to account for many writers' expressed preference for writing stories, because narrative offers the possibility of following your own interests and directions. One girl liked creating characters in narrative 'because then you can make them do anything you want'; for others, the freedom to create new worlds and engage in imaginative thinking were important in shaping their enjoyment as writers:

- I don't mind writing when I'm using my imagination.
- I enjoy creating a whole story of a whole different world.
- I like writing stories . . . where I can do my own ideas.

Even those writers who preferred argument often explained that preference in terms of being able to develop and express their own opinions, using the writing as a vehicle for addressing ideas and viewpoints that were important to them:

- I really like expressing my opinions.
- I like putting my views and what I believe.
- I quite like writing my own opinion . . . getting my opinion across.
- Arguing you can put your own opinion across and I find that a lot easier . . . . Arguing is more personal.
- In speeches you just write about what you believe in and give reasons for your opinions and I try to get my opinion across and change people's minds about something.
- I quite like argument writing, because you can put a bit of feeling into it as well, especially if it's something you feel strongly about.

This growing interest in using writing to communicate personal viewpoints is perhaps an indicator of the teenager's emerging identity as an active citizen moving towards adulthood. It is also a salutary reminder that autonomy is not simply about the classically 'creative' genres of narrative or poetry, but embraces all writing. These writers want to write for a purpose, be that creating imaginative worlds or crafting a structured argument expressing their views – the common denominator is freedom.

Teachers, too, in our studies have highlighted the pleasure they find in writing for and about themselves, and in exerting the right to muse on possibilities and make their own choices, many expressed satisfaction in writing about their own lives and reflecting on people and places of significance to them:

I loved my beginning – when I did the opening paragraph, I thought: 'I like that.' I just liked it, it brought tears to me eyes – it took me back in time. And I could immediately hear my Mother and Brian's mother yelling at us, 'Get out of the gutter!' – because we were always in the gutter. So that's where it starts – in the gutter.

Writing about my family has brought folk back from the past, helped me meet them again. It's enriched my memories too, if you'd said you have to write about them I wouldn't have wanted to, but given the choice I found I gravitated back to my childhood, I've explored the fabric of my memories and enjoyed almost every minute.

The most commonly mentioned form of writing in the teachers' memories across several of our studies, regardless of their perceptions of the experience, was autobiographical writing (Grainger 2005b; Cremin, 2006). This is perhaps indicative of the high profile afforded this in their own schooling or because such writing allows the writer to make connections, revisit events and gain perspective.

Studies with preschoolers also suggest that they seek to pursue their own interests through writing and that these frame how they approach writing events and the topics they select to examine and explore (Kress, 1997). These topics and the materials they engage with emerge from their social and cultural experiences and home and community practices, as Rowe (2008) and Rowe and Nietzel (2010) have shown. Their work with preschoolers also demonstrates the agency and intentionality of young sign makers, who, as Kress also recognises, 'act energetically, intelligently, perceptively, out of theirinterest, innovatively making for themselves their means of communication and representation' (Kress, 1997: 113).

Whose writing is it anyway?

Without a degree of ownership, authorial agency or a sense of connection to their writing, young writers are less likely to be truly engaged or motivated, and this will have consequences for their attitudes to writing and their development as writers. Extrinsically motivated writers are likely to write to satisfy the demands of others – writing for recognition, for grades or for competitions, and writing to meet their teachers' or their parents' expectations for example. In contrast, writers who are intrinsically motivated are more likely to be writing for their own pleasure and satisfaction; and as such may write more frequently in recreational contexts and enjoy writing more.However,the relationship between intrinsic and extrinsic motivation is complex and young people are likely to write for their own pleasure *and* be obliged to write for others' purposes in school. There are parallels with reading, since, as Woods (2001) comments, what you read and the satisfaction you gain through reading can make a significant difference to your desire to read, although, as he also observes, 'it must be reading you do for yourself, at your own pace, in your own way, and that has a bearing on your own background, interests, values, beliefs and aspirations' (ibid.:74). Similarly, writers need to be encouraged and supported in writing for themselves, in selecting themes and subjects, forms and modes which suit their purposes, and they need to be enabled to compose at their own pace and in conditions which they find conducive.

In Sharon Creech's (2001) stunning prose poem published as the book *Love That Dog*, she explores one boy's perspectives about studying and writing poetry in school, written as if he is in dialogue with his teacher. Creech voices the boy's lack of interest in poetry, his fear of his writing being read aloud or displayed for others to read, and his discomfort around being obliged to write about imposed topics, which, whilst they align with the given curriculum, either have too little relevance or too much emotional connection for him. As he notes wryly at one point, he doesn't have any pets and so cannot write about one, and, although he used to have one, he doesn't want to write about it. Tensions between private and public writing can surface in our classrooms if we expect children to commit to paper on subjects which, with the best of curriculum intentions, we always prescribe.

Whilst we are responsible for offering writing instruction that increases writers' knowledge about written language, and enhances their skills and metalinguistic awareness, we are also responsible for supporting the development of authorial agency and finding ways to motivate and engage young authors; prompting their desire to write and enhancing their pleasure and independence as writers. Reading for pleasure and developing independence as a reader has experienced a renaissance in England recently, yet there is comparatively little professional discussion about writing for pleasure or fostering young people's independence as writers. If the writing classroom is predominantly teacher controlled, then young writers will develop little sense of what they are doing, or why, and will have little sense of their own agency as authors. Yet evidence suggest that teachers do not tend to offer much choice in writing, rather they let the specified learning outcomes dominate the school writing agenda (Grainger et al., 2005; Fisher, 2006).Set schemes of work and the pressure of internal and external assessments may further reduce the degree of choice offered.

This issue of a lack of opportunity for developing independence and choice has been a concern expressed by Ofsted over the years. In 2002 it noted that in underperforming schools, young people have 'little notion of themselves as writers in control of the process, rather writing is seen as performing, the content, audience and purpose of which has been determined externally rather than internally' (2002: 146). More recently commenting:

> When teaching writing, teachers tended to dictate both the form and context of the work, such as instructing pupils about the features of narrative writing in a particular genre and then closely structuring the required response. They therefore missed the opportunity to encourage independence. Yet pupils, especially boys, responded more enthusiastically when they were given some choice about the topic.
>
> (Ofsted, 2009:18)

However, it is not enough for writers to be occasionally allowed to choose their topics. They also regularly need to be offered the chance to select their audience, purpose and form, since if they become too dependent on the required learning outcomes, their freedom and voice as writers will be constrained. Conversely, it is not always desirable or possible for young writers to make all their own choices, as they need to become acquainted with written conventions in order to control them and to realise their intentions in a piece of writing. It is a real challenge 'to balance the potentially opposing demands of creativity and correctness; prescription and individuality' (Fisher, 2006: 197). Though this is achieved in some schools, as Walsh (2007) shows in his study of young people as web designers, in others, a deep disconnection between the worlds of home and school remains, and writing is seen as school focused and somewhat irrelevant (Hall and Thomson, 2005).

As writers we are never entirely free to choose: our words are always framed by our audience and purpose, our knowledge, experience and resources and the contexts in which we write. Furthermore, writing is part of larger social and political contexts, 'an act of self-definition' (Rowe, 2003:264). Recently, for example, I was asked to compose a response to the new National Curriculum remit, which, whilst a reasonable request,was a somewhat rhetorical one and certainly a time-limited task. My summary, in which I was expected to critically evaluate the remit and raise questions for debate, would be available to others, so whilst the content and views expressed were mine (influenced, of course, by my stance, my reading, experience, conversations and email discussions with others), the audience, purpose, and the task itself were all externally imposed and set within the wider context of my work. To write the response I had to make a number of authorial decisions, some of which were at the level of the text, including, for example: which of the many contradictions in the document to highlight; how to communicate my views most clearly; whether bullet points or subheads were more suitable; what was the most appropriate tone, and so forth. At home later that same day, I chose to add to my weekly diary. After a particularly heated row with my daughter, I found myself unusually carefully and hesitantly choosing my words, conscious that if they were read, even in the distant future, they might be misunderstood and taken as a permanent position, not an expression of momentary frustration. My language choices, even in my private diary, were constrained by the possibility of a future, unknown readership, again highlighting writing as social ideological practice.

Developing authorial agency and ownership

As we discussed in Chapter 1, writing is not just a cognitive process. From the earliest years, young writers learn ways of making meaning through drawing and print, according to the culturally situated literacy practices they take part in and experience at home, in the community and in school. In these different contexts, they exercise different forms of agency as writers, variously accepting, resisting and rejecting as well as transforming their practices and positions around texts. Dyson's research (1993, 1997, 2001) highlights the shaping forces of the official and unofficial worlds of childhood on young people's writing and reveals how the young both appropriate cultural materials and flexibly recontextualise texts in ways that demonstrate their agency as authors. It also shows the influence of peer relationships and how, whilst often placed as apprentices of the official textual agenda, they remain playful intentional beings in the writing classroom, moving across social, symbolic and ideological boundaries.

In school, teachers can seek to foster the authorial agency of the young, nurturing a sense of ownership and independence through, for example, recognising and validating their writing beyond school; increasing the real-world relevance and use of writing; creating more space and time for writing that is co-created and followed through to 'publication' and establishing regular opportunities for choice. They can capitalise on genuine reasons for writing and seek out other audiences beyond the learners' peers and themselves as teachers – for example, family and community members, professional writers, local politicians, charities and societies, as well as visitors. Furthermore, teachers can engage young people in local and national issues, in voicing their views through writing to newspapers and local magazines, as well as creating individual, class and school publications (e.g. newspapers, newsletters, magazines, anthologies, web pages, PowerPoint presentations, brochures, books). In enabling young writers to follow through and make public their work, a sense of responsibility for it is likely to develop, particularly if a response is expected and sought. Other opportunities which can offer increased agency to the youngest writers include: well resourced writing tables, role-play areas in which writing can be modelled and is often child-initiated, and the use of fictional toy characters who can be written to and who always write back!

Additionally, professional writers can help young authors explore issues of agency and ownership through discussing their own desire to write, their fascination for different subjects and their urge to explore and create. This can be coupled with consideration of the wider cultural context, the challenge of getting published, the expectations of publishers and the need to work with others, such as editors, web managers or illustrators for example. Exploring the tensions, dilemmas and compromises involved in such work can be useful, as can discussing the ramifications of being commissioned to write texts for particular purposes; such 'writing to order' may stultify some writers, whilst others live their professional lives engaged in such practice. Bakhtin (1981:144) argues that whilst novelists are relatively free to select from the 'voice strewn landscape', most authors' aesthetic intentions are compromised by having to sculpt a piece of writing in a particular form. Through working with professional writers who write in the workplace, this issue can be examined as part of an exploration of authorial agency. Journalists, for example, may be assigned to particular stories and required to deliver articles for particular papers (and readerships) on specified subjects in set time periods. Their agency in such contexts is likely to be compromised, although this will not necessarily influence their pleasure and satisfaction in developing their own angle and asserting their ownership of the article. Exploring the audiences which professional writers and their publishers choose to target, and the reasons for these choices, can also be interesting in relation to their authorial agency; some will acknowledge they find this problematic. As poet Tony Mitton (2010) observes: 'I don't write for schools, I write for myself and the children and their parents – but my books go into teachers' hands to mediate.' As we highlight in Chapters 8 and 9, working alongside a range of professional writers, who assert their need for space and time to compose and who are prepared to discuss their perceived rights and sense of agency and ownership as writers, can be a valuable opportunity for young writers.

Out-of-school writing

In the world beyond school, young people often write for and about themselves, so exploring learners' everyday literacy lives, their routines, practices and preferences as writers and designers can help us recognise the diversity of their culturally situated writing practices, and acknowledge their agency in these out-of-school contexts. In one of our studies, teachers from eight primary schools collected 310 children's perception surveys about writing (Grainger et al., 2006) and followed some of these up with interviews. They were astounded at the breadth of writing being undertaken out of school and acknowledged that they had tended to assume that children hardly ever wrote at home, except for homework. But as the results for the children aged 7–8 and 10–11 (ibid.) indicate, considerable diversity is evident. With increased access to mobile technologies, it is likely that such self-generated lists would look very different today, although the extent to which such home writing is recognised or built on in school may not differ so markedly. Children's 'virtual school bags', as Thomson (2002:2) argues, are full of different interests, narratives, knowledge and understanding which will be reflected in their out-of-school writing; but such knowledge is not always recognised, counted as valid or valued in class. Many today will be involved in texting, tweeting, adding to their Facebook profiles, emailing and blogging, as well as making notes and lists, doodling and drawing, writing stories and song lyrics and much more besides.

In another project, through carrying out a case study of four children's out-of-school writing, we found that the diverse texts they produced offered them considerable satisfaction and were highly purposeful (Earl and Grainger, 2007). In tune with Burnett and Myers'(2002) findings, we found their texts were useful organisationally, valuable as a way of maintaining and reinforcing relationships, and constituted a rich resource for learning. Most of the extended texts they composed, on paper and on screen, were also forms of identity exploration and connected to salient events and people in their lives, although these were often fictionalised. Another frequent theme was the use of toys, television and computer games as cultural resources for identity exploration. For example, Hattie, aged nine, spent several months writing a series of stories and drawing pictures which connected to her baby sister's exploits; some were real, whilst others were imagined, many made use of ideas from Spy Kids films and Nintendo games. In most, Hattie played a role either as herself or as a fictional older brother for example. Through these tales, which she chose to compose in her own time at home, Hattie appeared to be considering the possible identity options available to her in relation to her new baby sister. In demonstrating the transformational potential of language and making multiple connections to popular cultural texts, Hattie was exerting her agency as an author. She was clear this was not the same as school writing, since in her view the latter was 'mostly focused on the SATs' and 'the kinds of things you need to include to get a level 5'. All the case study children were emphatic about the differences between writing at home and at school; they tended to see school writing as 'work' which had been assigned and home writing as more volitional, over which they had more control. Their views, expressed in different interviews, indicate this perspective:

- Writing is not about what you are forced to do, but it's about what you really, really want to do. That's what I like about writing a lot – you just write down all your stuff and even your feelings in some of them.
- Well I don't like doing homework at home because that's something you have to do and it's like a job you have to do. But writing you want to do at home that's different.
- I like doing literacy and we're doing persuasive and balanced arguments and I like writing them, that's normally for work, but normally at home I like to free myself a bit and I do what I want.
- Writing at home, that's for me – my own writing.

The gap between the authorised writing curriculum in school and the children's text production at home was however partly bridged for these youngsters by the practice of offering 'writing journals'. In these personally covered and often precious books, they made more of their own choices as writers. Their journals were not marked by their teachers, and as some travelled between home and school, the journals represented an in-between literacy practice – a kind of third space in which, in their drawing and writing, they made use of both home and school literacies (Pahl and Rowsell, 2005).

Exerting choice in journal writing

Writing journals are seen by many as a practice which foregrounds authorial agency and allow writers to draw on their cultural capital from home (Bearne, 2003; Graham and Johnson, 2003; Grainger et al., 2005). In such journals, young people can write about subjects which matter to them, play with ideas, follow some through, abandon others and experiment with the production of texts which might not, in the course of 'normal' classroom practice, ever be suggested or required by their teachers. For example, over the course of one term, Zak, aged ten, worked on the following texts in his bulging journal with commitment and interest:

- A list of favourite pop songs
- Character 'studies' in preparation for a story – listing age, date of birth, weight, height
- Lists of possible character names for a story
- Three stories focused on the pop world, football,and animals
- A poem on Zombies
- A fact file on Tottenham Hotspur
- A set of designs for football kits
- Reviews of football matches
- Newspaper articles aboutplayers being transferred
- Drawings of football players in action with labels
- Football score summaries
- A list of Premier League fixtures
- A poem on loneliness
- Lists of best friends and personal belongings
- Christmas list
- Quiz questions about the world (with a friend)
- Sales information about a new Nokia mobile phone
- A review of the film *Avatar*
- A rap about school food
- Song lyrics about life

Through journal time, which complemented writing instruction time in his classroom, Zak appeared to experience writing as a meaningful activity. He was writing for himself and for his friends about issues of common interest;his texts operated as 'tools of identity' (Holland et al., 2001). Although he was more committed to and pleased with some pieces of this writing than others, he tended to write at greater length and with more concentration in this context than in literacy lessons, and was rightly proud of his journal, which was covered in a collage-like manner with pictures of his football heroes. Like several of his friends, Zak was experimenting with writing long stories in instalments and sometimes took his journal home to extend what he had begun. In contrast, nine-year-old Kiera much more frequently chose to write about members of her extended family, although make-up, friendships lists and fictional stories also figured in her choices. She had always struggled with writing, was dyslexic, wrote very little and worried about spellings, but her attitude towards writing shifted significantly when offered more choice and privacy in this context where her work was not marked and her spellings not commented on. Over time she shared some pieces with her teacher and chose to read extracts to the class, including the account of her older brother's entry into the cadets (see Figure 5.1) in which she reflects proudly on his achievements.

Journals or notebooks are often popular with young writers, particularly when teachers foreground ownership and the opportunities they provide for students to exercise their rights as writers. This may involve them in experimenting and playing around with issues that matter to them, abandoning one piece and starting another, retaining their right to privacy as well as their right to share, writing alongside chosen others and keeping lists of possible future topics and ideas. In offering writers' notebooks and providing dedicated time for young people to work in them, teachers shift some of the responsibility for writing to the writers; this often fosters increased commitment and may help seed new possibilities for writing. As novelist Diane Samuels (2010) notes in relation to her journal writing practice, 'This is the raw material that feeds a developing piece of work, like gathering clay from the riverbed. It also serves as regular practice to keep tuned.' Diane argues that the gap between writing in schools and writing as a profession can, in part, be bridged by offering journals, or writers' notebooks, as she calls them:

> What I offer as a writer is a model of creative practice based on the use not of exercise books but of writers' notebooks. These have brightly coloured covers and are never scrutinised or marked. Every child from Year 2 to Year 6 receives one and I work with each year group for half a term, more if necessary. In his or her notebook the emerging young writer is encouraged regularly to practise the method of free writing without stopping to liberate whatever voice wants to speak, experiment, splurge, and play. In order to keep writing, they can abandon all concern for correct spelling and punctuation, make no corrections, avoid crossing out. There is an invitation to write nonsense, and if it happens to make sense, then that'll do just as well. Trust that intuition. The children flex their writing muscles regularly and find authentic voice. Most importantly they develop true confidence and flexibility of expression.
>
> (Diane Samuels, 2010)

Many professional writers attest to keeping notebooks or journals which often capture possibilities or observations that might be used later. Young writers, too, may find that keeping a section of their journal as a notebook, or a separate notebook, can represent a rich resource if they add quotes from books, notes of films, cuttings from newspapers, glimmers of ideas, plots, visuals, or observations. They may also map out options or create collages, project briefs or outline plans, as web designers do for example. Such notebooks encourage observation, an awareness of possibilities and an alertness to the unexpected, all of which may feed into their writing. Kevin Crossley Holland observes that he uses notebooks for 'keeping brief impressions of all sorts. Scraps of conversation, pressed wildflowers. Lists of things to do' (quoted in Gamble, 2008:22). David Almond, in his prequel to *Skellig*, *My Name is Mina*, gives his protagonist Mina a journal. When she takes it up for the first time, she ponders:

My big brother has become a Curdet and he is gowing to go to war when he is alood to go.

When he was being tested he got A * for showting and for target! The rest he got a bit below but he still passed sowe he was happy. He is sweet.

On Sunday he had to get his unforme and he was gowing to meet Prince Chils but he had to do some think. So he is gowing to meet him on 30th march so he is very very exsited!

Evry whun was so kind like the bus driver let him go on the bus for free and all the old ladeys whur smiling and trying to talk to him. I am pleesed for him.

Figure 5.1 One of Kiera's journal entries

Then what shall I write? I can't just write that this happened then this happened then this happened to boring infinitum, I'll let my journal grow just like the mind does, just like a tree or a beast does, just like life does. Why should a book tell a tale in a dull straight line?

Words should wander and wander. They should fly like owls and flicker like bats and slip like cats, they should murmur and scream and dance and sing.

Sometimes there should be no words at all.

Just silence.

Just clean white space.

(David Almond, 2010: 11–12)

Mina mostly writes her journal in the privacy of her bedroom or in the safety of her favourite tree, and in a parallel manner the environment of the classroom needs to be considered if journal writing time is to be the young people's own time to write. If we are seeking to foster ownership and engagement in writing, we need to explore what conditions are conducive to writing. An informal atmosphere may assist some writers who, like Sally Nicholls (quoted in Gamble, 2008: 13), may wish to play music to 'block out the rest of the world', although others, more in alignment with Michael Morpurgo's practice, may wish for silence; he notes 'I don't like noise around me when I'm trying to weave a story inside my head' (Fox, 2004: 241). Likewise, Kevin Crossley-Holland (ibid., 2008: 14) prefers peace, as he believes 'the rhythms and pitch work against the music of the language I hear in my head'. Discussing the young writers' practices, preferences and habits around writing can be revealing, although this may depend on the nature and challenge of the writing, and compromises will have to be borne.

Some may want to work with others on their journal writing, so they can seize the initiative and collaborate over the production of a single text or multiple articles for a magazine or website for example. Teachers can encourage such self-directed learning in other contexts too if they foreground relevance, ownership, control and innovation, and offer open-ended activities (Jeffrey and Woods, 2003). As we argue in Chapter 2, writing is not a solitary activity and through working with others on production briefs and in response to new challenges, groups of young writers can come together to invest time and energy, take collective responsibility, and reposition themselves as expert text producers in different contexts (Dyson, 1997; Merchant, 2003; Walsh, 2007).

Conclusion

Students can feel distanced from the act of writing if teachers retain too strong a grasp on the curriculum reins and profile writing instruction at the expense of developing the desire, commitment, ownership and agency of young writers. A shift in the locus of control is needed to foster an enhanced sense of autonomy and authorship. Space, time and choice need to be made available to help students exercise their right to write about what is meaningful to them in literacy and across the curriculum. As teachers we cannot offer choice in writing all the time, but we can negotiate activities and take responsibility for developing their pleasure and independence as writers. In widening our own conceptions of writing and being a writer in the twenty-first century and in documenting young writers' practices beyond the school, we can blur the boundaries between writing at home and at school; creating a third space where young writers make connections and draw on artefacts, life narratives and resources from both contexts and developing positive identities as writers in the process. In this way and through increasing the real-world relevance of writing in school, we can foster a growing sense of young people's agency as text creators and meaning-makers.

Writing has never been my strong point so therefore I always feel that I don't really want to write so usually I don't look forward to having to write an essay or even an imaginative fiction task. Although I don't enjoy it and aren't particularly good at writing I still try my best whenever we have to write essays in English using quotes to back up points and structure answers well to get my point across. I think that my teachers help me a lot with writing because thy show me examples of how to write and always give me pointers to help me write to my best ability which is useful because I know how important it is to get a good grade in English as it is a main subject which without it you wouldn't get too far. Once I get into a writing task if I understand it and I have had helpful input I do seem to enjoy writing because I feel successful at it and I know without being able to write I wouldn't be as successful through life at structuring letters to anybody such as employers or a complaint letter. In the future I expect I will use writing and enjoy it more because I can sense the reason for it however at the minute I don't see the purpose as I don't plan to continue English though college or university so why should I do it now?

I think a lot of teenage boys feel this way because it seems almost pointless. I think I used to enjoy writing more when I was in primary school because it was more fun rather than having to do it so I could see the enjoyment whereas now we are forced to write as it is a good base for all learning being able to write essays and reports for all subject areas you have to structure writing well with good English if you are looking to get a decent mark you have to learn how to write well. Personally I don't find anything in particular hard about writing I just generally find it hard I cant explain why but It seems as though you either have a natural knack at writing or you don't and its hard to learn how to unless you have some natural talent for writing. All writing is hard no specific type of writing but the hardest for me is fictional because as I am a talented science and mathematics student my mind is more practical and I can see a definitive answer to things whereas I find it hard in English not having a definitive answer so writing isn't easy to so when my mind wants a definitive answer. I would like to be a good writer and enjoy it but I'm not and I don't so I will just have to hope i get through with my other strengths.

Benjamin – student

Chapter 6

The role of metacognition in writing

Introduction: what is metacognition?

Metacognition, at its simplest, can be defined as thinking about one's thinking. It is one level beyond the act of thinking itself as it stands outside it, looking in, and reflecting on it. So if you are tackling a difficult mathematical calculation and are trying to remember what 6 x 9 is, that is an act of thinking; but if you are mentally noting to yourself that you always have problems with the 9 times table, then that is an act of metacognition. You are thinking about your thinking. Flavell (1976) is commonly given credit for developing the concept of metacognition. He describes it thus: 'Metacognition refers to one's knowledge concerning one's own cognitive processes or anything related to them, e.g., the learning-relevant properties of information or data. For example, I am engaging in metacognition if I notice that I am having more trouble learning A than B; if it strikes me that I should double check C before accepting it as fact' (Flavell, 1976: 232). One key feature of metacognition is that it is a conscious process which gives a learner more active control over his/her learning, and as such it is a higher order form of thinking. Because it is conscious, it allows learners to become more aware of their own thinking and learning processes, and so to have some influence on them. Nelson et al. (1990: 368) called these 'self-awareness judgements' which are part of metacognition. In particular, such awareness allows you to monitor how you are managing a particular activity; 'it can lead you to select, evaluate, revise, and abandon cognitive tasks, goals, and strategies in light of their relationships with one another and with your own abilities and interests with respect to that enterprise' (Flavell, 1979: 908). If you are reading a difficult text and you decide to highlight the most important passages, you have made a decision about how to manage the reading task. If, as you are reading the text, you realise that you haven't understand what one paragraph means, then you are monitoring your comprehension. When you have finished reading the text, if you decide to reread all the highlighted passages and make notes from them to see if you have made sense of the text, you are evaluating your progress in the activity. All these decisions are metacognitive.

Some research has suggested a direct link between metacognition and intelligence (e.g. Sternberg, 1986). Given that notions of fixed quotients of intelligence are now strongly challenged by more recent research and that we now know that our ability to learn is strongly influenced by social contexts, this link is probably not worth pursuing. However, because of its relationship to thinking and the possibilities it offers for learners to manage their own learning, there is a close relationship between metacognition and learning: metacognition helps learners benefit from classroom experiences (Carr et al., 1989) and helps develop independent learners. The current interest in ideas such as Learning How to Learn, Building Learning Power and Philosophy for Children all draw on metacognition, thinking about thinking, as an important element in vibrant learning environments. Teachers, working with Robert Fisher on his Teaching Thinking programme, came up with the following definitions of metacognition to help inform their own classroom practice:

- thinking about thinking and developing the process of solving problems and answering questions;
- the examination of how we think about how we do things, how we go about finding solutions, how well we can understand and analyse the systems, strategies and techniques we use to think to do things;
- an awareness of the process of how an answer is found, what strategies and type of thought has gone on and the previous experiences that have been used;
- to *consciously* apply a process, a procedure to a problem or activity, and to be aware that the result is satisfactory or otherwise. To be able to 'unpick' that strategy/those actions and so improve performance;
- awareness of the different processes involved in thinking;
- the ability to take out our thinking, and examine it, and put it back, rearranged if necessary;
- thinking about thinking, rather than just remembering facts and recalling events.

(Fisher, 1998: 13)

Becoming an independent learner demands what psychologists call self-regulation. Self-regulation is the monitoring of progress towards a goal, the evaluation of success and the development of alternative strategies if progress is unsuccessful (Berk, 2003). It is a powerful aspect of metacognition – it moves the learner from self-awareness of a problem to being able to solve the problem. So, for example, it is good if a young writer has the metacognitive awareness that she struggles with spelling and always has problems with double consonants in the middle of words, but it is even better if she has a strategy to tackle that spelling problem. There has been a considerable amount of research, especially in the UK and the US, which suggests strongly that teaching children to think about their own learning and to regulate how they manage their work is very successful in raising both motivation and attainment. In science and maths, Shayer and Adey (2002) have shown through their Cognitive Acceleration programme how teaching thinking can improve understanding. In literacy, Oakhill et al. (2005) have shown how important comprehension monitoring is in the development of reading skills. Good readers are 'disturbed' if what they are reading does not seem to make sense, and will stop and reread to clarify, whereas weaker readers do not notice they have a comprehension problem.

But how does this relate to the teaching of writing? In Chapter 1, we emphasised how demanding writing is for all writers, from the early years to expert writers. There has long been a realisation that metacognition is particularly significant in writing (Martlew, 1983) because it is a highly sophisticated and reflective activity which requires a myriad of choices and judgements to be made at every stage of the process. Writers need metacognitive knowledge to develop 'a model of their audience, for reflecting on rhetorical and content probabilities . . . for monitoring their progress . . . ' (Kellogg 1994: 213); revision is always a conscious activity requiring metacognitive decision-making (Alarmargot and Chanquoy, 2001: 108); and, of course, planning requires strategic advanced thinking about the task and your intentions as a writer. Metacognitive knowledge includes the 'knowledge we have about ourselves as learners in relation to a subject area (writing); knowledge we have about particular writing tasks and the context within which we will be working; and knowledge about the kinds of strategies which might help us to reach our goal' (Fisher et al., 2010: 109). Before I wrote this chapter, both authors collaborated on planning the shape of the chapter and creating a bullet-point outline of the chapter. As I am writing this chapter, I am imagining what sense you might be making of it as a reader and grappling with whether I am successfully explaining complex abstract ideas in a meaningful way. And as I write, I repeatedly reread what I have written as the chapter develops to check that it is coherent and doing what we want it to do. I also write little notes to myself, highlighted in lurid yellow in the text, which capture my thinking about problems in the chapter as they occur. Fortunately, these are edited out of the text you are reading! All of these processes are metacognitive processes.

Young children are less able to engage in metacognitive thinking during writing because of the cognitive demands that writing places on them in terms of shaping letters, knowing how to spell words, understanding where to put punctuation marks and their social understanding of texts in their writing communities. We know that more mature writers move recursively through planning, creating text, and revising processes but young writers are unable to do this. However, this is not to say that young writers are incapable of metacognition, as was once believed. Jacobs (2004), amongst others, has demonstrated how very young writers can be helped to think about and reflect on their thinking and composing processes.

For writing, metalinguistic understanding is also important. Metalinguistic awareness is a subset of metacognition, particularly related to knowledge about language, and it is the ability 'to take language as the object of observation and the referent of discourse' (Camps and Milian, 1999: 6). It is all about looking at words, and sentences and texts, and being able to make choices or talk about how they are working in the text. Writers of all ages are capable of metalinguistic talk at some level. In one of our research studies with Year 1 children, many of them could talk about language choices, such as this boy, who had problems with his partner's phrasing: '"Whizzing harshly past my face" doesn't make sense, does it?' In a different study, with teenagers, they demonstrated a growing facility for looking at text and reflecting on its effect. This writer is commenting on the effect of a short sentence: 'It's sharp, so it just, like, hits you. When you're reading a big long sentence, and it's just dragging on, but then one comes like that, which stops you and makes you think about it.' If we can summarise metacognition as thinking about thinking, then we can also summarise metalinguistic activity as thinking about language. Both are higher-level processes of critical importance to the intellectual development of writers.

'Me as a writer' – metacognitive thinking about the writing process

Perhaps not surprisingly, given that their livelihoods often depend on it, many professional writers, particularly novelists and poets, have written extensively about how they write, showing a strong sense of metacognitive awareness of themselves as writers. Many of these writer reflections highlight the hard slog of writing, as we noted in Chapter 1. George Orwell memorably wrote that 'Writing a book is a horrible, exhausting struggle, like a long bout of some painful illness. One would never undertake such a thing if one were not driven on by some demon whom one can neither resist nor understand' (Orwell, 1946: 11). Many of these metacognitive reflections illuminate the conditions which writers find conducive to writing and the disciplines they impose on themselves in order to get writing done. In the extract below, from an interview by Ben Opipari, novelist Susan Henderson, author of *Up from the Blue* (2010), talks about how she writes:

Interviewer: How disciplined are you as a writer?
Henderson: Right now, the publicity process for the book has been distracting, but when I am really disciplined, I block out about eight hours a day. Probably an hour and a half of that is really useful writing. But if you define writing more broadly, I've learned that I don't produce as much as I want. So the night before, I decide the theme or the characters or the question I'm trying to figure out, and I write it down with no expectations for what the answer is going to be. I pin it to my board and when I go to work the next day, I spend probably two hours working on nothing but that thing. I've learned that if I try to wait for a zone, when it feels like God is moving the pen, that works for me maybe twice a year. So I have a much more blue-collar approach: I have a job to do and a goal to achieve each day. It's OK to write it badly, because I know I can go back and revise. Most of the day, I am sharpening the writing pencil or my brain: I'm reading, blogging, thinking about writing.

Interviewer: But that's still part of your process. So you have a very, in your words, 'blue-collar approach'. When is quitting time each day?

Henderson: I try to stop about a half-hour before my kids come home from school and shift gears. My office is in a little room in our garage, and I found that when I wrote in the house, I never really stopped. I had to separate the writing from the rest of my life, instead of writing while I was cooking dinner. I needed a place to physically leave.

Interviewer: Back to the discipline idea. Is there anything you must have with you when you write in order to put yourself in the right frame of mind?

Henderson: I did the Squaw Valley writers' conference a few summers ago, and Ron Carlson kept saying, 'Keep your ass in the chair. That's the way to write.' I thought about that, and I realize that's dead wrong for me. I am a restless person, and I hate to sit down in a chair. So my new thing is an iPhone, and I use the voice memo. Now I do almost all of my writing while walking. For my first draft, I go to the woods and hike for two or three hours. I'll go with a specific question, scene, or dilemma, and I'll just talk it into the voice memo. I pretend like I am talking on the phone, so when I pass people I pretend to have a conversation on the phone, like 'Hey honey, I'll be home at five.' Then when they pass, I continue composing. But I realize I have to be walking.

In this brief extract, we can see that Susan Henderson has to impose on herself a discipline of writing regularly (a commonly reported practice amongst professional writers) but also that she is aware of the rarity of inspiration, 'when it feels like God is moving the pen', and that she has to really work at developing her ideas. She is also very aware of the physicality of her composing process; that she needs to walk to think and create. This kind of metacognitive awareness gives writers more ownership and control of the writing process to the point where Susan Henderson can confidently reject the advice of others because she knows it does not work for her.

In the writing classroom, there are many things teachers can do to help writers of every age to develop greater metacognitive knowledge and awareness. For example, children can be encouraged to think about their own autobiographies as writers, reflecting on their own experiences, interests and preferences as writers. This is often helped by some form of scaffold, perhaps the teacher talking about his/her own writing biography or by hearing the biography of a visiting author. Another strategy is to invite young writers to create a spidergram which captures their autobiographical thoughts. A prompt such as the one below, adapted for the age group, can help stimulate autobiographical thinking.

Because historically the teaching focus on writing has been on the product, the writing produced, rather than the process of writing, many teachers have not thought about themselves as writers in this way. Despite the popularity of the process approach to writing, described in Chapter 1, genuine metacognitive

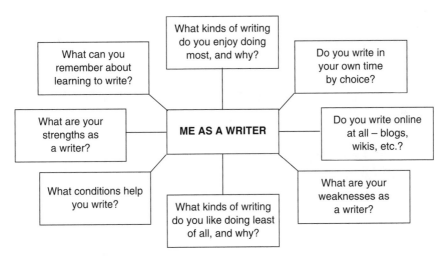

Figure 6.1 A prompt diagram for 'Me as a writer' spidergrams

thinking and reflection on how we write is still rare. Teachers and children do often talk about the process in terms of planning, drafting and revising as linear stages, but not so frequently about their own composing processes and preferences. This is one of the benefits of ensuring that teachers have experience of writing workshops themselves as writers, as it encourages this kind of reflection. Please see Figure 6.2 for two examples of 'Me as a writer' diagrams produced by two PGCE students thinking about their own writing biographies. These reflections often prove to be a rich starting point for further discussion about how we write and what helps us write.

Another way to develop metacognitive knowledge is to create classrooms where talk about and reflection on each aspect of the writing process is a regular aspect of practice. This can help both teachers and students develop shared understanding, and sometimes provides the teacher with important developmental information. Bereiter and Scardamalia (1987) used children's metacognitive reflections on their composing processes to develop their model of how novice writers move from a knowledge-telling strategy to a knowledge-transforming strategy. More immature writers tend to treat the composing process as chaining ideas together sequentially by writing one idea, then pausing and thinking of the next one and generating their text in this way. By contrast, more mature writers have a better sense of the whole when they start writing and are attending both to what they are writing now and also how this relates to their plans for what will follow. One child in Bereiter and Scardamalia's study reflected on how s/he writes: 'I have a whole bunch of ideas and write down until my supply of ideas is exhausted. Then I might try to think of more ideas up to the point when you can't get any more ideas that are worth putting down on paper and then I would end it' (Bereiter

Figure 6.2 Examples of 'Me as a writer' diagrams by two PGCE students

and Scardamalia, 1987: 9). This is a classic description of the knowledge-telling strategy and the teacher could use this reflection to engage the writer in thinking about how to approach the writing process differently to allow for more advance planning and more purposeful revision.

In one of our research projects with teenage writers, we found that students were very perceptive and articulate about their writing process and thinking about their writing. For example, in terms of generating ideas, students were confident talking about how they got their ideas for narrative writing, with imaginative empathy and visualisation being common idea development strategies:

- I like to have a picture in my head of what I'm supposed to be rewriting.
- Well, I think that I'm going to see, for instance . . . today, I was going to choose to write about Simon going to the woods, I think . . . I just think where he's starting from and I just start describing where he's going and that, I just sort of do it from my head as he's walking along.
- I like to think that I'm like the main character that's there and I might think what I'd be feeling if I was that person . . . if I was in that situation. I'm thinking about that most of the time and walking myself through the story line that's happening.
- I would put myself in their situation, you know, the character's situation in the story. I just think, you know, how I would feel, how I would react to the situation that they're in . . .

Some students are aware that they plan before they write, often mentally rather than on paper, whilst others are aware that they begin writing with no sense of where they are going:

- I know roughly what I'm doing at the start. I think before I write.
- Yeah, it wasn't really that I'd run out of ideas, I sort of had a clear idea about what I was trying to bring across the whole time. It is just thinking about how I'm going to phrase it so it's not . . . it doesn't seem awkward in any way on the page and stuff.
- I need to think of the whole story, I can't just start a story and carry on, I have to think of it first.
- I'm not very good at planning too far ahead.
- Sometimes I'll write a first paragraph and I don't really . . . say if it's a story, I'd write the first paragraph and then I wouldn't really know what's going to happen next, then I'd think about it after that from the first paragraph.

Young children are equally capable of developing metacognitive thinking about their writing. In a different study exploring the role of talk in supporting writing in 5- to 7-year-olds (Fisher et al., 2010), one of our aims was to create classrooms where children talked about the writing process and where metacognition, or reflecting on writing, was a key part of the process. We created a classroom poster

Figure 6.3 Classroom poster to support metacognitive thinking about the writing process

which all the teachers used, which gave a structure to thinking about the planning and generating stage (getting ideas), about the text creation stage (say it, write it) and the reviewing stage (thinking about my writing).

Teachers routinely encouraged children to ask themselves questions, such as 'Where did I get my ideas from?'; 'What did I do when I got stuck?'; 'What was I thinking about when I was writing this?'; 'What was I feeling when I wrote this?'; and 'Could I have done it differently?'. The children were also encouraged to collaborate together during writing to help each other with strategies for managing the writing process. In the extract below, a girl and a boy discuss how to approach the writing task they have been given and collaboratively arrive at a solution. This is metacognitive talk because they are talking about *how* they write, not just about the writing itself.

Girl: [watches boy writing in the grid] I don't know how to write it.
Boy: [pointing to the grid] You can write them in there.
Girl: But you have to draw the animals.
Boy: Yes, but we can draw the animals later. You can start with these ones [pointing to the grid] and then go down or you can start here [pointing to the left-hand side] and go across. I started from the top.
Girl: OK I'll do this line then.

Boy: We need to do some.
Girl: OK I'll do this one and this one [pointing to different places on the grid].
(Fisher et al., 2010: 118)

A series of sample lesson plans were created for the project which exemplified the fostering of metacognitive reflection, and one is included below (see Fig 6.4).

Reflection activity – thinking cap

Purpose: To encourage reflection about the process of writing

Summary: Children wear a 'thinking cap' to help them focus on reflective questions about their writing.

Resources/preparation:
- A class set of thinking caps or hats
- A recent piece of individual writing

Activity
- The thinking cap is an actual cap that the teacher or a pupil can wear. The teacher explains to the children that wearing the cap can help you think about your writing.
- Each child has a recent piece of writing.
- n pairs they take turns to wear the thinking cap and talk to their partner about their writing. The aim is to focus on process rather than product.

Ideas for focus questions
'What kind of writing is this?'
'Where did you get your ideas from?'
'What were you trying to write about?'
'How well did you write about this?'
'What did you do when you got stuck?'
'What were you thinking about when you were writing this?'
'What were you feeling when you wrote this?'
'Could you have done it differently?'

Class-based example
Graham has been working with his class of 25 Year 2 children. They have been writing kennings about jungle animals. Graham returns to the shared writing they completed in the last session – a kenning about a monkey. He shows the children the thinking cap and explains that whilst he is wearing it, he is able to think really carefully about his writing. He has three prompt questions on cards: 'What kind of writing is this?', 'What did you do when you got stuck?' and 'What were you feeling when you wrote this?'. Graham models wearing the thinking cap, explaining his ideas carefully. He then asks children to return to their desks. They will be working in pairs talking about their own kennings. Each pair has a thinking cap and they take it in turns to talk about their writing whilst wearing the cap. At the end of the shared talk activity, each child writes down one

---

Figure 6.4 Sample lesson plan to encourage fostering of metacognitive reflection
Source: Fisher, Jones, Larkin and Myhill 2010: 148

thing that the thinking cap helped them reflect on. In the plenary Graham looks at the children's written reflections and reinforces the importance of reflection.

If this is the first time you have tried this activity . . .

Remember that children are often unfamiliar with this level of reflection. Begin by using the thinking cap as part of shared writing sessions. Model the things *you* might say whilst *you* are wearing the thinking cap. Next, ask children to wear the 'thinking cap' and help them reflect on their writing. When you are happy that they are gaining confidence with this activity then move on to using the thinking cap in pairs.

Teachers who use this activity successfully might say:
'Tell me about. . .' rather than 'Why?'
'How was that the same as. . .?'
'When you said . . . it really helped me understand your thinking.
Who else found that?'

Figure 6.4 Continued

At the end of the project, in classrooms where teachers had confidently developed metacognitive talk, the teachers believed that this had an impact on children's learning about writing. As one teacher reflected:

> The children have all learned to work better co-operatively, recognizing their partner's strengths and weaknesses and providing support for each other. They have become more aware of their own strengths and areas for development. They know what helps them to learn and can find or ask for specific support, becoming more independent learners. Through talk and reflection the children have become far more aware of what they need to do in order to improve their writing.

'My writing' – metacognitive and metalinguistic thinking about written text

As noted earlier, metalinguistic thinking is a subset of metacognition and it focuses specifically on thinking about language, as an object or artefact in its own right. We are interested here in how to develop metalinguistic thinking about written text. At its core, metalinguistic thinking is fundamentally about learning to look critically at writing and to make language choices, or as Coleridge expressed it, creating text 'in which every line, every phrase, may pass the ordeal of deliberation and deliberate choice' (1817: 485). The Romantic notion of writing, especially poetry, is that, if inspired, the writing will flow effortlessly onto the page. But all too often, for experienced and inexperienced writers alike, this doesn't happen. It is good to have one of our greatest Romantic poets remind us that composing text is an act of creative slog!

Of course, there are strong links here with writing as design, as discussed in Chapter 4, as language choice is one key element of text design. Developing young writers' ability to talk about their language choices and the reasoning behind those choices helps make visible the richness and the possibilities of language, and at the same time allows writers to see that they have agency and ownership of the texts they create. Wheeler argues that 'teaching children to consciously reflect on their linguistic varieties and to choose the appropriate language variety for a particular situation provides them with metacognitive strategies and the cognitive flexibility to apply those strategies in daily practice' (Wheeler, 2010: 138). An active and engaging writing classroom provides plenty of opportunities for this kind of discussion to occur and ensures that discussion about writing does not just address what to write, the content of the writing, but provides planned, quality time for talking about language choices.

We have called these moments of discussion about language choice 'meta-linguistic conversations', partly to stress the idea of dialogue and shared negotiation of meaning, and partly to stress the participatory, rather than regulatory, role of the teacher in these conversations. Developing metalinguistic thinking is not about directing young writers to 'correct' choices or formulaic patterns of writing; it is about enabling the kind of thinking that will help writers to become independent and creative decision-makers in their own right. In a study we have just completed, investigating whether purposeful teaching of grammar can help writing, one key principle of the design of the teaching materials was to create the maximum number of opportunities for students to engage in discussion about writing possibilities; in other words, to participate in metalinguistic conversations. In one lesson, looking at writing persuasive political speeches, the focus was on modal verbs and how the choice of modal can influence the relationship with the reader/listener and how you position yourself as writer/speaker. The students were given the extracts below and the questions which follow to stimulate their thinking about the effect of modal verbs in these speeches.

Winston Churchill

'We shall fight on the beaches', Speech to the House of Commons, Second World War: 4 June 1940

[. . .] We shall go on to the end, we shall fight in France, we shall fight on the seas and oceans, we shall fight with growing confidence and growing strength in the air, we shall defend our Island, whatever the cost may be, we shall fight on the beaches, we shall fight on the landing grounds, we shall fight in the fields and in the streets, we shall fight in the hills; we shall never surrender, and even if, which I do not for a moment believe, this Island or a large part of it were subjugated and starving, then our Empire beyond the seas, armed and guarded by the British Fleet, would carry on the struggle, until, in God's good time, the New World, with all its power and might, steps forth to the rescue and the liberation of the old.

John F. Kennedy

Inaugural Address: 20 January 1961

[. . .] Let every nation know, whether it wishes us well or ill, that we shall pay any price, bear any burden, meet any hardship, support any friend, oppose any foe, in order to assure the survival and the success of liberty.

George Bush

Operation Iraqi Freedom, Address to the Nation: 19 March 2003

[. . .] The people of the United States and our friends and allies will not live at the mercy of an outlaw regime that threatens the peace with weapons of mass murder. We will meet that threat now with our Army, Air Force, Navy, Coast Guard and Marines, so that we do not have to meet it later with armies of fire fighters and police and doctors on the streets of our cities. [. . .] And I assure you, this will not be a campaign of half measures, and we will accept no outcome but victory.

My fellow citizens, the dangers to our country and the world will be overcome. We will pass through this time of peril and carry on the work of peace. We will defend our freedom. We will bring freedom to others. And we will prevail.

May God bless our country and all who defend her.

1. Which modal verbs can you see? What feeling or effect are the speakers trying to create by using them?
2. Do you think that using 'shall' has a slightly different effect to using 'will'?
3. Can you see any other similarities/differences between the speeches?

This provoked considerable discussion over whether 'shall' or 'will' was a more assertive modal, as well as debate about language change, since for many students 'shall' was an option they rarely used. One teacher preceded this activity by asking his class to re-punctuate an unpunctuated version of the Churchill speech, the results of which generated some very lively metalinguistic conversation. Some of the students did not punctuate in the way Churchill had written it, but instead punctuated it as follows:

We shall go on to the end. We shall fight. In France, we shall fight. On the seas and oceans, we shall fight. With growing confidence and growing strength in the air, we shall defend our island, whatever the cost may be. We shall fight. On the beaches, we shall fight. On the landing grounds, we shall fight. In the fields and in the streets, we shall fight . . .

Perhaps surprisingly, very few students knew the Churchill version so they did not have a 'correct' model in their heads. This version stimulated a lot of discussion about the different impact of placing 'we shall fight' at the beginning or end of the sentence and about how putting the prepositional phrase at the start of the sentence emphasised the sense of place, and that the fighting would be taken to all places. The critical thing about this metalinguistic conversation is that the teacher had not expected the punctuation activity to bring up this possibility, but he used it expertly as an opportunity to pursue their thinking and choice-making. At no time did he suggest any idea that there was a correct version, and even when Churchill's version was revealed, he raised the question over which they felt was the more effective.

It is perhaps worth observing here that sometimes metalinguistic talk is less constructive, usually when it focuses on a grammatical feature without any accompanying discussion about purpose or effect. In our interview discussions with secondary writers, many talked about the fact that they needed to use more complex sentences in their writing. But when we probed this, no students were able to explain why they might want to use more complex sentences in their writing, other than that they had been given it as a target or it would get them a better mark in the examination. In many cases, when asked, the students could not identify a complex sentence in their own writing! This is using metalanguage in a hollow, meaningless way, giving writers no support for metalinguistic thinking and decision-making. In primary schools, as discussed in Chapter 4, we have seen a similar thing happening with adjectives. Young writers are often encouraged to 'add' more adjectives to their writing to make it more descriptive, but with no parallel consideration of what descriptive images they want to convey and how best to do that. Very often powerful description is more effectively accomplished through better noun choice, rather than additional modification of the noun.

Our observations of writing lessons in primary classrooms suggests that sometimes even when adjectives are not the learning focus, teachers tend to draw attention to adjective choice. In particular, there is a tendency to encourage unusual choices without discussion of appropriateness or effect, often implying that using adjectives is inherently good and using an unusual one even better. In one lesson observed, the teacher held a sustained discussion about better words for grass than 'green', and offered 'emerald' as an improved substitute: there was no discussion of why 'emerald' might be more appropriate or what the connotations of 'emerald' were that supported the communication of the text. Ironically, the teacher began this teaching episode by misquoting Coleridge, saying the writing poetry was about 'the right words in the right order': the message of the discussion of adjectives was that 'emerald' was the right choice as a substitute for 'green', even if many writers might have suggested it was not the best choice!

Conclusion

The examples of metalinguistic conversations given in this chapter highlight how crucial the role of the teacher is in stimulating metalinguistic thinking and capitalising on all opportunities to foster metalinguistic decision-making. Peer reviewing of writing can also be used very constructively to generate metalinguistic talk, and collaborative writing, where two writers co-construct a text, is a particularly valuable approach to making visible linguistic decision-making. When a text is written collaboratively on screen (or using a wiki), two authors have to cooperate and negotiate the shaping of the text, and need to articulate their metalinguistic thinking in order to explain their choices to their partner. The study, referred to earlier, investigating the impact of purposeful grammar teaching on writing shows strongly significant positive effects – and the qualitative data, drawing on observation and teacher interviews, suggests that one of the factors influencing this success was the considerable amount of metalinguistic talk in the teaching materials. Of course, both metacognition and metalinguistic thinking focus on the deliberative elements of writing: this does not ignore the fact that not all writing is the outcome of a deliberate choice, and that just the right image, or metaphor, or phrase sometimes springs onto the page without deliberation. Both the unbidden and the deliberate are important in becoming a writer. However, the thrust of this chapter is to signal the importance of thinking and talking about writing processes and writing choices: as Kellogg argued, 'to be successful, the instructor must teach the student how to think as well as write' (Kellogg, 1994: 213).

My Writing Biography

The home I grew up in was governed largely by what my mother was reading or writing, and how well the writing process had gone, from day to day. She had me when she was 21 and just starting her MA, and so from the beginning I was aware that her writing was the thing that was most often on her mind if I wasn't. I didn't resent this; rather, I was intrigued by this activity into which a person could retreat, and ultimately, find some self-definition. My brother and I spent a large part of our childhood sitting under Mum's desk while she wrote her PhD, articles and papers, listening to her composing sentences aloud. She would ask me if sentences sounded OK, or which words sounded better in a sentence, and even pretended to take my advice, and so I too became immersed in this thing called writing.

Despite the academic influence at home, I had some trouble with eye-hand coordination which affected how quickly I was learning to write at school, and my year 1 teacher recommended that I see an occupational therapist. My mother was incensed, but eventually submitted, and carried me kicking and screaming to occupational therapy. As a result, I remember feeling a quite ashamed and confused, and hugely anxious about my handwriting. My anxiety to 'get it right' slowed me down even more in class, confirming my teacher's suspicions. Eventually, my parents decided that enough was enough and that I would develop in my own time, and somehow, things corrected themselves and my confidence eventually returned.

At primary school I enjoyed creative writing most as it offered me the chance to be a storyteller in my own right, and to play with language in ways that I felt couldn't be judged and assessed. I guess I really appreciated the unique combination of play and expertise that creative writing exercises offer. However, I think I really started to enjoy and stretch my writing skills when I was given opportunities to do critical writing. Funnily enough, my first opportunities to do such writing were provided by my parents in response to episodes of bad behaviour. When I had been naughty, I was charged with writing little essays analysing the choices I had made and stating what I thought was an appropriate punishment. My efforts to argue my case, or admit delinquency graciously, really did shape my writing ability.

Secondary school and university, with their increased emphasis on critical writing, meant that I found myself becoming more comfortable with written argument than I was with creative writing. My inclination and ability to write stories and poems has diminished significantly since secondary school, and today I feel the need to re-activate that side of my writing identity, mostly because I am seeing how much fun it is in schools, and I want to give it a go again myself! However, my true love will always be critical writing. My university career cultivated in me a special geek-dom and a real love of essays. I think that a certain kind of creativity is active when I write critical essays. Essay writing requires a certain combination of flourish and restraint, eloquence and precision, that I really enjoy practising. I would say that the amount of essay writing I have done in recent years has really shaped the way I think about things.

I guess that writing has influenced my identity more than [I] would originally have imagined, probably because my identity is tied to academia. Of course, this isn't – and needn't be – the case for everybody. But what I do think is important is that people get the opportunity to play with language in as many different ways as possible. As a trainee teacher I'm really keen to get kids writing in lots of different critical and creative ways because ultimately, the ability to play with language does increase the ways in which one is able to articulate one's own thoughts. It's this opportunity for self-articulation that, for me, is the most beneficial aspect of writing.

Bianca – PGCE English student

Part II

Teachers as writers

Chapter 7

Writing teachers

Introduction

Do you see yourself as a writer? Do you choose to write in your own time? What kinds of writing do you enjoy most and why do you think this is? What do you think are your strengths or weaknesses as a writer? Does your degree of assurance and confidence as a writer shift according to the form, the purpose and audience or the extent of volition or choice involved? These are some of the many questions we can ask ourselves as writers as we consider how we use, or might use, our personal experience of writing and being a writer in our teaching. This is the focus of the two chapters in this section, which both connect to the work of Commeyras et al. (2003: 4), who coined the phrase 'Reading Teachers – teachers who read and readers who teach'. In these chapters we are exploring teachers' writing identities and the potential of developing Writing Teachers – teachers who write and writers who teach.

Writers' identities matter: influenced by multiple histories and experiences, our identities as writers influence the way in which we approach writing and deserve more recognition and development in schooling. In recent years, concerns have been expressed about young people's attitudes to writing and their low self-esteem as writers, an issue discussed further in Chapter 5. Home, peer and institutional practices all shape children's writing identities (Bourne, 2002) and the way we as teachers view writing and ourselves as writers will impact on the modes of participation and writing identities made available to young people in school. Teachers who write in their personal lives, Yeo (2007) argues, develop their writing identities and transmit the benefits of such practice in their teaching of writing. So it is important to develop a richer sense of our own identities as writers and consider how we position ourselves and our students in the writing classroom.

Teachers' writing histories

Do you remember learning to write at all: the challenge of holding a pencil correctly, the opportunity to make up fictional worlds, learning to spell and punctuate, or receiving early critical acclaim? Our work with teachers in various writing projects has repeatedly shown that those whose early memories were predominantly positive often recalled specific occasions in their childhood when pieces of work had been praised or made public (Grainger, 2005a, b; Grainger et al., 2005; Grainger et al., 2006; Cremin, 2006). For example, having a head teacher read aloud a piece of work, making a picture book which friends read, having a PowerPoint presentation selected for demonstration in school, or winning a poetry competition. Significantly, most of those who noted such positive feedback, either in their early years or later in life, also tended to rate themselves positively as adult writers. Although they did not always find writing easy, they retained a sense of positive self-esteem as writers; feedback had clearly been influential in shaping their perceptions of themselves as writers. Sue's poem on this subject and her insightful reflections on the impact of feedback offer an additional perspective (see p. 152, Chapter 8 //Sue vignette//), as do comedian and comic scriptwriter Miranda Hart's comments at the 2011 British Comedy Awards. On receiving an award for her scripts, she declared unequivocally, 'I hate writing', yet in describing the labour and challenges involved she reflected a positive sense of herself as a writer and was proud of her work.

Some teachers in our studies had strongly negative memories of learning to write; remembered the fear of having nothing to say, being worried about spelling, punctuation and handwriting, and the disappointment of rarely finishing any writing due to the struggle involved. Many recalled being given almost no choice and being told to do better, but not knowing how one noted: 'Once a poor speller, always a poor speller, my teacher used to say'. Several others also retold specific incidents of a challenging nature. For example, one was slapped across the wrist with a ruler, another said that her writing was often crossed out because it was so untidy, and yet another recollected the day a teacher ripped up her work in front of the class. Such strong early experiences impact on current perceptions and the practice of teachers in various layered ways (Cremin, 2006; Yeo, 2007). For example, some teachers with negative childhood memories talked with passion about how they sought to make writing a more positive experience for young writers than it was for them, whilst others who still reflected low self-esteem as writers, avoided risk-taking in school and reported doing minimal demonstration writing in case their perceived lack of competence was revealed.

Reflecting on our writing histories and sharing early memories of writing can help us gain distance and perspective on ourselves as writers. You might want to record significant memories of writing – from home, primary or secondary school and/or university – and then perhaps consider them:

- Where were you, who were you with, was it completed over time or in one setting? (Context)
- Who read this writing and did you receive any feedback? (Audience)
- Were you asked to do it and why did you write it? (Purpose)
- What did you feel about this writing then and how do you feel about it now? (Response)

As you reread your memories, you could also ponder on whether there is anything in common across these experiencess. For example, was there an important figure in your writing life, was any of your work made public, did you have a favourite form of writing at any time, which texts (e.g. poetry, songs, narratives, computer games) might have influenced your compositions? Do you think your reflections on yourself as a writer have any bearing on how you teach or view writing now? Children, too, find recalling their significant writing memories and creating collages and 'writing rivers' of these recollections can help them gain a sense of their own journeys as writers. See Brandon's example on page 64, Chapter 3.

Teachers' contemporary practices, habits and preferences

Our current practices and habits as writers can also help us develop an awareness of ourselves as writers, and how our writing shifts according to our intentions and the wider social context in which it is produced. Today, for example (a cold Sunday in January 2011), I made myself record all the occasions on which I put pen to paper or fingers to keyboard; the resultant list is noted below, in no particular order.

Form of text	Audience	Purpose	Medium
Texts, one with an emoticon	To my daughter	To confirm train arrival times	Mobile phone
Emails	To colleagues regarding the White Paper	To suggest ideas about coordinating a response	Computer
Emails	Work colleagues	To share my views about the non-word reading test	Computer
Emails	Work colleagues	To remind others about writing workshops	Computer
Note	Myself	To record an address in a phone call to my mother	Post-it note
Letter in a card, note on a gift tag, address	My niece	To send birthday greetings	Pen, card, gift tag, envelope
Diary	Myself	To reflect on the week	Special embossed book
List	Myself	To be an aide memoire	A4 notepad and biro

Form of text	Audience	Purpose	Medium
Testimonial	Judges in the UKLA John Downing Award	To promote the excellence of a Newham teacher	Computer
Text and emoticons	To friends	To arrange a weekend away	Mobile phone
Text	A work colleague	To rearrange a meeting venue	Mobile phone
Form	Myself	To apply for a Network Railcard	Computer
Email	To co-author	To respond to chapters sent and discuss use of voice in this book	Computer
Form	The OU Research School	To record my publications in the Research Audit	Computer
Notes	Myself	To redraft this chapter, sharpening up the argument	Pen and paper copy

All these different texts are highly specific, tailored according to purpose and my relationships with those to whom I wrote/sent information; each was also afforded different amounts of time, effort and engagement across the day. I appear to have been using writing as an organisational tool, as a mode of communicating information, as a prompt for thinking and shaping my understanding (in writing this chapter, for example), and in order to maintain and reinforce relationships. My text to a particular group of friends, for example, whilst focused on arranging a weekend away, was playful and cryptic, using 'in-house' phrases and references which no one else would understand. In contrast, my defence of Ellen as a creative teacher of literacy was much more formal in tone, although hopefully enlivened by vignettes from the classroom. Based on her data, McClay (1998) argues that teachers undertake little 'recreational writing' – writing undertaken for the personal satisfaction of the writer – although for me, and perhaps for many of us, most of my everyday practices offer me a degree of satisfaction; even applying for a railcard, whilst tedious at one level, represents a job completed, and crafting Ellen's testimonial has recently proved to be highly satisfying since she has now been shortlisted for the award. It is evident that many of the texts produced were brief in nature, but in each I had to make choices as a writer and consider my audience, purpose and form.

You could use the frame above to record the different kinds of writing you engage in over a day or a weekend, and perhaps reflect on what made some of this writing more or less pleasurable or satisfying. Was it time and space, the audience, and/or the presence or absence of immediate response or feedback? Much of your writing, like mine, will be read by friends and colleagues who primarily respond to what we say, not the way we say it; little will be judged or immediately evaluated, as young people's writing in school often is, by lesson objectives, the features of a form or in relation to set targets. Clearly, little of our writing will be graded. Through considering our different practices and the values attached to writing in different contexts, we can come to appreciate more fully the socially constructed and culturally validated nature of writing, and examine the consequences for teaching writing in school. It may also cause us to consider our students' writing practices beyond the classroom, the breadth of their practices and the relevance of 'school' writing to young writers, an issue explored further in Chapter 5.

Students' perceptions of their teachers as writers

In one of our projects we invited the learners to comment on whether their teachers were 'writers'. The youngest voiced the view that their teachers were writers, yet with increasing age across the primary phase they appeared considerably less sure. Most of the 10- to 11-year-olds did not see their teachers as writers, although this may tell us more about their conceptions of writing than their teachers (Grainger et al., 2006). Several of the older children observed that their teachers did not like writing: 'I think he finds it boring', 'She doesn't like writing and says she is no good at it', 'I don't think she would choose to write because she doesn't like it', 'He hates writing, he says we do too much of it', 'She doesn't really like it much, she says she's no good but that's not true', and 'He does write stuff, but I think it's because he has to, he doesn't really like it'. When asked what they think their teachers write, the overwhelming majority of the 310 children (from the 9 schools) listed writing that was school-/work-related; their experience of their teachers as writers appeared to be confined to this context and relatively few listed kinds of writing which might be contextualised beyond the school, such as emails, shopping lists and letters. The young people recorded a plethora of school-based teacher writing, which only occasionally included writing in shared or demonstration contexts and predominantly related to evaluation and assessment. Typically, they commented on teachers using writing to evaluate and grade their work or behaviour, also noting other forms of evaluative writing such as report writing, for example:

- She writes how good we've been.
- She writes our names on the board if we're in trouble.
- He grades our work and writes what we need to do next.
- She writes the lesson objectives up so she can check.
- She comments on our work and gives us levels.
- She writes reports for my parents.

Do you think the children and young people you teach see you as a writer in this predominantly evaluative manner? What might the consequences be for their conceptions of writing and understanding of its use and real-world relevance? You could share your everyday writing life with your students, demonstrating that adults write for personal and professional purposes, and have their own habits, preferences and practices which connect to their interests and roles. Young writers can become 'writing detectives', recording examples of writing in and around the school and through everyday classroom practices, then categorising these in terms of their purpose, form and audience. You may also find that in sharing some of the challenges of writing in demonstration contexts and in writing alongside younger writers, you begin to build a more reciprocal community of writers.

Are teachers assured writers?

Despite the fact that we are all writers, some commentators and researchers question whether the profession is sufficiently confident, assured and well informed enough about writing to teach it effectively (Rosen, 1981; Geekie et al., 1999; Andrews, 2008a; Horner, 2010). On the basis of their surveys of primary and secondary schools, Oftsed too assert that teachers lack confidence as writers, and observe that, as a result, students are 'not able to see how ideas and language is created, shaped, reviewed and revised' (2009: 48). Furthermore, it seems that secondary teachers are drawn to teach English not by a love of writing but of reading, and whilst many identify reading with personal pleasure, satisfaction and fulfilment, relatively few view writing in the same way (Peel, 2000). An Australian study with student teachers confirms this view, revealing that a love of literature or an inspirational English teacher prompted most of them to teach English, not an interest in writing (Gannon and Davies, 2007). In the primary phase there is less research focused on this issue, but a Canadian study by Yeo (2007) suggests that teachers tend to see reading, not writing, as the core of literacy and that they see themselves primarily as readers, not as writers. Yeo argues that this has considerable impact on their classroom practice, where reading is profiled over composition. Andrews (2008b), in agreeing that teachers are neither as keen nor as experienced writers as they are readers, calls for a UK National Writing Project (NWP) for teachers to support their development as writers.

Teaching writing is arguably an artistic event, involving creativity and artistry, but if few teachers see themselves as writers or write alongside their students then the teaching of writing may be constrained by a lack of awareness of the complexities of composition and the significance of writers' identities. Too many teachers, Geekie et al. (1999: 219) observe, 'are not writers in any but the most superficial sense'; they may not appreciate that 'writing, as much as music or art, exists in a tradition of its own which is a resource for generating meaning'. They suggest that we do not understand what it means to be a writer, or maybe we have simply never considered this issue or reflected on our identities as writers and the connections between writing identities and teaching writing. Perhaps too we have not stopped to make explicit to ourselves our conceptions of writing, nor sought to develop our metacognitive and metasocial awareness of compositional processes, nor investigated possible synergies and differences between ourselves and young people as writers.

Teachers' confidence as writers, it seems, is not something that can be taken for granted; in several of our studies, teachers have expressed considerable discomfort and uncertainty when composing and sharing their work (Grainger, 2005b; Cremin, 2006), and some expressed low self-esteem as writers. This is likely to influence their writing identities and may restrain their enthusiasm and motivation to teach writing effectively. Young people's motivation too is related to their 'self-perceptions and beliefs about themselves as writers, their writing competence, and their ability to manage writing tasks' (Boscolo and Gelati, 2007: 204). Our identities are context-dependent and fluid, maintained and developed through our literacy and interaction with others (McCarthey and Moje, 2002). Maintaining our multiple identities involves considerable work as we position ourselves and are positioned as writers in different contexts and with different people. As teachers in school we construct our writing identities in relation to the young people, other teachers, teaching assistants and parents, for example. In one of our recent studies (Cremin and Baker, 2010), we observed two teachers, Elaine and Jeff, who engaged in ongoing writer-identity work in their classrooms as they sought to compose authentically and write alongside younger writers. These practitioners talked of their dual personas and positioning as 'writers' and as 'teachers', and stressed the struggle involved as they shifted in a moment-to-moment fashion between these two positions. At times both wrote for explicit instructional purposes, demonstrating the knowledge and skills laid down by the National Strategies (DfES, 2006a); on such occasions we argue they were positioned more as teacher-writers at one end of a writing continuum (see Figure 7.1). At other times, their writing in school appeared to have more personal resonance and emotional connection for them as individuals; on these occasions we perceive they positioned themselves more towards the writer-teacher end of the continuum. It appears that for these teachers there was a constant oscillation between more conforming identities – teacher-writers writing for the system; and more liberating identities – writer-teachers writing more for themselves.

This work highlights the tensions and challenges for professionals who, in order to support young writers, position themselves/are positioned as writers in the classroom. The impact of interaction with others and wider institutional factors, such as the National Strategies and school expectations on the identity positioning of these teachers was significant. Additionally, their situated sense of themselves as writers, their emotional engagement in the subject matter, degree of personal authenticity and authorial agency all impacted on their identity positioning in the classroom. Pondering on the struggle, Elaine and Jeff wondered whether the children were positioned by them to 'write for the system too often' and whether they afforded enough space for the young writers to write for themselves.

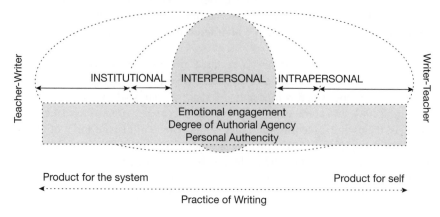

Figure 7.1 A diagram to represent a teacher-writer, writer-teacher continuum (Cremin and Baker, 2010: 20)

Teachers engaging as writers – a historical perspective

The notion of teachers positioning themselves as writers in the way Jeff and Elaine try to do can be traced back to the process writing movement (Graves, 1983; Calkins, 1986), it has been the focus of debate for many years. Graves (1983: 5) argued that the teaching writing 'demands the control of two crafts, teaching and writing' and that neither can be avoided nor separated. Whilst his work has been heavily critiqued as being anecdotal and unsystematic (Martin, 1985; Smagorinsky, 1987; Beard, 2000a), there is no doubt Graves raised the profile of teachers' roles as writers, and helped teachers see how their own writing could be used in class as a teaching tool. His work has prompted a number of small-scale studies, which collectively suggest that as teachers develop their confidence and adopt the identity of writer in the classroom, their attitude to teaching writing changes (Atwell, 1987; Draper et al., 2000; Hansen, 1985; Murray, 1982). Some studies also claim that when practitioners demonstrate writerly behaviour and share their challenges as writers, younger writers benefit (Root and Steinberg, 1996; Susi, 1984). However, still others suggest that teachers' perceptions of the importance of writing and their faith in their students' ability are more significant indicators of their efficacy than their involvement as writers (Gleeson and Prain, 1996; Robbins, 1996), and some express concern that by writing authentically teachers not only become susceptible to exposure but lose teaching time.

Graves' argument also underpinned the work of the Bay Area Writing Project (BAWP), now the US National Writing Project (NWP), which is a national non-profit-making professional development initiative with more than 200 sites. One of the central tenets of this work is that to teach writing, you need to be able to write, and that teachers should write alongside young people, undertaking the same tasks as they set their students. On the basis of a two-year study of NWP sites, Wood and Leiberman (2000) conclude that by encouraging teachers to discover themselves as authors, the NWP fosters the development of voice and ownership in writing, and contributes to teachers' sense of agency in their professional lives. Influenced by the US work, New Zealand also set up a NWP, funded by the Department of Education, studies of which additionally support the premise that it is beneficial for teachers to develop their identities as writers (Pritchard, 1989; Prichard and Honeycutt, 2006a). Whilst NWP-type professional development has considerable potential, the degree to which it impacts on young peoples' identities or achievements as writers is less well documented. Indeed, as Andrews (2008a) and Whitney (2008) have both commented, considering the size of these national projects, the research base is not that strong. It tends to rely on small-scale studies and self-reports from 'exemplary writing instructors' who often write extensively in their private lives (Brooks, 2007; Susi, 1984), or on larger scale quantitative data drawn from NWP evaluations which measure student outcomes but do not offer detailed analysis of classroom interaction (Buchanan et al., 2005). In the UK in recent years, in response to the call for an NWP for teachers, several projects focusing on teachers, student teachers and teaching assistants as writers have developed, some involve working alongside professional writers (e.g. in Bath, Bedfordshire, Berkshire, Essex, Newham, Bury, Worcester, Medway, Kent, and Hampshire). Whilst not all of these have produced published papers, many have been presented at conferences (Grainger et al., 2006; Cremin, 2006; Ing, 2009; Goouch et al., 2009; Cremin, 2010; Rooke, 2010; Wilson and Metcalfe, 2010). Together they suggest that increasing teacher assurance and understanding of the processes of writing has considerable potential in developing younger writers, but more research is needed.

Teachers positioned as expert writers?

As the poet Philip Gross (2010b) observes, 'the world is not divided into the people who know [how to write] (authors, grown-ups) and (children) who don't'. We continue to give ourselves writing lessons, albeit often unconsciously, as we read and write for new purposes and in different forms. We all make mistakes and can encourage ourselves to take risks, experimenting with new ways of working and alternative ways of conveying and developing our thinking. Yet framed by traditional conceptions of instruction and authority, teachers in England have tended to be positioned as highly proficient writers. They have been required to demonstrate considerable skill mastery and genre knowledge and model their expertise; the National Strategies assert that this involves the teacher as the 'expert', demonstrating how to do something and 'making explicit the thinking involved' (DfES, 2006b: 4). Such a conception of modelling is rather limited however as it appears to focus on performing the construction of perfectly formed individual pieces of writing and does not appear to involve teachers modelling *being* writers, engaged in the struggle to compose. Further, it does not suggest teachers might explore the relationship between their own writing lives and conceptions of writing and those of younger writers. To offer an authentic model of a motivated and socially engaged writer, teachers need to do much more than model the act of composition: arguably they need to adopt a number of roles, including:

- engaged and reflective reader
- authentic demonstrator of writing
- scribe for class compositions
- fellow writer, writing alongside younger learners
- response partner
- editor, co-editor and adviser
- publisher of their own and their students' work
- writer in their everyday lives.

Teaching assistants can also be involved in this more extended approach, modelling being writers and seeking to develop their own identities as writers in order to support students. In this way we can explore the potential synergies between being teachers who write and writers who teach. As Spiro (2007) demonstrates, we can plan, share and review our work as genuine members of the classroom community of writers, but in order to do so we need to engage as writers ourselves. Horner (2010) prioritises this in a recent review of writers working in schools, and suggests that in terms of teacher development:

> The first priority is the need for *teachers to be writers* themselves. Only in this way do they learn empathy with their pupils, which enables them to give more space to pupils when they are writing and respond more. They are also then able to model writing 'live' rather than repeat what has been rehearsed.
>
> (Horner, 2010: 30, original emphasis)

Writing alongside younger writers

Teachers of writing who are involved as fellow artists in the classroom and who place themselves physically alongside learners, sitting next to them as they engage in their own writing, often become personally involved, thinking and feeling their way forwards as they compose. In a recent project, Writing is Primary (Goouch et al., 2009), which sought to prompt such teacher positioning, the teachers wrote alongside the younger writers and assumed the role of fellow writer. In direct contrast to their previous practice during independent writing, which the teachers described as moving around, troubleshooting and intervening in response to need, during the project almost all of the teachers regularly sat alongside children and undertook the same writing tasks. This offered new insights, since on several occasions teachers observed that the task they had set was too difficult for them as adults, let alone the children. Some came to interpret themselves differently in this context: as writers and learners, not primarily as teachers and instructors. They often invited the young people to read and respond to their own writing critically and reflectively, and worked as response partners, listening to their partners read their work aloud and sharing their views. In addition, dissatisfied with responding to children's writing as professional assessors of specific skills/targets, the teachers sought to resist this particular positioning and refashioned their responses, offering feedback from the arguably more personal position of an interested reader of the children's writing. Many perceived this made a significant difference not only to the way they were perceived, but also to their responses, which were more focused on the content and meaning of their partner's writing.

These subtle shifts in the teachers' professional positioning provoked some intriguing reactions from the children, who, in interviews with the visiting researchers, commented on how it felt to have their teachers writing alongside them. Most appeared to value their teachers' writing and openly sharing their drafts. For example, one case-study group of 10- to 11-year-olds commented:

- It's only fair that they write with us because we're all writing and the teachers aren't just standing around talking.
- I like it when she writes with us – she does the same thing as us, so she's one of us.
- It makes it easier – she doesn't interrupt.
- When she walked around, it made me feel uncomfortable. It's like I couldn't write what I was thinking.
- We don't feel like we're the only ones doing all the work.
- Sometimes she finds it hard, sometimes writing is.
- It gets us more involved – we're all writers.

The teachers reported increased motivation and commitment on the part of the children during the times in which they were writing alongside them, and subsequent work has affirmed this, suggesting that young writers settle more quickly and remain focused for longer when their teachers are similarly engaged (Goouch et al., 2009; Cremin and Baker, 2010). As Celia Rees (1999: 200) notes, before she became a professional writer she worked as a secondary English teacher, and when she wrote alongside young writers in class she found they responded to this very well; she perceived this was 'because I'd opened up to them and shared my experiences with them'. Often the teachers in our projects joined their students in journal writing, and in this context chose to share some of their writing. In the process, like Celia, they shared something of themselves, and the issues and themes dear to them. Many were honoured and pleased when the younger writers did likewise. Such writing alongside students may provide a temporary bridge between teachers and children, perhaps in part because the self-disclosure necessarily involved in the sharing of writing creates a web of connections which draws writers closer together.

On one occasion, Sarah, a young teacher, sitting with a group of 10- to 11-year-olds, was struggling to move from her mind map of ideas on the flip chart to a coherent text. Mentally she considered various options but, as she reported afterwards, none of these seemed quite right, so she kept on turning the possibilities around in her head. After a while, Adam, sitting next to her, interrupted her reverie and, looking at her blank page, observed somewhat candidly, 'I see you haven't written anything yet, Miss.' Sarah tried to explain, but the 10-year-old retorted, 'It looked to me like you were just looking out the window – daydreaming.' This conversation and the spontaneous role reversal which it prompted, since as Sarah herself noted later:

> I was caught – I needed the time and space – yet to be honest I rarely offer them much time – and if the shoe had been on the other foot I'd have said, 'Adam – stop staring out of the window and get on with your work!'

She realised the terms of participating as a writer deserved more attention in her classroom and began, in conversation with her students, to consider the role of silence and the different ways in which writers can and may need to play with and mull over ideas. The teachers in our projects have found this simple step, if undertaken regularly and authentically, to be an extremely useful one. It has involved the development of new knowledge and understanding and new positioning in the classroom. In their view it appeared to foster an atmosphere of shared ideas and more positive attitudes to writing; a more participatory pedagogy built on teachers' insights into the social process of writing. As some typically noted:

- I was always unsure how to reflect or to engage the children in this task. However, now the discussion comes automatically as I'm engaged in the task with them.
- Writing alongside has made me more confident in understanding just what I've asked of them.
- When they see you struggling, or fiddling with your pen, they're able to see that that the words don't just come straight to me either, it's all about choices and choices are about thinking.
- We face the same kind of challenges – I mean I know I am more experienced, but writing is still hard and we all need help and strategies to move forwards.
- We talk about the process more now, writer to writer, if you know what I mean.

Demonstrating writing authentically

In relation to demonstrating writing in school and spontaneously composing in class in front of students, our small survey of teachers and student teachers revealed that this was relatively rare (Grainger, 2005b). Instead the pieces for demonstration were assiduously prepared at home, prior to composing them 'authentically' in school. The practice of preparing writing at home was particularly marked in those teachers who expressed low self-esteem as writers, since they were worried about their ability to model specific literary features to order, they reflected a degree of insecurity about writing. Working with student teachers (Luce-Kapler et al., 2001) also found a marked reticence towards demonstrating writing authentically in class, due to the trainees lack of assurance as writers. Many attested to preparing their writing at home. Yet in the comfort of our own homes, we may procrastinate and make a coffee first, ponder on possible subjects – consciously and unconsciously – read, view and talk with others, and even check the features of the form, searching the Web perhaps for examples of kennings or cinquains to support us. In this way we are offering ourselves incubation time, preparation time and percolation time before we write, yet we may not afford the same degree of preparation to younger writers who, after observing an apparently impromptu compositional performance, may then be required to compose their own poetry with considerably less time, space and support.

In addition, we can capitalise on authentic demonstration writing to share our thinking as we compose, revealing that we too find blank spots, encounter problems, feel hesitant and keep changing our writing as we write and as the piece evolves. As Bruner notes:

> Written language is a problem space in which hypotheses and the capacity for self correction are present in abundance. It should be treated as such rather then as some sort of mysterious assembly line of bits and pieces to be put together.
>
> (Bruner, 1984: 200)

In seeking to model being a writer, teachers in a recent local authority project sought both to demonstrate more spontaneously in front of the class and to reflect on the problem-solving nature of writing and the difficulties they encountered; their cognitive and emotional responses (Cremin, 2010). Over time, through voicing their internal thought processes more publically and revealing some of their vulnerabilities as writers, several also found that the children began to talk more about their own thought processes as writers, and began to appreciate that all writers, whatever their age and experience, encounter challenges and frustrations as they write. When they sought to demonstrate authentically as writers, rather than as teachers playing the role of a writer for instructional purposes, the teachers perceived they learned more and offered stronger support for younger writers in the process. Additionally, the younger writers were prompted to offer them advice more readily and seemed to discern their teachers were authentically engaged and on occasion genuinely struggling and thinking through their writing. As some of the teachers commented:

- Modelling authentically can be a difficult and messy process. But working through the process in front of children clarified things for me. I've been having conversations with myself and the children help me.

- When I demonstrate writing on the spot, complete with mistakes and thinking things through, I find they ask more and contribute more, it's a much more open process.
- I used to prepare and plan all my demo writing beforehand and write in a very prescriptive way without explaining my thoughts to the children. Now I write more authentically and honestly – I show them that it's organic and unfolding and not tidy and neat!
- I try to show them how I solve my problems, though you never know what problems you're going to encounter, you have to work at them and find a way round and often now they offer me ideas to help me out.

Writing spontaneously in demonstration contexts is challenging, since the purpose of such a composition is complex and time constraints tend to mitigate against personal authenticity and our ideational fluency; but as these teachers indicate, it is important to declare our doubts and demonstrate to young writers the dialogic nature of writing and the essential struggle and perseverance required to craft effective written prose.

Conclusion

It is argued that both teachers and student teachers can benefit through considering their experiences and identities as writers and as teachers of writing. Reflecting on ourselves as writers, our writing histories, and current practices, we can widen our sense of self as writers and may come to reconceptualise writing in the twenty-first century. We may also choose to adopt new positions as teacher-writers and writer-teachers in the classroom. An examination of our identities and positioning can also prompt consideration of our students as writers and the ways in which our conceptions and practices may frame and limit their identities as writers. Through recognising the diversity of our writing lives and composing authentically in the classroom, we model being a writer and demonstrate the everyday nature, purpose and relevance of writing in all its many modes and media. Furthermore, through examining the relationship between our own writing practices and our classroom practice, we may come to develop more authentic tasks which offer a higher than usual degree of congruence with writing in the real world. Through re-positioning ourselves we may come to create more genuine and reciprocal communities of writers within and beyond school.

Black Cat stirred in his purring sleep, stretched his long soft, black as night body and busily began to lick lick with his pinkish sandpaper tongue.

Suddenly Black Cat became still, gazing intently in the direction of the open window where the moonlit curtains blew in the silver rays of the midnight full moon.

There came swiftly in the night's silence a tinkling of bells, faint at first, but louder and louder as the sound neared the open window.

Black Cat was ready, his yellow eyes searching searching for the sign that would set him free. His ears pricked up and from the open window he heard his name 'Black Cat, Black Cat, come fly with me. Black Cat, Black Cat, come fly with me. The moon is bright, we must away before the day'

With a giant sprawling leap Black Cat flew through the window soaring upwards into the night sky. Long flapping arms caught him. Black Cat was home. He purred with happiness as he nestled under his mistress' cloak peering out at the starry sky as they flew thorough the night.

'Say the words, say the words Back Cat' whispered whispered his mistress.

'OIYA OIYA OIYA OIYA' howled Black Cat, 'OIYA OIYA OIYA OIYA'

From far away and all around darting and diving through the midnight sky, appeared swathes of silver glinting broomsticks with black as night cats, laughing witches and the DANCE BEGAN . . .

Later, much later when the sun came up and the birds began to sing in the new dawn, Black Cat jumped numbly, nimbly onto the window pane of the open window and with a giant sprawling leap leapt into his wicker basket. Black Cat stretched stretched his soft furry body purring out a long yawn.

Curling up like a tight black coiled rope, Black Cat slept the sleep that only a witch's cat can do.

May 17th – Log entry I am finding this really difficult, I am not sure how to start or what to write about. I have put it off all week and think it's because I am feeling very stressed with schoolwork and this is affecting me more than I thought it would. My brain feels cluttered. MY IDEAS JUST DON'T COME!

May 18th – Log entry I am still desperately searching for some kind of inspiration/where/how do I begin?

About 10 pm something begins to gently 'tinkle' in my brain, the minutest speck of an idea and so it began. Me staring at my black cat sleeping curled up under the dog's lead in a wicker basket (not hers) on my work table. Her name is Isis and she's pure black with clear yellow eyes, she looks like she belongs to a witch . . .

Some of the responses from Elaine's fellow readers in the teachers' writing group:

I really like the last line – I don't know why it just sounds as if there is something about a witch's cat's sleep that is mysterious and different. Would like to read more!

the repetition makes the whole story sound like an incantation – like the spell that's being cast. I like that his "mistress" is a shadowy figure and her 'cloak' hints at witch before we're finally told she's a witch. I wanted to know what happened in the dance — it's description heavy and the plot is slighter.

Love the description and what is said to the cat to make him go – very enticing.

fantastic description – creates powerful imagery and loved the repetition of words and phrases.

The images created in this story are wonderful. I particularly like 'darting and diving... swathes of silver glinting broomsticks'

Elaine – teacher

Chapter 8

Teachers reviewing writing

Introduction

When we write we participate in a set of social practices which are shaped by social and historical understandings about what writing is, what it is good for in particular contexts and what forms it takes. As discussed in the last chapter, in our personal lives we write for a myriad of reasons, yet in school as teachers of writing we may tend to constrain students' reasons for writing, tether these to the curriculum and accept the version of school literacy and composition defined in current policy documentation. This version of writing is so persistently repeated and reinforced through curriculum requirements, assessment, training and teaching materials that it can remain uncontested. It is likely to frame and limit our practice and young people's learning about writing unless we seize opportunities to re-view writing and widen our subject knowledge, our pedagogy and practice.

In this chapter we explore some of the insights about writing which teachers develop when they write and reflect on the experience. In taking a more consciously reflective role as a writer, we can come to understand the complex recursive and creative compositional processes more fully. Additionally, we may develop a more nuanced understanding of the cognitive and emotional demands involved in generating, shaping and evaluating ideas. In re-viewing writing we may also come to review our classroom practice (Bearne et al., 2011).

Learning from an insider's perspective

One useful strategy to deepen understanding about writing is for teachers to learn about it from an insider's perspective and to consider whether this knowledge enables them to know the subject in a way that helps them teach it to others. Such 'pedagogic content knowledge' (Shulman, 1987: 8) has been described as the 'special form of professional understanding' that teachers use to transform their subject knowledge into the content of their instruction; although, as Johnston and Ahtee (2006) argue, relevant and in-depth knowledge of a subject is a prerequisite for developing pedagogic content knowledge. Arguably, the National Strategies (DfEE, 1998; DfES, 2006) in England widened teachers' subject knowledge of genres and their features at text, sentence and word level, but writing is far more than the sum of its textual parts: a writer's ideas and intentions, and their sense of an audience/reader also play a critical role in the creative process of composition.

> The acquisition of subject knowledge in praxis is essential to developing a more informed view not only of how texts are constructed, but also of the emotional and cognitive engagement of the writer . . . . Knowledge of the creative process by which texts come into being needs to be a key part of the teacher's repertoire of subject knowledge.
>
> (Gardner, 2010: 26)

Professional knowledge of text structures and language features and how texts work to achieve their purposes needs to be augmented by insider knowledge of the writing process and the experience of writing; particularly since pedagogical content knowledge also encompasses 'the ability to articulate and make accessible to developing writers that which is implicit and often at a level below conscious thought; to unpack what writers are doing as they engage in the writing process' (Parr, 2009: 147). In order to bring to conscious awareness our implicit knowledge about writing, we can seek to write alongside our staff colleagues or peers in teacher training, composing more reflectively than usual, focusing on the process and perhaps even recording reflections in a notebook and discussing these. In this way we can expand our metacognitive awareness of the experience of writing and our knowledge and understanding of the process of composing. We can also learn through writing alongside younger writers, experiencing the often time-limited demands and developing our grasp of the inherent challenges and possible scaffolds. In such contexts, we can expand both our subject and pedagogical content knowledge for the learners' benefit. Additionally, there is the potential to develop one's own assurance as a writer and to find increased pleasure and satisfaction in writing.

Over the last two decades, as noted in Chapter 7, a number of projects in England, the United States, New Zealand and Canada have encompassed attention to teachers' development as writers, and several have documented the subject knowledge that they developed (Pritchard and Marshall, 1994; Grainger, 2005b; Grainger et al., 2005; Cremin, 2006; Domaille and Edwards, 2006; Grainger et al., 2006; Pritchard and Honeycutt, 2006b; Goouch et al., 2009; Ing, 2009; Whitney, 2009; Cremin, 2010; Rooke, 2010; Wilson and Metcalfe, 2010). Some have also noted resultant shifts in pedagogy and practice. These studies variously sought to give teachers and student teachers the chance to consider, articulate and share their learning about composing and the social and emotional demands of the experience. Taken collectively they reveal that there are benefits to be gained through making one's implicit knowledge about writing more explicit and considering the pedagogical consequences of this new subject knowledge.

Learning about the compositional process

In exploring how teachers conceptualise composition and literacy at the primary phase, Yeo (2007) established that through their multiple histories, experiences and enactments, teachers develop a uniquely personal take on composition. In her study, undertaken in Canada, she found, however, that the teachers' conceptualisations were not connected to what they had been taught during teacher education, nor to the kinds of composition and literacy that operate in the twenty-first century. Rather, they reflected their own childhood experiences of writing and later 'induction into *school* literacy and *classroom* composition, which is very specific in its form and content' (2007: 125, original emphasis). Teachers, Bailey argues, will only teach writing effectively if their practice is deeply informed by 'an understanding of the complexities of composition processes' (2002: 26). Yet we will not necessarily develop our understanding through increasing our exposure to writing or by simply writing more; much will depend on our degree of reflexivity and openness to recognise our own compositional experiences and our discussions with others. I doubt I would not have been able to bring to the surface what I am now stretching to convey without having written, reflected, discussed and researched my own as well as others' compositional processes. In school, it may be inevitable that at times we set written tasks without having gone through the activity first ourselves, but we can also seek to explore the potential of writing alongside younger learners. For example, we can engage in writing a short story across a three-week unit or compose a persuasive advert and publish our work next to our students in the termly broadsheet. If we challenge ourselves to compose over time, working on pieces in class and at home, then some of the tensions, contradictions and complexities involved in writing may be revealed.

A complex recursive process

More than 30 years ago, the cognitive psychologists Hayes and Flower (1980), using 'think aloud' protocols, suggested that writing involves the interrelated processes of planning, translating and reviewing. Furthermore, as discussed in Chapter 1, they made it clear that their model did not reflect a chronological sequence; rather, it sought to capture the recursive nature of composition as described by able writers. The planning element refers to the generation or retrieval of ideas and the sorting/selection of these; translating refers to the process of committing ideas to paper or screen in the act of composition; and reviewing refers to any aspects of evaluative revision, such as rereading and making changes to the text. They also recognised the shaping influence of the writer's prior knowledge of the topic, the genre and the intended audience on these dynamic composing processes.

Whilst their work has been developed since, and there is increased recognition that these processes may develop at different rates (Beringer et al., 1996), it is evident that this conceptual understanding of the complexity of composition is in sharp contrast to the simplistic linear notions of planning, drafting, revising and editing, which tend to hold sway in the classroom. Such a simple model of the process of writing, like the 'simple model of reading' (which merely features decoding and comprehension), can short-change more complex and layered conceptions of composing, and may limit both teaching and learning about writing and the development of young writers.

Yet through writing regularly, talking about the process, making compositional collages and keeping composing logs, teachers can come to challenge previously accepted notions of the writing process. Our research (Goouch et al., 2009) revealed that with support teachers can re-review the writing process, develop new knowledge and understanding about the complexities involved, and question their reliance on this practice, even when the simple sequential process may have under-pinned their teaching from the beginning of their professional careers. As some noted:

- I've always taught it in stages and made everyone kind of move together to the next one, but it's not been like that in the group, and at home I'm much more eclectic – moving all the time between planning, reviewing and editing and so on. I couldn't have done it in the order I've always imposed on the children. It wouldn't have worked.
- I don't know why we've let ourselves accept the simple sequential approach. I've been teaching it like that for years, and never once questioned it really, I just assumed it was *the* writing process!
- Understanding the complexities and the constant shifting around and reviewing as I write has made a huge impact on me. I realise now the writing process is an individual thing; there is no set process to go through.

Divesting oneself of the notion that there is no one process to be followed creates its own challenges however, especially with a class of 30-plus young writers to teach. Yet if we hold too closely to a linear model, we may be in danger of ignoring difference and diversity in terms of the ways writers write. The teachers in the Writing is Primary project (Goouch et al., 2009; Ing, 2009), like the teenage writers in Myhill and Jones's study (2009), were involved in reflecting on their journeys as writers and considering their own composing processes. As outlined in Chapter 1, some of them could be described as 'discovery writers', who establish what they want to say as their writing unfolds before them, whilst the composing profiles of others were more attuned to those of 'planner writers', who revise and reflect throughout the process (Sharples, 1999). As children's author Tony Bradman observes:

I'm an obsessive planner. I spend a lot of time developing my stories from the initial idea to a full-scale outline, It's a way of feeling my way into the story and characters and working out how everything connects.

(Tony Bradman, quoted in Gamble, 2008: 16)

In contrast, Elaine, the teacher of six- to seven-year-olds who wrote the prose poem 'Black Cat' (see page 136, Chapter 7), composed this rhythmic verse one winter's night after considerable procrastination and assiduously not planning anything; instead she let the tune find itself on the page. As a discovery writer, she is more in harmony with Helen Cresswell, who, having published dozens of novels, maintains that she does not plan:

> With most of my books I simply write the title and a sentence and I set off and the road leads to where it finishes . . . . I used to have this saying by Leo Rosten pinned up on the wall that went 'When you don't know where a road leads, it sure as hell will take you there'. When I first read that I thought, that's exactly it! That's what happens when I write – I really don't know what's going to happen; it's quite dangerous in a way. I often put off starting because it seems a bit scary, yet at the end of the day, I feel that a story has gone where it's meant to have gone.
>
> (Helen Cresswell, quoted in Gamble, 2008: 118)

Whatever the approach to composing taken by individuals, teachers are better positioned to support young writers if, through first-hand experience, they are cognisant that, as Jackie Kay (2010) asserts, there is 'no one "correct" method. The right method is the one that works for that person, and produces the goods'. Teachers who appreciate this are more likely to encourage and celebrate different ways of approaching writing, and may support young writers in reflecting on their own processes in order to develop self-knowledge and understanding.

A process of rereading at the point of composition

Another aspect of the recursive nature of writing which teachers in several of our projects commented on was rereading at the point of composition (Grainger, 2005a; Grainger et al., 2005; Cremin, 2006). As they wrote, revised, reshaped and developed their ideas, many of them found themselves reading and rereading their emergent texts internally and/or sub-vocally. Many observed that, to some degree, they were noticing this apparently automatic part of the composing process for the first time, and came to consider the role of constantly rereading their unfolding writing. They remarked:

- I find I need to reread as I write to feel where my voice is going . . .
- I never realised how crucial rereading is, particularly in shaping writing and deciding the direction one is taking.
- Rereading is a vital strategy, not just for drafting, but in order to hear my own voice and reinforce my angle.
- It's automatic, isn't it? Well for me anyway – it's all about flow – how does it sound, how does it flow?

Multiple purposes for this practice of constantly reading back and forth through writing were identified, including clarifying meaning, shaping the text and ensuring a sense of direction, as well as reviewing the tune and tenor of their writing. This reflective interaction between the writer and the developing text is described by Murray (1982) as a dialogue with self:

> The self speaks, the other self listens and responds. The self proposes, the other self considers. The self makes, the other self evaluates. The two selves collaborate: a problem is spotted, discussed, defined; solutions are proposed, rejected, suggested, attempted, tested, discarded, accepted.
>
> (Murray, 1982: 165)

Significantly, however, very few professionals from these projects reported having discussed such rereading with young people; most were sure they had never done so beyond asking them to read their work through before handing it in. Yet this is not the same as pausing to evaluate one's text during the process of composing, and considering where the piece is and where it is going, both at the level of the sentence and in relation to the 'whole' text at that moment. This weighing of words and phrases, hearing their pattern and evaluating whether they suit the intended meaning (which itself will shift as decisions are made), demonstrates again the recursive nature of writing.

If we recognise that an understanding of this interactive process counts as relevant subject knowledge then this should prompt us to consider how we can transform it for instructional purposes. We could try to raise young writers' awareness of the practice of rereading and sub-vocalising as they compose by sharing some of the questions we ask ourselves as we write. One group of teachers shared the following list of 'questions to self' with their classes:

- What am I trying to say?
- How effective is what I have written?
- How does it sound?
- Why did I choose . . . ?
- What do I want to say/do next?
- How could I say/do that?
- What will my reader be thinking/feeling as they read this?

In this way, they became writers then readers and writers again as they shuttled back and forth inside the compositional process: writing, rereading, reflecting on their messages (intended and conveyed) and reshaping their work as a consequence. Many sought to model this dialogic process in the classroom and used metacognitive asides to share the process of voicing, listening and attending to their unfolding texts. They sought to show that such monitoring is a crucial part of the compositional process. Additionally, many began to encourage the students to reread their drafts to one another several times during a lesson as their writing evolved. Whilst this inevitably interrupted the flow, some perceived it helped avoid the piece spiralling out of control and heightened the young people's awareness of the meaning and flow of the text, particularly in poetic writing.

A personal meaning-making process

Reflecting on the process can remind us that writing, like painting, dance and music, exists as an artistic tradition, a resource for generating meaning. In adult workshops or when writing alongside young writers in school, teachers can experience writing as a means of creating and expressing meaning both in their own lives and the lives of those they teach. The heart of writing, Moffett (1968) claims, beats deep within the subjective inner life of the writer, and some of the teachers in an early project (Grainger, 2005b), and many since, voiced deep satisfaction when their writing helped them make dynamic sense of their lives. The workshops appeared to represent an opportunity to take time out of the rush of teaching, testing, and life, and became a personal space in which they could pause, reflect, and connect to the people and the issues they cared about. Many chose to revisit their childhoods both explicitly and metaphorically, and explored their identities as mothers, fathers, siblings, campaigners, and friends. As one typically observed, 'I feel I've met myself again through these writing sessions, I hadn't realised writing was so much about oneself, even when I'm writing in role I can see myself, my life, my views in the writing' (Grainger, 2005b: 83).

'The artist's interpretation of experience', Britton (1982: 21) suggests, 'is concrete; sensuous, emotional and intellectual. Yet it is not mere re-enactment either – it is a work of the creative imagination'. This was borne out in much of the writing in which the teachers appeared to be in dialogue with themselves, often about issues of angst. For example, in one session of the Writing is Primary project (Goouch et al., 2009; Ing, 2009), one colleague revisited a childhood friendship foreshadowing a friend's death, another reflected metaphorically on an affair, and yet another retold her daughter's birth. Yet another, in reviewing Shaun Tan's *The Red Tree*, reflected on her son's depression, ending her review with the following words:

> Not only will I use it in my classroom, but every now and again, when I find myself waist deep in fallen leaves, I will open its pages quietly in my bedroom and reflect on its quiet message of hope.

In coming to appreciate the layering of life, texts and issues beneath their writing, the teachers were prompted to consider the pedagogical consequences of these more nuanced insights. They considered how in the classroom they often insisted that personal writing was restricted to units of work on autobiography and that choice was limited. They discussed how to validate more explicitly the practice of leaning on one's own life, and some developed work on personal stories and oral storytelling, whilst others explored activities such as holiday timelines, family trees, and 'autobiographical boxes'. Such resources and activities were used to prompt the retelling of significant memories and could be added to the learners' options lists for journal writing.

Making intertextual links

When we write and document the influences on our writing and the rich seedbed on which we draw, we often come to recognise more fully the interplay between life experience and our reading and writing. As adults we know that writers are magpies and mine their own lives and others for incidents and episodes, and that Shakespeare used others' stories and poetry as the source of his plays. But do we make this implicit knowledge explicit in the classroom, and encourage young writers to borrow ideas from life and the myriad of vicariously experienced incidents and issues, characters and themes in books, music, television, film and the Internet for example?

In several projects, we made composition collages with teachers to help reveal some of the influences on our texts. Using cuttings from magazines and newspapers, and connecting to a composing log or notes made during the composition, we created collages and later talked through possible connections, invariably finding more traces of other texts in our writing in the process. As Vicky's example in Figure 8.1 subtly indicates, in her extended five-verse poem 'Bluebell Woods' she draws

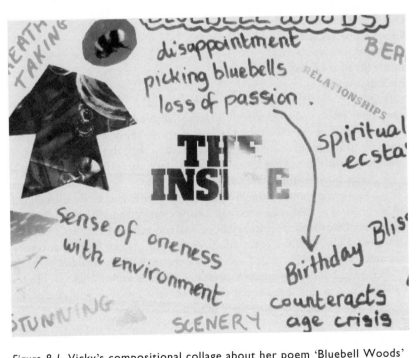

Figure 8.1 Vicky's compositional collage about her poem 'Bluebell Woods'

on a walk in the woods to explore what she later described as 'difficult personal issues' and a 'niggling worry about growing old'. Her first verse begins in hope:

> There is blue in the woods
> Where the still scent lingers
> As close as breath
> Where joy throbs in hope
> Distilling the silence
> Repeating now repeating
> The rhapsody of birdsong
> Pause the day

In later verses the imagery Vicky uses suggests the tension she feels as the bluebells weep, those picked become limp and frail, bruised by the hands of humans, and their colour seems to fade. Yet as she walks on, following a bee's hum, she comes upon 'a glade conceiving light' where the blue seems to negate the night and ravish the day, restoring a sense of balance and solace which she evokes in her last verse:

> Blue, blue in the woods,
> Flooding through the grey,
> Of that clay of yesterday
> Free falling thought seeds
> Germinating rain drops
> Find wisdom and solace
> In the life beat of that hour
> Redeem the day.

Some of her emotional engagement with the subject matter is captured in her compositional collage, in which she places the words 'the inside' in the centre, commenting, 'this is more about me than the woods – though I tried to make the blue shine through'. In talking about her text, Vicky also referred to reading a friend's birthday poem entitled 'Growing Old' in the last workshop, her memory of Robert Frost's 'Stopping by the Woods on a Snowy Evening', which she had learned by heart as a child, and watching a nature programme recently. In such collages, some of the diverse life incidents, personal concerns and interests, televisual experiences and film and text connections drawn on in a text's production are brought to the surface and recorded as echoes; some are richly resonant of the text, whilst others remain more distant. As Vicky noted through writing, making collages and keeping a composing log, she felt she had become much more aware of the influences on her writing, and the source of some of her ideas:

> I've always said that talking and reading contribute to children's writing, but
> I guess I hadn't known it for myself and it's not just that either, it's life

experience, looking, listening, thinking creatively, combining ideas and incidents and being determined too.

Experiencing the social and emotional demands of composing

In drawing a parallel between beginning to write a story and fishing at night, Philip Pullman (2002) observes: 'There's a lot you can't predict . . . the fears and delights of fishing at night have nothing to do with rationality'. This experience of fishing in the dark – waiting for a pull on the line, navigating the open seas, and wondering if one will go to shore with a huge catch, a few sprats or nothing at all – was encountered by many of the teachers in our projects, each of which has demonstrated that whilst teachers can develop their subject knowledge about writing, this is often a socially and emotionally demanding experience.

Initially at least, many of the teachers lacked confidence as writers, and despite the scaffolds and assurances offered, worried that their writing would be compared and negatively judged. This issue of teachers' perceptions of themselves as writers is examined more fully in Chapter 7, although it is worth noting that the concerns of those in the We're Writers research (Grainger, 2005b) have been heard repeatedly over the years:

- Why am I so hopeless at this?
- I've always been awful at writing.
- I never understand instructions, I feel thoroughly thick when I'm asked/told to write.
- I bet everyone else will have better ideas.
- It'll be embarrassing if we have to share, mine will be the worst.
- My fear of being shown up makes me feel rebellious – perhaps my boys feel like this too.
- I hope we don't have to read it out, everyone else's will be better than mine.

This fear of failure and possible exposure raises issues of security, ownership and self-esteem. In one project, the teachers' self-set challenge to write a short story for children was almost halted by their head teachers who, unbeknown to the staff, perceived they were so stressed by this that they requested it should cease (Cremin, 2006). After vigorous discussions however, the activity continued, although the time to complete the narrative was extended well past the May assessment tests. In all the groups, as trust between the professionals gradually developed, some of the tensions between private and public writing eased and most of the teachers became more comfortable writing in the company of others and sharing writing. Nonetheless, the compositional process was experienced as difficult at times; the teachers variously learned more about the uncertainty involved, the value of writing as a resource for making meaning, writing in role, and working collaboratively.

Uncertainty and discomfort

The work indicates that the lived experience of composing represented an ongoing struggle for many of the teachers, despite their gains in confidence over time. The sense of uncertainty never entirely ceased; they set themselves new challenges and found the open-endedness of the creative process fostered a sense of continual uncertainty. The metaphors employed by one group help make their perceptions apparent, namely that the compositional experience was at times like 'a maelstrom', 'being on a roller coaster and not knowing when you can get off', 'being at sea without oars', 'swimming without arm bands' (Grainger et al., 2006). It was evident that, often as a consequence of the emotional discomfort created, the professionals were obliged to take risks to find ways forwards, yet this too was demanding. As France (2008) observes, writers 'inhabit the instability between text and meaning, and are thus constantly without sure footing and become more vulnerable as they attempt to forge new paths between language and reality as it is perceived by the reader' (ibid.: 61).

This instability and unpredictability were experienced as a struggle, as was the openness and sense of possibility involved. As writers, when the teachers sought to select the most effective option, many found their decisions led to further possibilities, which meant the process remained open and unstable. This struggle to generate ideas, find the 'right' words, select from the alternatives, and convey their desired meaning was common. The wealth of options available to reshape a poem or tighten up a newspaper article was also experienced as emotionally draining. Notes from their composing logs indicate the degree of disquiet experienced:

- I can't seem to make it say what I want it to. It's always just beyond my grasp and I have to keep trying other ways to say it, to see what happens when I do this or that. It keeps changing and I find that infuriating.
- Sometimes it's like a total mess of writing in my mind. As I write and rewrite, I change and debate things with myself and that's confusing and messy – more messy than I realised.
- It's like an endless stream of new possibilities, new decisions to be made – it's exhausting me – I'll never get it finished at this rate – not how I want it anyway.
- When I came back to this today, I reread it and started making immediate changes. I added more about the old man's thoughts, but then when I read it again it seemed to be saying something different – seemed to be weaker somehow, less focused. The ominous image of the night sky got lost in all this other stuff and I'm not sure how to get that sense of underlying threat back. It's exhausting this business and I'm not sure where it's going any more and that makes me uneasy.

Although negative emotions are widely recognised as being part of any creative process, the challenge that engagement in composing represents for teachers (and younger writers) should not be underestimated. There is unquestionably risk-taking involved, although if teachers experience a 'pedagogy of discomfort' (Boler, 1999) in creative endeavour, arguably they will be more empathetic to the feelings and concerns of their students may be better placed to help them handle their own worries and compositional uncertainties. Recognising the affective dimension, the writer's self-esteem and their response to the process and content is an important strand of subject knowledge about writing.

Writing collaboratively

The teachers in our projects were surprised to find that writing together and composing one piece in pairs or small groups was often enabling and satisfying. Many came to appreciate the conversational context and mutual support which such writing engendered, as one observed: 'Until we did it ourselves I never knew how valuable writing together is – for me it was like a breakthrough – I felt more supported and less judged'. In the Creativity and Writing project, Sally, who had very negative memories of writing and spelling at school, reflected a continued sense of low self-esteem as a writer (Cremin, 2006). Over six months, she wrote little, separated herself from her colleagues and, whilst keen to develop her teaching of writing, continued to find composing difficult. However, a few weeks before the sharing of the group's stories, she invited a friend to compose a story with her. As she explained:

> I felt under pressure to create a decent story but couldn't get started, I did feel guilty not writing, but the longer it went on the harder it became. I did a plan, but it was embarrassingly basic and wasn't worth writing. I began to think about just not doing it, refusing, but everyone was talking about their work, drawing the journey and that and I knew I'd got to do something. Then a friend at school asked me how it was going, she'd had my class last year and I thought why don't I risk it and ask her to do it with me. She agreed and we focused on the kids and did it together. I read it to them this morning and they really listened and clapped and clapped. They even asked us to write a sequel! It was amazing. (Late-phase interview)

> (Cremin, 2006: 425)

As the extract below demonstrates, their tale not only perceptively connected to the audience, but also metaphorically explored some of Sally's own concerns:

"A Year Six child who cannot spell!"

Terry sat down quickly, a little embarrassed but trying not to show it.

"You!" his finger pointed straight at Julie. He had never asked one of the younger children before. Julie stood up nervously.

"I-n-f-o-r-m-a-t-i-o-n" she said quietly.

"Very impressive!" smiled Mr Lovett, but Julie wasn't smiling. She could feel the other children's eyes burning into her.

"You should've got it wrong even if you knew it" whispered Sophie as they went back to class. "You're such a goodie goodie! No one wants a friend like you."

Julie thought about how true that was. The one thing she wanted was a friend but she never seemed to do anything right when it came to the other children.

(Extract: *With a Smile*)

(Cremin, 2006: 425)

For Sally, the collaborative compositional process supported her as a writer, alleviating some of her insecurities and allowing her to experience the satisfaction of children's and colleagues' positive responses. As a consequence of writing together, some of the teachers offered such opportunities in class, and one, working with 10- to 11-year-olds, set up foursomes who wrote in pairs and then reviewed one another's collaboratively produced writing. Such collaborative evaluation was also explored by Domaille and Edwards (2006) in their work with trainee teachers, who also found it a highly effective tool, especially when reviewing quality writing.

Writing in role

Writing in role offers significant support to teachers as well as children who often that writing in the midst of a dramatic context and in the voice of another helps them push the boundaries of their own language use, and write with more conviction and a stronger voice. Empathetic writing in role, which often emerged during the various projects' drama and writing workshops, was seen to emerge with relative ease, in complete contrast to writing in more solitary contexts. The teachers often became so engaged in the imagined experience that the transition to writing appeared to be seamless, undertaken in a 'state of flow' (Csikszentmihalyi, 2002), which enriched their writing. This was evidenced in their comments:

- When I was in character, it just flowed onto paper. I couldn't be wrong, it was what I felt, what I believed.
- Putting myself in someone else's shoes and experiencing their dilemma really helped me form what I wanted to say.
- I was able to experience the place – it became present/not past – real not imagined.
- My anger was real, I would not stand for this injustice – I wrote from the heart.
- I felt like the old woman and needed to write it all down quickly before the feelings went away. As I wrote, her pain seemed to ebb away. I suppose I was sharing her loss and remembering mine.

(Grainger, 2005b: 84–5)

The consequences for the classroom of appreciating the support for writing which drama offers were discussed by the teachers, some of whom sought to offer their students more opportunities for 'innerstanding' (Heathcote and Bolton, 1995) and inhabiting the voices of others. The teachers sought to avoid confining writing to an 'after drama' slot and worked to 'seize the moment for writing' (Cremin et al., 2006) when the context was tense and challenging, and writing could be used as a meaning-making tool. In this way, the younger writers were offered extended opportunities for oral rehearsal through imagined experience. This is discussed further in Chapter 2.

Conclusion

The process of composing is neither fixed nor predictable, and teachers and student teachers deserve to experience this in supported contexts, to enable them to learn through reflective involvement and come to voice an insider's informed perspective.

We concluded Chapter 6 with Kellog's (1994: 213) observation that teachers 'must teach the student how to think as well as write', yet this is not possible unless teachers themselves are metacognitively aware of composing processes and open to exploring the relationship between thought and writing. Through becoming personally involved, thinking and feeling their way forwards as adult writers, they can deepen their subject knowledge and understanding.

However, whilst the examples offered in this chapter highlight that teachers can expand their subject knowledge, it is not an easy task to transform this knowledge into pedagogic practice and the basis of instruction. Furthermore, most research in this area focuses on teachers' understanding of composing continuous prose; there is little work examining teachers' digital text production. What needs to be understood, Yeo (2007: 127) asserts, 'is the relationship between teaching, composition, and life', and this requires openness and connection-making as well as a desire to learn about compositional processes in different modes and media. Diversity and complexity are key; it is not a case of 'do as I do' but a case of recognising both the uniqueness and the shared understandings of being a writer. Considering one's compositional journeys and the social and affective nature of writing can help us review writing, develop new understandings, ask different questions, and consider whether our practice builds on this knowledge and connects to the world of writing beyond school.

Positive Feedback

Seeing you
recently
took me back
thirty years
to when I sat
in your class
and first tussled
with
ideas
which led me
to a new world.

At first it was
blurry and fogged
but slowly
brought into focus
by words
which I found
hidden, waiting
and half formed,
tentatively there
inside myself,
oozing from pen to paper.
I never knew their power
until you showed me.

Thirty years on
I have learnt
more of the magic.
And I am still in awe
of those like you
who unlocked its pleasures
and sent me into a future
where anything became
possible.

This was my original draft - initially it didn't have a title.

Seeing you recently
Took me back 30 years
To when I sat in ~~your~~
Your class
And first tussled ~~with~~
With ideas
Which took me to a
New World.
At first it was
Blurred and ~~foggy~~ fogged
But slowly brought
Into focus
By words
Which I found
Hidden & waiting
Half formed
Tentatively there
Inside myself
Oozing from pen to paper...
I never knew their power
Until you showed me.

30 years on
I have learned
More of their magic.
And I am still in awe
Of those like you
Who unlocked its pleasures
And sent me into a future
Where anything
Became possible.

I changed the capital letters at the beginnings of the lines to lower case — I think it makes it sound less formal & 'poetic' — more direct?

It was a chance meeting with my A level English literature teacher, who I hadn't seen since I'd left school, that gave me the motivation to write this poem. I hadn't really written much poetry since I was a student and it wasn't until I'd done some mind-mapping and spent some time in discussion with other people about my memories of writing that I recognised that I had something that I wanted to write about.

Putting pen to paper honestly felt a bit like diving into deep water - murky, unfamiliar territory and with no certainty of re-surfacing with anything. But actually, once I'd got the first few lines down, it flowed quite easily and quickly. I don't remember making a specific decision to use a poetic form - that's just how it came out. Maybe it was a sub-conscious choice - after all this was addressed to the teacher who had introduced me to poetry. In those days it was Keats and Wordsworth but since then I've particularly enjoyed the works of TSEliot, Robert Frost and Carol Ann Duffy so perhaps they too had an influence?

I suppose, once I'd finished, made a few alterations (not many) and reflected on what I'd written, I realised that I had 'surfaced' with something. I had expressed some of the emotions that had been invoked by that chance meeting, exploring en route what it meant for me now, having this new understanding. And it had also seemed like a way of articulating a sense of gratitude.

So yes, I did send her a copy...

Sue – literacy consultanat

Part III

Professional writers

Chapter 9

Professional writers
Working in schools

Introduction

Working with professional writers can be an inspiring experience for both teachers and young people alike. In school-based residencies and on visits to heritage sites, museums, galleries and other venues, writers of all ages and experience learn through creative engagement, through composing and considering the art and craft involved. Many different writers, including novelists, illustrators, playwrights, poets, journalists and non-fiction writers are involved in such partnership projects. Such writers not only demonstrate that they are passionate and enthusiastic about writing (and reading), but they privilege time for creating and completing texts. Many also work towards making public the work of young writers, creating real audiences for their compositions.

This chapter, in recognising the potential of these partnerships, briefly reflects on some of the benefits and challenges involved and then attends to the voices of three writers: Philip Gross, a renowned poet and Professor at Glamorgan University, Mary Medlicott, a well-known storyteller of oral and written tales, and Linda Newbery, a novelist and popular teenage writer. Their reflections offer a rich resource for pondering on compositional processes and the dissonance between these authors' experiences of composition and the way it tends to be taught in schools. There are no easy answers, but opportunities for intriguing insights abound, some of which I have sought to tease out, while others are left for you as readers to discern and debate.

Young people, as the National Literary Trust (NLT) survey suggests, may have somewhat limited views of what a writer writes. The 8- to 13-year-olds involved in this study perceived that 'writer' produce stories, poems, plays or screenplays and thought that they 'will do well in life', although some saw writers as solitary, 'boring' individuals (Clark and Dugdale, 2009). As Dave Smith, a comedian who works in schools, comments:

> Many pupils have a picture of a writer as a fusty, dusty, grey-haired bore, hunched over an ancient, cobwebby typewriter, ploughing through the fortieth chapter of a worthy, heavyweight novel. Not me. OK, I hardly go marlin-

fishing like Hemingway, or live the *louche, roué* existence of Noel Coward, but I do ride a Triumph and go to the pub sometimes.

(Dave Smith, 2010)

Despite evidence to suggest that professional writers make an impact on the motivation, confidence and achievements of young writers (Coe and Sprackland, 2005; Owen and Munden, 2010), a recent review for the Arts Council England notes that opportunities are unevenly spread and many young people, particularly in the 11–14 range, never experience working with a writer (Horner, 2010). It is also argued that the influence of such creative experiences is constrained, in part because of the teaching profession's apparent lack of assurance/desire to sustain and develop the work begun by writers, and in part because of writers' lack of awareness of the curriculum. Nonetheless, as Horner notes:

The introduction of an artist, who has a different relationship with the pupils from their teachers, opens up possibilities for a form of authority based on expertise in an artform rather than institutional authority. This means the writer responds differently to children and helpfully dislocates the learned patterns of classroom interaction.

(Horner, 2010:13)

Additional evidence suggests that when young people work with creative practitioners of various kinds, they are often inspired and develop creative skills such as risk-taking, improvisation, resilience and collaboration (Ofsted, 2006). Writers in particular can help young people see with 'new eyes' and explore imaginative possibilities. They often use different strategies from teachers, share their own practices and experiences, and frequently follow through to publication and celebration. However, as Thomson et al. (2006) indicate in their case study of a failed arts partnership, issues of ownership, perceived appropriateness of the material produced and teachers' perceptions of the role of writers in schools can also lead to censorship and disappointment. Part of the challenge in this instance appeared to emerge from the teaching role being delegated to the writer, with little involvement on the part of the teachers; positioned to one side they separated themselves from the work of the writer, which is sadly not uncommon in creative partnerships (Galton, 2008). A recent UKLA professional development resource pack, *Writers in Schools* (Cremin et al., 2010), offers examples of how to negotiate residencies and visits in order to ensure that when we work with writers in school, this becomes a rich learning experience. However, much will depend on the ways in which writers position themselves, as Philip Gross observes:

One of the jobs of good writers in schools is to remind us, adult and child alike, that:
- *poets* are not different from *people*
- *people-in-print* face the same choices as learning writers

- writers are not different people from *readers/listeners*
- *adults* writing – and especially teachers – are as worried, often, as the children . . .
- and can/should be as playful.

Gratifying as it is to be an entertainer and a small celebrity, the best poets in schools leave pupils and teachers with a sense of alongsideness, too.

(Philip Gross, 2010: 234, his emphasis)

Philip Gross: poet, novelist, playwright and short-story writer for radio

Philip is Professor of Creative Writing at Glamorgan University and a writer of many parts – poet, writer of thought-provoking fiction for young people, science fiction, haiku, schools opera libretti, plays and radio short stories. His poetry up to and including the Whitbread Prize-shortlisted *The Wasting Game* is collected in *Changes of Address* (2001), since when Bloodaxe has published three more collections, the latest of which, *The Water Table* (2009, won the T. S. Eliot Prize. *Deep Field* is due from Bloodaxe in 2011. Collaboration with arts, dance and music has been a source of energy in his writing life, and *I Spy Pinhole Eye*, with photographs by Simon Denison (Cinnamon, 2009), was the English-language winner of Wales Book of the Year. He is the author of ten teenage novels – most recently *Going for Stone*, *The Lastling* and *The Storm Garden*. His children's poetry includes *The All-Nite Café*, which won the Signal Award, and *Off Road To Everywhere*, a PBS Children's Poetry Bookshelf choice (Salt, 2010).

Creating space: Reflecting on writing

Knowing, not knowing

Looking into one's own workings as a writer . . . There's a fascination to it, and a sense of danger. Some writers, poets especially, keep well away, for fear of tampering with what feels like a gift. I've committed myself to the risk by teaching Creative Writing in universities, where 'knowledge' is the name of the game. I had been a working writer for ten years before I set foot in a university. For ten years after, I kept a boundary between the two parts of my working life. Now, another ten years on, I find myself wearing the title of Professor, i.e. the person who should know what that Creative Writing knowledge is. Not every bit of the knowledge, of course . . . but who should know, if anybody does, just what sort of knowledge it is, as distinct from what, say, media or literary studies know.

In case this seems, literally, academic, let's acknowledge that any writer who visits a school to encourage writing has implicit thoughts about what s/he knows and how it might be shared.

One thing I do know is that creative means working with elements we can't, or can't yet, know. This seems a fruitful paradox, and quite different from being precious about 'inspiration' or the visits of the Muse. I feel more hands-on about it, like a cook knows that there are stages when not to take the cake out of the oven to check if it's rising.

But all this starts from my own writing, both for adults and for children – no distinction there – and I see no reason why children's writing should be fundamentally different. What follows from this is that predictable outcomes, the kind that education policy demands, might sit uncomfortably with the genuine creative life.

Showing our workings

Conceptualising process might not, for young writers, be the best place to start. Letting the process be visible on the page, or in the things we do together . . . that's another story.

To be honest with children when I ask them to write with me it seems the most important thing of all. Each starter-pack or exercise I offer aims to give an outward and visible/audible form to something that I know that I do. Am I claiming that all other writers work the same? Of course not. Young writers should meet a range of us, with a wide range of tools. The most vital knowledge they gain about writing, gradually, will be self-knowledge (metacognition, if you like) of the most practical kind.

So writers in schools – who include teachers brave enough to write alongside children – need to show their workings. The children need to see a not-too-precooked glimpse of how the process really goes.

For me, some of it can be glimpsed in my notebooks – the small black police-style notebooks that slip in a pocket and come with me almost everywhere. This is where a large part of my poetry, at least, begins . . . and a vital germinative part of the scripts and novels too. This is what I return to day after day, often with no intention or project in mind. This is mulch.

What you might see in there, as educator, looks dismaying: almost unreadable ravellings of tiny writing, slapdashed at different angles, disconnected almost wilfully. It would be a rare teacher, in my own school life, who could have looked over my shoulder and said Yes, Philip, that looks promising.

Tearing up the book

I said wilful, and I meant it. I have shelves of linear, diary-style notebooks at home, and for years I chafed against them. Even I knew that the dogged recording of what happened (and, worse, what I thought and felt about it) would be too dull for me ever to read it again. One test of the liveliness of Creative Writing for the reader is whether the writer is being surprised at all by what they're finding as they write.

At a certain point, then, I lost patience. I ripped the pages out and shuffled them. I made myself a loose-leaf book in an A5 ring binder and began to write fast, almost too fast to watch myself doing it, and dealt the fragments into the book in any order.

I began to play a game (or should I say, to use a meditation-style technique) that involved letting a thought form, holding it a moment, visualised as clearly as I could . . . then dismissing it, clearing the mind like bursting a bubble or wiping a screen . . . before the next. Or else I would walk and spot a detail here . . . and there . . . and there . . . for as long as it took to jot it, then walk on.

In all these self-set exercises I was saying Don't Look Back. When I finally did look, weeks or months later, not only was I surprised by some of what I found, but I had the uncanny feeling apparently unconnected passages were snuggling up against to each other in interesting and suggestive ways. Potential characters turned up together, though I had imagined them for different stories if any at all. Even stranger, they seemed to have been having conversations while my back was turned, and hints of their possible clashes and comings together seemed to be hovering in the space between them on the page.

Putting it this way is playful, and at the same time perfectly serious. Those two terms never seem like opposites to me.

Cultivating chaos

I did not go on with the loose-leaf notebooks indefinitely – that too could have become a mere habit. But the sense of a page being fluid, of being a space where molecules of thought could move around and recombine, into which I could work back . . . that stayed with me. I suspect it is an outward image of what occurs inside us, generally too fast to perceive. So much of creativity is not so much a new creation as recombination, spotting a slantwise association that brings new life to both the terms involved. Poetry tends to foreground this in the form of unexpected similes and metaphors, but inventing/discovering a plot line for a story functions much the same.

Look at my notebooks today and space might be the first thing you notice, deliberately-left white spaces inviting me to come back weeks or even years later, saying It's not finished. Think again. You might spot me choosing not to think a thought through to its logical conclusion – to leave it fragmentary, loose-ended. Meeting the tiny Japanese verse-molecules of haiku was an education to me, because part of that art is to create a verse that feels unfinished to the Western ear. The reader has to think on, to 'complete' it in his or her mind.

This did not come naturally to me. It is a way of working I have learned, originally as a self-prescribed corrective – self-education, if you like – for an anxious and exhaustive habit of mind. Later I did it simply because . . . well, it's fun, and seems to work for me.

It is hard, maybe, to explain this carefully cultivated discipline of encouraging disorder to young writers. It is hard to explain to adults sometimes too. But explanations might not be the point, not before they have experienced the feeling for themselves. Most of the writing games I like to use are explained as little as possible in advance, so the facilitator's role is to say Trust Me . . . These are often to do with relaxing one's hold on the work, on one's ownership even. Trust me, says the facilitator (and s/he has to be trustworthy, or this is a criminal thing to say) and find out where the process leads.

The confidence of our uncertainty

Describing this at all could sound like just another prescriptive method. Rather, let's be aware that we vary, not just from each other but from ourselves in different moods and stages of our lives. At some ages, children may need all the urging they can get to cohere; at others, they may be so much in the grip of the need to conform that some cultivated chaos is the only hope for creativity. The experienced writer learns to do this for him or herself – often with the help of friends and mentors (some of them living, some in books or dead five hundred years ago).

Gradually we learn – as hopefully we can help others learn – to have the confidence of our uncertainty.

If that sounds like playing with yet another paradox, fair enough; I'd guess that paradox lies at the heart of all creative process. To be disciplined and free-form; to work fast, on the impulse and to come back, nag away at it, if need be, for years; to put your mind to it and to trick yourself out of too much thinking . . . The challenge for the educator is to hold this shifting balance for each different class, each different child.

Having and letting go

The visible space across which words can move might not be private. The ideas I bring to work in schools are frequently collaborative. I have always revelled in working with other writers, artists, dancers and musicians for myself. People commonly fear that collaboration means compromise, watering down or losing something precious to yourself. How revelatory is it, then, to have an experience in which you find yourself writing something that is both intensely you and also surprising as you each watch it form, semi-independently, in the space between you and someone else. To experience that, you have to take a risk. By learning to let go of your hold on an idea you discover that it can come home to you sea-changed. (Yes, I want to win that Shakespeare reference back from the political cliché it has become!) I said found yourself just now advisedly; the experience is of you-plus, not you-minus.

That letting it go, across the physical space between people, across the spaces on the notebook page, across time between me-now and me-later, was an essential part of self-learning for me, and probably the most distinctive single thing I can pass on. No one writer-in-schools should offer to be a whole curriculum. The teacher has the training and the skills to hold that wider view. For each of us to offer something close to the heart of our own work, in practical shareable form, is the truest thing we can do.

What we can also share – what we must model, too – is the taking of risks in writing, and the ability to recognise and to manage our fear. This applies especially to teachers, many of whom might have absorbed all kinds of anxiety about writing when younger and now find it redoubled by the responsibility of standing in front of a class as the person-who-knows.

One last paradox

Reading all this talk of space, you might be imagining a writer with a relaxed working life, clear routines and boundaries. That writer is not me. Much of my writing takes shape in snatched moments, on a crowded train. My space is often an interior experience, invisible from outside. That is, ultimately, where a writer needs to have their space . . . and this might be increasingly urgent and rare for young writers who live in an extrovert, performative, Facebookish world. Creating small visible pockets of it on the page or in the air between us is itself an education, a step on the way.

Mary Medlicott: professional storyteller and writer

Mary worked on the National Oracy Project in the late 1980s and in 1990 devised *By Word of Mouth*, a Channel 4 series on the revival of storytelling in the UK. She has carried out hundreds of residencies and visits to UK schools and has also made storytelling trips abroad, including to Ireland, New Zealand, South Africa, Tobago, and the United States. As well as working in performance and with community groups, she has a special interest in supporting teachers as storytellers. Her one-woman shows include *Travels with My Welsh Aunt*. Mary has been Chair of the Society for Storytelling and edits its publications in the Papyrus, Oracle and Artisan series. She has published two books on storytelling with children, *The Little Book of Storytelling* and *Stories for Children and How to Tell Them*, as well as two children's novels, *Open Secret* and *Elephant Luck*. Her most recent publication is *Shemi's Tall Tales*, set in her native North Pembrokeshire area.

Making out: Reflections on writing

'Making out' was how the Brontë sisters described visualisation. It was a way of working they all used to employ, sitting together through the Yorkshire evenings in front of their small glowing fire. For me, the method is one of two key processes that bring together the writing side of my life and my oral storytelling work. On one occasion, a 10-year-old girl who had just tried out the technique for the first time described it to me as difficult to begin with and then very good – 'like going further back in your brain'.

My other key process has to do with listening: it's the habit of listening to what I'm writing or saying even while I'm in the act of producing it. I think this is part of the double-sidedness, the conversation that lies at the heart of both writing and storytelling, which are after all kin processes. It is the very essence of creating. Not that I read stuff aloud when I'm writing or even after I've finished. Yet even as I am composing phrases, getting them down on paper or up on the computer screen, I am sounding them out in my head, my inner voice performing as vital a role in the editing and shaping as when, while walking round my local park, I am 'making out' for a story I am preparing for telling.

Visualisation is the crucible. But what ignites the process, where initial ideas come from, is almost entirely mysterious to me. In preparing to retell a traditional story, there is already a story to work on; so the process of preparation is one of remaking. Creating a story from the beginning, however, as for instance in writing a novel, is more a matter of digging over the ground, then leaving it open to ideas to take root and hopefully flourish. Once or twice while taking a walk I've realised that a whole short story has suddenly arrived in my head, apparently fully formed. With my two children's novels, it was rather different, a case of becoming aware that various ideas which had been previously lurking around in my mind had now combined and come alive in my brain. A secret eco-farm had been found and made public. But how could it previously have remained a secret and what was now going to happen? A precious object was lying hidden down the back seat of a car. But how did it get there and who did it belong to? Quite quickly the problems created characters – Charlie, a shy London boy who felt guiltily responsible for the secret existence of the eco-farm being exposed; Catrin, a girl from the town where I myself grew up, who was determined to find answers to impossible questions. Once such characters exist, they won't leave me alone. They demand to be seen and heard in my head.

It's all fascinatingly different when I'm writing a think-piece, an article or book review – or, for that matter, this piece. On those occasions, after a period for subliminal thought, it's straight to work on the computer, usually with a plan of action being created if not at once, then pretty early in the process. With fiction, nothing may visibly happen for months. Only when the life of the story seems securely established in my mind am I able to begin. Then it's out with the fountain pen, ink-rag and blue-black Quink ink (actually they all sit permanently on the desk) and it's reaching down for the story notebook (large, hard-backed and lined). The scratch of the pen is part of the pleasure, so is the forming of words and the movement of the hand down the page, the sense of something growing beneath it. I also love the brisk crossings-out when I feel dissatisfied. When I finally sense that the thing has enough brio, but maybe not for many weeks, what has so far been created will go onto the computer. It's not that there's no planning. At some point a mundane list of chapters or summary of the plot will emerge. At some point, too, there's the hard-headed moment when I think about numbers of pages. Publishers have strong ideas about what different ages of children can cope with and the former freelance journalist in me remains alert to totals of words.

With oral storytelling, opportunities to discover what happens when a story meets its audience are ample and immediate. With written work, the prospect of response is potentially far more nerve-wracking. In my experience, once a publisher has said yes, (phew!) a good editor makes a vital contribution. I always try to remember just how important they are, and why, when I'm working with children in schools. Prickly feelings are prone to arise when words are challenged, meanings questioned. Put them aside, as I long ago learned to do, and you can discover a lot, not only about the reader's response but about what you had hoped to express. At the centre of the dialogue is the plain fact that nothing is more delightful to the creative ego than to feel you have been 'heard'. The editor is a crucial mediator between the work and its prospective audience. In my case, I have been doubly lucky. In the person of my husband, himself a former journalist, I have someone at home who is as willing to suggest improvements as to respond to a story. He is also extremely patient: when writing fiction, I confess, I never breathe a word about it until a first draft is completed. Call it obsessive secrecy or just paranoia, to my mind such privacy is a precondition of the creative process. Perhaps this has to do with the failure which has been a crucial factor in my own writing history.

What got me into oral storytelling, now a good many years ago, was struggling and failing to complete a book I was writing. A study of stories of feral children (the associated myths as well as the historical accounts), my subject proved as engaging as it was demanding. Ever since I feel I've been fed both by the research it entailed and my struggles to find a way to write it that would do justice to it. When the struggles became most desperate – and, dogged by bad luck, the book remains unpublished – was when I first came across oral storytelling, then just beginning to make its revival. Here, I discovered with feelings of joy, was a pathway to fluency, a way to liberate the words on my tongue and an accompanying free-dom never to have to arrive at a final fixed way of telling a story but to be endlessly able to re-explore it.

One of my foremost aims with children (and teachers) is to inspire in them a similar feeling of fluency. It starts by attempting to show them that they do have something to write about and continues by giving them time and techniques to enjoy the flexibility of different ways of telling. Oiling the desire then to write what they've discovered is the next major challenge. At the younger primary ages, there are going to be children who simply don't want to write. There are any number of reasons why. They can't concentrate long enough. They don't have the ability to put down the words. They don't have words in their head to get onto the page. To inspire such a cross-section of pupils while giving space to the more advanced to let rip: this is hard. Similar problems are likely to apply at upper junior levels and, in my experience, these often worsen in Year 7 and beyond. By then, I find, many pupils have lost the nerve for writing if ever they possessed it. I understand this. Writing is a form of exposure. It takes great courage to do it unless there is a generally positive and sharing atmosphere where what is revealed is noticed, encouraged and rewarded. From my outsider's point of view – for I am generally a visitor, not a long-term part of a group – I want writing sessions to be as open and flexible as possible with opportunities for participants to receive the kind of feedback that shows they have been properly heard.

So oral storytelling is the way I encourage the desire and enthusiasm for writing in schools. There is a downside to the work. It comes when I feel that teachers with whom I am working are either too strained by curriculum pressures or insufficiently confident to trust the methods involved to be able to take them on themselves or to give them enough time. A general tendency in the teaching of writing is to move too quickly into the formal writing task and to fail to dig over the ground beforehand, seeding it with images and words and stories. Understandable hesitancy about the act of telling a story without a book – even when it involves something as simple as telling a small personal anecdote in order to kick-start some work – can spill into a reluctance to take on the rich panoply of associated storytelling techniques – visualisation, image-sharing, questioning, story-boarding – which can so powerfully inspire and enhance children's writing.

Another challenge about working in schools is my personal resistance to the 'beginning, middle and end' approach, which is probably the most common approach among teachers. To me, a story does not operate like this. A story is what happens. It's the change that comes about in the course of the story, the way a problem or dilemma is resolved. This is the driving force of the story. Working backwards or outwards from it is how you begin to develop such aspects as the story-setting or your first and concluding sentences. For me, it's obvious that, before starting out on the writing, it's vital to get some sense of the core of your story, be it a character, a problem or an atmosphere. With reluctant writers, this is a good reason to give children plenty of practice in the oral retelling of those previously created stories that are categorised as traditional tales. Traditional tales have simple patterns. As Betty Rosen (1981) so marvellously demonstrated in *And None of It Was Nonsense*, they give children something to work with. Initially relieving them of some of the burdens of sequence and structure, they give rich opportunities for the development of language, the reinvention of plot and character and the expression of individual creativity.

Writing and storytelling arise from the same deep source. You don't make either your career if you want an easy life or, for that matter, a guaranteed income. Some of the reasons I do them myself are identical with the reasons I also spend time working with children in schools. It's not – or not centrally – to inspire them to become writers or storytellers too (although I certainly hope that some will and often see signs in some that they might). It's essentially to communicate a passion for life and a love of the world around us and to turn them on through sharing that with them. Beyond that, what is involved necessarily means a lot of hard slog, a persistence and patience that I've learned a good deal about from my various close friends in the arts. Pianists or painters, poets or translators, knowing them over the years has shown me that at the heart of all this activity there has to be a sincere devotion to your chosen art or craft. It's not even a choice, it's a need, a need to continue a conversation that, once begun, you don't want to end.

Linda Newbery: novelist

Linda Newbery has published widely for young readers of all ages, with work ranging from a picture book, *Posy,* to young adult fiction. Her books for juniors include *Catcall* (Nestlé Silver Award winner), *Nevermore,* and *Polly's March* and *Andie's Moon* for Usborne's Historical House series. Amongst her older novels, *Set in Stone* won the Costa Children's Book Award in 2006, and *The Shell House* and *Sisterland* were both shortlisted for the Carnegie Medal. Her latest publication, for readers of about seven years and older, is *Lob,* published by David Fickling Books. She regularly tutors for the Arvon Foundation and is a frequent visitor to schools, libraries and festivals.

Letting it grow: reflections on writing

When an idea for a new book presents itself, I start collecting things – postcards, cuttings from newspapers, sayings, poems, pieces of music, and sometimes specific items like marbles, pebbles or green men. A book in a second-hand shop might jump out at me, or a news item chime uncannily with something taking shape in my mind. During this time I might write nothing at all, but the selecting and hoarding is an enjoyable time of anticipation – a gathering of ingredients, as I think of it.

Authors vary greatly in the amount of preparation they do. Some work from a chapter-by-chapter outline, and won't start until every twist and turn has been plotted. I'm not a great planner. What comes to me first is usually a sense of place and atmosphere; then I wonder whose story it is and what's been happening to them. The tone begins to suggest itself: the refined veneer of well-heeled Victorian society in *Set in Stone,* or the mild eccentricity and slightly larger-than-life characters of *Nevermore.* Soon I start to make notes. I always have a sense of how and where the story will end (though that might change) but what I don't know, or even want to know, is most of the middle. I might have two or three key episodes in mind, but no more than that.

It's the setting off with questions but not answers that keeps me hooked. Exploration and discovery is a large part of the enjoyment; for me, there's only so much that can be planned. This seems to relate to the 'left brain, right brain' theories developed by Richard Sperry in the 1960s, for which he was awarded a Nobel prize. According to Sperry, the left brain controls rational, logical thought, whereas the right side is more intuitive and spontaneous. With no detailed knowledge of brain function, I know that my mind works differently when I'm planning, or trying to plan, from the way it forms ideas and connections once I'm engrossed in the story. My best ideas occur some way into the writing, not when I'm staring at a synopsis.

Writers are often asked whether they have to feel inspired in order to write. Jan Mark once said, 'Inspiration does come – but rarely at first.' The initial impulse can come from seizing of an idea and seeing its possibilities, but there's also the deeper inspiration that comes later, when characters have begun to interact and assert themselves, and when settings and dilemmas feel more tangible than the real world. Authors often talk about characters taking over and making their own decisions; I think this too relates to the 'left brain, right brain' dichotomy and to the intuitive feelings that arise when immersion in the story takes over.

When I talk about this to a group of children or adults, I emphasise that there's no right or wrong way. Because I don't plan very much, I do copious amounts of revision, dropping a hint into an early chapter, or striking out whole episodes which have proved to be redundant. As I enjoy revising – reliving the story, knowing that everything I do will improve it – I don't mind that.

There are decisions to be made about viewpoint and structure, and the 'voice' of the story must be found. This is different each time, and might involve experimentation. In my most recent novel, *Lob*, for young readers, it wasn't until the second draft that I found the right 'voice'. The moment I heard it, it felt right; a kind of simple but poetic directness was what the story needed. Every book presents its own challenge, a set of puzzles to be solved. Children sometimes ask, 'Once you think of a story, doesn't it get boring just writing it down?' Just! That *just* is everything. You haven't got a story until you've written it, in the same way that you haven't got a drawing or a painting until you've made marks on paper or canvas. You can't tell how it will turn out. It might surprise you. One of the delights of writing is that you never quite know where your thoughts will lead you, if you let them.

It's hard to produce this slow, unmeasurable and unobservable experience in the classroom, where everything is time-limited and requires an 'outcome' (how I dislike that word!), but I think it's important to try. Many a time I've heard teachers expressing regret that children's imaginative writing is squeezed out by the demands of the curriculum. There are teachers who take every chance to provide such opportunities, but it's all too easy for the playfulness and experimentation of writing to be crushed beneath the weight of assessment objectives. It's difficult for English or literacy teachers – with everything else they have to cover – to put themselves in the role of practitioner: to know first-hand how it feels to be immersed in the world of a story to the exclusion of the real world, to feel that it's an unmanageable mess that will never be good enough, to find ways of keeping going; to experience the light-bulb moment when a plot kink unravels itself, to spend productive time doodling, or gazing out of a window. I think it's important that children meet authors to learn something about what drives them; to have the chance to talk, ask questions; and to write with them. And the most important part of this is to give children the sense of fun, freedom and surprise that is crucial to writing.

For more than twenty years I've been visiting schools as an author, giving talks and workshops; many times I've worked with groups away from schools on residential retreats over the space of a weekend or a whole week. My co-tutors have included several poets, from whom I've learned a great deal. I worked with the prolific and kindly John Cotton; observing his gift for encouraging children to explore the wonder and beauty of ordinary life; I watched Fred Sedgwick use Shakespeare's language as a starting-point, to magnificent effect. On courses run by the Arvon Foundation I saw Wes Magee give confidence, enjoyment and relish in wordplay through ideas ranging from the absurd to the heartfelt; from Michael Laskey and Dean Parkin, I absorbed ways of taking the possible threat out of writing, showing writers of all ages how to delight in their own inventiveness. Having taught English in a secondary school, I was used to working with teenagers, but these courses gave me my first experience of tutoring primary-age children. I found it exhilarating to tap into the freshness, energy and willingness of this younger age-group. They would seize any idea and run with it; they were funny and ingenious; they responded attentively to each other's work. They left those courses with notebooks full of ideas, and – I'm quite sure – a sense of themselves as writers.

Yes, it's a luxury far from classroom restraints – a whole weekend or more to devote to writing, in the company of other children and adults who share the challenge and the excitement of putting ideas into words. But I try to replicate something of that whenever I work with a group in a school.

Through working with the poets, I realised that story-writing is not necessarily the best way to encourage young writers, especially at first. Short poetry activities can give confidence and a sense of achievement to everyone present, for example through simple list-poems as warm-ups. Group poems can be produced by asking everyone to read out their best or favourite line, and at once there's a sense of creating something that didn't exist fifteen minutes earlier. Possible inhibition about reading aloud is also reduced, because everyone speaks at this early stage. Poetry exercises have the advantage, too, of leading to compact, manageable, complete pieces of work.

This may seem a strange thing for a prose writer to say, but I've come to the conclusion that the hardest thing for a child (or teenager, or adult) to write is a complete short story. Yet it's one of the commonest tasks set to children, even in exams. 'A story must have a beginning, a middle and an end,' children are taught, as if it's easy. Any group of children can recite this, when asked what a story must have. Yes, a story does need those things, but not necessarily until you get to them. Over-emphasis on planning can be inhibiting, and that's one reason why I rarely lead workshops that focus on plot. To ask for plot is to invite the sensationalism that dooms good writing in all but the most expert hands: vampire attacks, alien invasions, random slaughterings, and the like. Not unnaturally, children and teenagers used to fast-paced TV drama and whizzy action on computer screens tend to think that plot is everything – that you think of a plot and then write it down in whatever words come most easily.

To counter this, one of my workshop activities focuses on pace – so important, so crucial to the reader's involvement. Using extracts from my own and other stories, I show that the pace actually slows down at crucial moments; tension is lost if the reader is hustled through at a gallop. Sometimes the participants make a graph, plotting the rise and fall; tension can't stay high-pitched throughout.

Then, individually, they write a piece of a story where something tense happens – someone's being followed, or overhears a secret, or enters a dangerous building site as a dare. Because the whole emphasis is on building tension, and the episode will stop at this point, the temptation to hurtle on and finish the story is taken away.

I'm often asked in schools for advice for children who want to write. My answer is, 'Think of yourself as a writer – know that your writing is for you.' And, more practically, 'Try to write something every day – even if it's only for ten minutes at bedtime or when you first wake up.' Sometimes I ask a group, 'How many of you do any writing that you don't have to do, for school?' The number of hands that either shoot or creep up often surprises everyone present. There's a lot of writing going on – especially when I make it clear that I don't only mean stories or poems; song lyrics, diaries and blogs count too. Even when I ask this question to year eights or nines, there will usually be some kind of response, even if it's furtive, and preceded by embarrassed giggles or shuffling.

Another question I ask is how many of them have something they love to do, which they feel is important for themselves – it might be singing, gymnastics, playing football, acting, drawing or painting, running, playing an instrument, making up songs, swimming. Usually a majority will raise their hands, albeit slowly, and depending on the group feeling I might ask some of them to tell us about their special thing – how it makes them feel, and how they feel if they don't or can't do it. That's what writing is for me – a crucial part of myself, my self, so that if I'm not writing or at least planning to write, I feel fidgety, irritable, and lazy; the only cure is to get to work. Often I talk about ambition – my dream, from the age of eight, of seeing my own book on a shelf next to E. Nesbit – and setting out to achieve something that I knew would be difficult. Many children can relate this to their own dreams of film sets or football stadiums; and from an early age, most recognise the satisfaction that comes from extending their reach beyond the easily graspable.

The most effective workshops, wherever they take place, are those in which everyone present takes part – teachers, classroom helpers, senior staff, everyone. It's crucial that no one in the room presents themselves as knowing the answers or a set of rules. Children are encouraged by seeing adults having a go, reading bits of work aloud like any other member of the group, admitting that this or that bit doesn't quite work yet. For it to feel like real writing, they need to see we're all the same – we're all writers, playing about with words, seeing what we can make them do, finding satisfaction in the making of something uniquely our own.

Commentary

Diversity and difference resonate across these reflections, demonstrating the uniqueness of these writers, and reminding us of the uniqueness of each of us as writers, as we draw on our cultural experience, knowledge and understanding, in different contexts. For me, Philip Gross's reflections highlight his deeply playful attitude towards writing. A sense of focused experimentation and improvisation runs through his thoughts on composing, although this is not a game without rules and he knows he can trust this 'carefully cultivated discipline of encouraging disorder'. He eschews predictable outcomes and seeks to be surprised by his writing, encouraging each of us to have the 'confidence of our uncertainty as writers' and find strategies which foster this. His stance reminds me of the work of Gurevitch (2000) who, in examining the serious play of writing, distinguishes between disciplinary seriousness, in which the writer takes on the responsibilities of an adult expert, and poetic seriousness, revealed from the point of view of the child whose play has been exposed. Philip it seems, integrates the two with ease, and suggests that as writers we need to carve out interior spaces for connecting and generating, for pausing, thinking, and for being.

Mary Medlicott, by contrast, uniquely highlights what she experiences as a particular kinship between oral and written storytelling. She attributes her written fluency to discovering a deep sense of the oral – words, sounds, gestures and embodiment – and seizes opportunities to listen, to visualise, revisit and inhabit traditional tales, tales which are never replicated and which are made new in each retelling. She draws intriguing parallels between the oral and the written, noting that her inner voice performs a critical role in the editing and shaping of written text, while in preparation for orally retelling a tale she is involved in visualising – 'making out' in the manner of the Brontë sisters. Perhaps most potently, at least for me, Mary voices a deep sense of self in and through her writing, and, in a manner reminiscent of Vygotsky (1978), reveals an intrinsic need to write, to communicate and to share with others, although she candidly acknowledges this involves devotion, persistence and 'sheer hard slog'. In working with teachers and younger writers, Mary talks of 'oiling the desire to write'; and demonstrates considerable empathy for the risks involved. She describes writing as 'a form of exposure' and through her reflections we appreciate that the journey has been, and often still is, a journey of angst as well as pleasure.

Linda Newberg also recognises the trepidation and vulnerability involved and the feeling that 'it's an unmanageable mess that will never be good enough'. Helpfully she shares some of the strategies she employs as a writer in schools. These focus on pace, plotting the rise and fall of tension on graphs, reading aloud, writing poetry collaboratively, using notebooks to capture ideas and discussing writing at home. In this way she demonstrates how she positions herself as a writer and a learner whilst working with young people, and reflects on her identity, as she says – 'that's what writing is for me – a crucial part of myself, my self, so that if I'm not writing or at least planning to write, I feel fidgety, irritable, and lazy: the only cure is to work'. In considering her own practices around planning, Linda recognises that whilst she 'doesn't plan much', she does enjoy collecting potentially related artefacts. Later, as an archetypal 'discovery writer' (Sharples, 1999), she takes particular delight in revising and polishing her work through deep immersion in her richly imagined worlds. Additionally, she draws our attention to compositional spaces and places, and reflects on how residencies and retreats can offer productive periods, interactions and dialogues as well as headspace for thinking. She seeks to recreate this in her work in schools, in order to help others experience the satisfaction of 'extending their reach beyond the easily graspable'.

Despite their distinct emphases and unique contributions, there are also observations in common, areas of convergence which Philip, Mary and Linda share about their experience and understanding of compositional processes and of working in schools. Their voices ring in harmony as they consider the unpredictable experience of constructing fiction and poetry; that essential element of exploration and discovery, of not knowing and accepting not knowing and delighting in this position, trusting it will lead somewhere. Philip reveals that not only headspace, but literal page space in his notebooks is important to him, allowing him to revisit, reread and find new pathways as he seeks to actively cultivate chaos and foster a degree of disorder, in order to 'find out where the process leads'. For Linda, a large part of the pleasure of writing appears to arise from never quite knowing 'where your thoughts will lead you, if you let them' as, she observes, 'It's the setting off with questions but not answers that keeps me hooked'. Mary also refers to such exploration, and suggests that writing a novel involves 'digging over the ground and then leaving it open for ideas to take root and hopefully flourish'. For her there is also pleasure in the act of writing, the tactile feel of her pen, the sound of its scratch on the paper and 'the sense of something growing beneath it'. In their various ways they each trust that, given time, space and activity of various kinds, the text will uncover itself and reveal an initial direction which can be followed.

Also in common, these authors gently critique the teaching of writing in schools, observing that the processes of assessment, curriculum expectations and objectives-led practices tend to constrain young writers. As Linda comments, 'It's hard to produce this slow, unmeasurable and unobservable experience in the classroom, where everything is time-limited and requires an "outcome" (how I dislike that word!), but I think it's important to try'. From their frequent forays into classrooms and residencies in schools, both Linda and Mary observe that the profession has an obsession with story structure and the 'beginning, middles and ends' of tales. They believe this focus is in direct contradiction with the unfolding nature of narrative which, as Mary states, simply 'does not operate like this. A story is what happens'. Philip too expresses concern that predictable outcomes, structure and policies might be at odds 'with the genuine creative life'. Is this inevitable? Surely as educators we should seek to foster the will to write as well as the skill, and find ways to balance creativity and accountability, freedom and structure. Much will depend on our knowledge and understanding of the social, creative and cultural act of writing and our involvement as teacher-writers in the classroom, which again our three authors see as significant.

Each, unprompted, refers to the potential of teachers writing and taking risks, sharing their challenges and developing, 'practice/self knowledge' of themselves as writers. Linda argues for the full involvement of teachers, teaching assistants and all others present; 'it's crucial that no one in the room presents themselves as knowing the answers or a set of rules'. This represents a real challenge when teachers are positioned or position themselves as 'expert writers', ready to demonstrate skill mastery at every turn, yet, as we have argued in Chapters 7 and 8, there is considerable potential in repositioning teachers as writers, both writer-teachers and teacher-writers. Unsurprisingly, Philip, Mary and Linda also comment on writing alongside children in the classroom, of being writers themselves in situ, not just talking about the art and craft involved and enabling students to write. Another theme is the influence of others on their writing and the wider social context in which their writing is shaped, shared and developed. Mary recognises the role of her husband as an empathetic response partner, Linda values and credits the impact of her many co-tutors on writers' retreats, and Philip acknowledges his enriching collaborations with dancers, musicians, artists and other writers, suggesting, as John-Steiner's (2000) work also indicates, that creativity is often a collaborative enterprise, a 'you-plus, not you-minus' relationship, as Philip so aptly describes it.

These three highly reflective texts open doors into the minds of these writers, but they offer us no final word, no definitive view, no distinct way of working to emulate in school. Rather their insights and reflections are offered as provocations and complications; challenges which highlight the complexity of composing and the tensions, difficulties and dilemmas for us all as we write, teach writing and foster the development of young writers. Their voices resonate with one another, and have much to teach us about the significance of exploration and discovery, knowing and yet not knowing – but trusting – and the potential of positioning ourselves as writers, as guides alongside.

I write at home, in my study, which overlooks the back garden. The hours between 6 a.m. and midday are the most productive. I start before I eat, but I have a cup of coffee to sustain me. I write with classical music in the background, usually Radio 3, but if they become too triumphant or nationalistic I turn to Mozart or a Taizé Chant on CD.

How do I actually put words on paper? I spend most of the time not writing (at least not with ink and paper), but thinking and sometimes reading. If I need to work with other people's material then I spend a good few days gathering that together, reading it and making notes. During this time, I have in the back of my mind the article I want to write.

Then I do the writing. I compose in my head and often in my bed. I think about the topic, the structure and the length of the piece. I sometimes visualise the final published article, including subheadings, charts, diagrams, length of paragraphs and where direct quotations will be used. I use key words to remind me of what each paragraph will be about. I formulate complete sentences and write each paragraph in my mind. This process can take anything from a few hours to days or weeks. It is usually curtailed by a looming deadline. I fall asleep thinking of the writing and wake up with sentences formed and paragraphs organised. There is a danger that I might forget before I can commit this to paper, so I rehearse the text, saying it to myself as I get up. The key words help to keep me on track.

The process of putting the words on paper is a process of scribing what is already formed in my mind. I do this quickly. I am not creating anything at this point, it is all coming from memory. I leave the piece for at least a day, often more. Then I return to it to edit. The editing process is most often one of cutting in order to meet word length; sometimes changing sentence structures, but I rarely change the content unless new information has come to notice since I started.

For me, the most important part of writing is what goes on in my subconscious and it is about trusting that process to deliver.

Shirley – university lecturer

My writing process cannot be described as disciplined. I am a pathological reviser. I tinker and quibble from the outset: not in the systematic sense of drafting and redrafting, but in a messy proliferation of false starts and alternative possibilities. I try to plan. I use bullet points and subheadings to impose some order, but these get revised too. I rethink the structure, the content and the language all at once. As the writing snowballs, and the fragments multiply, keeping sight of the whole thing is the biggest challenge. I waste a lot of paper; there are Post-it notes everywhere; and it's often quite stressful.

In the initial stages, I still prefer pen and paper. It somehow helps if I can see the different layers. Scrubbing-out and annotating can be quite a visual exercise. I use highlighters, arrows and symbols, sticky labels, sometimes scissors and Sellotape: writing as collage almost. When I have something half formed, then I word-process. And then I revise some more, on screen and print-outs, ad nauseam.

I write best in the mornings, somewhere quiet, often before others are awake. Long train journeys are especially good, and driving helps me think about writing. However, the thinking and writing frequently spill over into less convenient slots. I find myself scribbling in car parks and traffic queues, or in the middle of the night. I'll write on anything that comes to hand – envelopes, cheque-books, or more Post-it notes.

When I'm really stuck, I seek out some new material and try a different angle. I read something obliquely related, browse the thesaurus, interrogate someone, or sleep on it. I'm always surprised how many problems resolve themselves overnight. If desperate, and given half a chance, I try to revise the word limit or the deadline. Possibly not the best role model for young writers!

I think my composing process is painfully slow. It has the advantage of allowing me to move beyond some half-baked first attempts towards something approaching satisfaction. On the other hand, it's all-consuming, a perpetual struggle and expands to fill the time available. In the end, nothing is ever really finished, just put aside. I wish I was a satisficer!

Lucy – teacher

Chapter 10

Professional writers

Writing in the workplace

Introduction

This chapter moves out of the classroom and into the commercial world of writing, where succeeding in writing is intrinsically connected with making a living. The principal voices in this chapter are the voices of three professional writers: Julia Eccleshare, a journalist; Pete Moore, a science writer; and Rich Osborne, a web designer and blogger. We have deliberately chosen to explore here the reflections and experiences of writers who are not in the conventional 'creative writing' sphere, in that they are not poets, novelists or playwrights. Professional writers outside the world of creative writing are often silenced and marginalised in discussions of writing, yet their perspectives illuminate writing in the workplace. Crucially, in this context, writing is not voluntary, but a required element of their working life. We asked these writers to reflect on their own writing experiences, using the prompts below:

The writing process

- How do you get started with a writing 'task' or a new piece of writing?
- Where do your ideas come from?
- Do you plan your writing before you start? If so, could you explain what you do?
- Do you edit your writing as you write or leave it all until the end?
- How do you approach revising your writing?
- Do you deliberately give yourself space away from your writing for any reason?
- What do you do when you get stuck?

The writing environment

- Do you write in a particular place? With particular resources?
- Do you write with a word processor or with pen and paper?
- Do you write to a time-plan?
- Does anything (physical/environmental) help you write?

Your writing community

- What are the features of the community in which you write?
- Do you write with others?
- Do you seek or receive feedback from anyone on your writing, either during or after a piece has been 'completed'?
- Do you think about your audience when you are writing?

The writers' responses are presented here unedited, exactly as they were written. We will introduce each author first, then offer their reflection, followed by a brief commentary. The end of the chapter will conclude with a more sustained overview of the implications of their contributions.

Julia Eccleshare: journalist

Julia Eccleshare writes for *The Guardian* as Children's Books Editor, and won the Eleanor Farjeon Award in 2000 in recognition of her outstanding contribution to children's books. She has written several books of her own, including *A Guide to the Harry Potter Novels* (Continuum, 2002) and *The Rough Guide to Teenage Books* (Rough Guides, October, 2003).

How writing happens

All writing requires a great deal of time to do it and space around that time. The space is for 'practice' and 'thinking time'; these may look unlikely and unconvincing as part of the writing but they help. The practice can be short – firing off a handful of emails before sitting down to the job in hand can feel like scales might for an instrumentalist: they get the flow started. The thinking is a longer process; for me, writing about books, sorting the books on the shelves, looking at them, handling them, re-acquainting myself with them, is a form of tidying but it is also valuable space in which to reflect and be reminded of things about stories and inspired by what, at their best, they can do.

One of the complications of writing is that it requires two almost contradictory mind frames – an energetic one and a reflective one – which must somehow be harnessed together. The balance of this can be done in a variety of ways: sometimes the fast flow allows the writer to set down the ideas in a rough and ready style which can be worked on later; reflection can be added later in justifying clauses and examples, but a kind of energetic and highly readable character of the writing may be achieved. At other times, trying to convey the complexity of an idea demands such careful phrasing and such a delicate stacking up of words to make the point in exactly the right way that the writing is very slow and very reflective. Both can work, either can fail. The former may sing off the page, the power of the words allowing it to fly without visible support, it may be rough textured lacking elegance or even substance; the latter may bring insight deftly and with subtlety or it can be just unreadable because too clotted.

With all writing you want to make it the best you can: this requires a considerable amount of rephrasing, restructuring, smoothing and the rest. The feeling is very much the same as if you are icing a cake and having to go over and over it to make it look exactly as smooth and shiny as you'd like. Or, it can be just as a potter does, feeling with their fingertips for the tiny imperfections and smoothing them all out to make a perfect whole. In other words, writing is a craft, and practice, time and patience all go into making it better.

One of the problems for all writers is the very variable time frames of each writing project. From books with a two-year time frame to news stories with a two-hour turnround from breaking to delivery; from 70,000 words on a single author to 50 words to sum up a 400-page novel.

As most of my work is journalistic, I tend to write to close deadlines and therefore at speed. There are advantages to this. Setting oneself to write something under exam circumstances may sound like an unnecessary torture but, surprisingly, it can be creative. The adrenaline to get it done in time can be very creative – not only in terms of getting started and finished but also in terms of being succinct, clear and to the point. Otherwise, the problem is that writing – all writing, any writing – can take an absolutely unlimited length of time. Once the bare bones are down, it is much easier to go back and edit them and often the energy is valuably captured in the stylistic flow.

Inventing exam conditions is also good practice for the times when the writing really does have to be under pressure. Even as an arts journalist there are news stories which need to be written up fast but with exactly the same principles of research, fact finding, drawing on previous knowledge as would be needed for a piece which might have been being worked on for weeks, months or years. Additionally for me, there is the writing of obituaries which need a very high level of information which has to be sensitively gathered and assimilated at speed. This is sometimes made even more complicated by the emotions which infuse such writing. Again, as with speed, these often begin as a distraction but can also be valuable and an enhancement to creativity.

But then there are longer pieces. Planning a whole book is a challenge of its own! A two-year time frame has to be carefully managed, with shorter deadlines for small sections put in place to keep up the momentum. And it is not only the time that needs to be broken down into manageable pieces; the content, too, has to be carefully mapped out and planned to make sure that arguments are properly constructed, properly supported with evidence and carefully maintained.

Knowing your audience and purpose: different kinds of writing

As a writer of information rather than fiction, some of the shape of my writing comes from knowing the purpose of the writing and the audience it is intended for. In terms of purpose, there is a vast difference between writing for selling and writing any form of criticism. The former is fairly one-dimensional: selling copy must do exactly that. The task is to sell either a product or an idea to the reader who is defined by the market for wherever the writing appears. The writing must be grabbing and upbeat. Key words, of the kind described above, are at a premium here – 'best-selling' and 'prize-winning' locate the book as being something already highly praised and therefore to be prized while glib phrases such as 'cliffhanging', 'page-turning', 'side-splitting', 'an emotional roller coaster' give the potential purchaser an immediate sense of the kind of book they are buying. The 'criticism' or 'judgement' is implicit in the fact that you've chosen the book to be there. It is not and cannot be explicit in what you write: no one wants to buy a book about which there are caveats or cavils. In selling books for children, the only possible explicit warning that might be appropriate would be about strong language or explicit sexual references, since parents tend to expect books to be a bastion of rectitude on such matters.

In writing terms, reviewing books is a more subtle art. As with many other fields, there is a language or phraseology attached to it which can make it seem facile or glib. Certain adjectives carry specific overtones in a particular context because they have been used repeatedly. This has the advantage of allowing them to be used readily and without explanation. It can, however, have the disadvantage of leading to lazy writing in which a few recognisable words are used without any substantiation or analysis. In reviewing books this is particularly obvious and while one needs to give the reader a sense of comfort about what they are reading and an ease of understanding – some familiar territory – it is also important to make sure that enough originality of language and phrase are brought to descriptions to capture the essence of the individual book. It is an art not to 'tell' the story but to 'show' what it is about and how that has been achieved.

For a specialist market of informed readers – as teachers or librarians would be in the case of children's books – some greater sophistication can be added by references to other famous books in the same genre. '*Lord of the Flies* for a new generation' gives a very quick indication of both story and how substantial you think its impact might be. For a knowledgeable audience, it is easier to convey more than it is to a general audience. As informed readers, they bring their own knowledge to what you write and enrich it.

Finding the voice in which to express your thoughts is a very important part of all writing. I began my writing career at a time when reviewers and commentators demonstrated their knowledge of a subject but did not necessarily reveal much about themselves in their writing. Now, readers like to know about the writer: personal reactions, reactions of others close to you and the particular reasons for them all shape how the writing must be. It adds a dimension to writing which can be hard to accommodate but has the advantage of encouraging writing that more closely matches the author's speaking voice, which is often more comfortable and less formal to read.

Self-editing

All writers need to adopt the advice which is most usually attributed to William Faulkner – '*kill your darlings*'. In longer and more free-thinking pieces of writing it is all too easy to come up with a phrase, sentence or paragraph of which you become particularly fond. Frequently, as the rest of the piece grows below and beyond it, this may become less pointful or even euphonious; it may need to be excised but it can be very hard to take it out. Trying to stand back, and take an overview as a reader who comes fresh to the work would do, is essential and, at that point, being very self-critical of all aspects of the writing is an important discipline to develop.

Editing

Fortunately, although self-editing is a critical part of the process, it is not the only one. One of the greatest merits of print is that it is 'managed', 'moderated' and to some extent shaped by an editor. The more experienced you are at writing for a particular audience, the less likely it is that your work will be edited just because you understand the unwritten rules of that space. But, even with a great deal of experience, I find it invaluable to know that what I have written will have a 'first reader' who will do all they can to make the writing work better. Even if one follows the most stringent rules of self-editing, it is easy to be self-indulgent. What may seem like a quaint stylistic device can become an annoying writer's tic to a reader.

Writing and its complexities is an endless source of fascination. How subtle it is, how delicate and how sophisticated never ceases to amaze. How boldness and confidence are almost always rewarded by the resulting clarity and intelligence is a thought to cling to.

Pete Moore: science writer

Pete Moore is principally a communicator of scientific ideas and thinking and he has written a range of books on science, including *Being Me: What it Means to be Human* (Wiley, 2004) and *The New Killer Germs* (Carlton, 2006). He has contributed to academic science publications, such as *Nature* and the *Journal of Biology*, and is a member of the Association of British Science Writers. He also runs his own company (http://www.petemoore.biz/index.php/), running workshops and helping people communicate with confidence.

***

Think of an author and what comes to mind? A person with passion and imagination; someone who is inventive and impetuous; an introvert who sits alone for hours and hours, hunched in a leather chair and pouring over a keyboard in a romantically dusty attic room, with a tall jug of coffee and the odd tumbler of malt as key friends. Without thinking too hard, this view starts to affect your notion of the nature and purpose of a book. Soon a book becomes a piece of work that is crafted by an author to serve his or her personal interests. How long it is, how many chapters, figures and photos are seen as matters of personal choice. The length of time taken to write it is the length of time it takes.

Quite possibly there are writers who work that way. For better or worse, when I write, I come from another model, a more business-minded model. Over the past decade and a half I've written around 15 books. The exact number is difficult to count as some of them appear in various editions with strangely altered titles and different number of chapters, but it averages out at around one a year. And writing books is less than a third of what I do. Why? Well, partly because most books make very little money, so if you are going to stay alive you need to do something else as well. Also, I'd go mad if I only wrote books, I need to get out a bit.

While a few of my books have been initiated entirely from me, the majority start life as a phone call or email from my agent. She informs me that a publisher is looking for someone to write a particular book that fits in with a pre-existing list, or set. A consequence is that before you start, various things are already established – the basic word and page count, an indication of the number of chapters, illustrations, etc. A small school book that I'm starting needs 20 double-page spreads, each with 400 words and 2 pictures. Not much room for flexibility in that case, though there is greater scope on other occasions. In addition, this book comes with a tight deadline. From the first approach by the agent, to handing over the final document, there is a gap of three months.

With a tight deadline, there is a need for efficiency. I usually set up an Excel spreadsheet and wipe a set of dates down the left-hand column. In the next column, I note any event that might get in the way of writing, such as business appointments, holidays or birthdays. I like to put a colour bar through weekends, as I try to keep them as free as possible. Next I mark the days that I'll give to background research at the beginning, and a few days for editing at the end. Now I'm in a position to count how many days are left for writing and work out how many words need writing per day. I know that I'm not going to rigidly write the same number each day, but it's good to know the average I need to achieve if I'm going to hit the deadline.

On a second Excel sheet I list the chapters, sections, and the basic content within the sections. I note an approximate word count for each area, based on how much emphasis I think each part needs. If a book needs illustrations or images, I record how many are needed within each section. In effect, a book becomes a list of deliverables, and this sheet lets me track how well I'm doing at collecting them in. I've often wondered if this is preparation or procrastination – a little like using the task of creating a revision-timetable as a way of delaying the task of revising.

For me, this part of the task of writing a book is where the majority of thinking occurs. I spend time in considering the overall message that I would like a book to deliver, and how each chapter and section within each chapter can serve as stepping stones to take the reader from ignorance to knowledge, to the point that they can see how I reached my message. I don't necessarily expect the reader to agree with me, but I hope they can see how I reach my conclusions. To do this well, I need to consider my reader in some detail. How much do they already know before they picked the book up? What is the overall standard of English and level of reading? Are they likely to have any interests outside the main zone of this book that I could potentially call on when creating examples and stories? The more tightly I can frame the nature of my target readers, the more capably I can serve their needs. Once thinking is done I can move on to the task of writing.

My approach here, the task of typing in the words, varies depending on how well I know that particular area of subject. If I am quite familiar with the territory, I will simply jot down a list of individual words that can act as milestones in my narrative. The sections of text covering themes with which I'm less familiar, I plan in more detail. Here I'll draw a diagram that in many ways resembles a mind map. However, instead of letting the map evolve as my ideas flow onto the paper, I start by drawing an empty tree-like structure in which the main stems represent sections and the branches that come off the stems represent paragraphs. Before going further I can check that I have basically the right number of sections and paragraphs for the part of the chapter that I'm working on. The task now is to put one or two words at the end of each branch, words that indicates the basic content of each paragraph. I'm now in a position to rehearse the basic argument that I am planning to put down and check its overall flow of content long before I commit to individual sentences. Once this branching diagram is complete, I can transcribe the words from it to a simple list and once again use the list of words to help guide my writing.

I'm not about to argue that this is either the best way to write a book or the only way to write a book and I have a feeling that this system would not work particularly well for writing an imaginative novel. It does, however, serve to be a highly efficient method of creating books that present balanced arguments and deliver specific pieces of information.

Having a really clear list of words and sense of direction enables me to start using a rather exciting new piece of software. Over the last five or so years I have bought numerous versions of voice-to-text software, all of which have been too inaccurate to be useful. Recently I have loaded 'Dragon Naturally Speaking' version 10, and so far, in creating this piece, my fingers are yet to touch the keyboard. I have a feeling that without a clear sense of the journey through which I'm hoping to lead the reader, i.e. my list of words, the voice-only keyboard would encourage you to ramble endlessly, no longer hard on the fingers, but probably excruciating to the reader.

Editing and revising the manuscript is my least favourite part of any writing task. I've never been professionally tested, but I share many symptoms of a dyslexic tendency. I'm not a fast reader, and when it comes to the written word I'm not the best person to spot typos and small mistakes, particularly in my own work. It's all too easy for my eyes to see what I think is there, as opposed to reading what I actually wrote. Fortunately, my partner does have that attention to detail, and in most cases it is much more efficient to invite her to look at the script, mark any typos and note areas that make no sense. With the bits of poor writing pointed out to me, it is a relatively straightforward task to tidy them up.

I am someone who tends to be much more interested and excited in the ideas that I'm writing about, than in the task of writing itself. I seldom sit at my desk and think, oh great, let's get on with some writing. This then is another place where my Excel spreadsheet timetable can come to my assistance. It is important to me to know how much text I need to deliver on any one day, and know that at that point it's perfectly OK for me to stop and do something else. This works best when the something else is pleasurable – some form of reward. It might be as simple as a cup of coffee, a short walk, or on occasion getting on with the DIY projects somewhere in the house.

I'm not someone who suffers excessively from writer's block, that inability to think of where to go next. When it does occur, there is normally one of two main causes. The first is that I do not know where to go next simply because I have done insufficient research; I'm trying to work out what comes next rather than concentrating on the sentence I'm trying to create right now. I'm much more comfortable when I've separated the initial task of thinking from the second task of writing the sentences, a separation that enables me to give my mind fully to each component of the writing process.

My second cause of writer's block may seem somewhat perverse, but it occurs on the occasions when I started too soon. I have too much time available. For me, words flow most fluently when I have sufficient adrenaline coursing through my blood vessels. The optimum level seems to be achieved when I know that I have a tight, but achievable, deadline. An unachievable deadline gives rise to panic and despair, and neither of those emotions is productive.

I never intended to be a writer, much less an author, but now I am, I recognise the privilege that comes with the role. You have the opportunity to study specific areas in great detail, to phone experts and gather their thoughts, and to visit exciting people and places. Very few people turn you down if you say you are writing a book and would like a few minutes of their time. And then there is the thrill of receiving the occasional letter from a reader who enjoyed the book or seeing your work on a library or bookshop shelf. I can't imagine I'm the only author who, driven by vanity or a desire to sell more copies, makes sure that their titles are in a prominent position on the shelf before they leave the shop!

The last thing to remember about writing a book is that the author is part of a large team of experts. Once you put your document in the post it will meet editors, copy editors, designers and layout folk and printers. Possibly, most important of all, there are the sales team, the all-too-often unsung heroes who place books on websites and chase around shops getting buyers to take a risk and try a copy or two on their shelves. Authors often complain about the low fraction of the cover price that they receive, but many other people work hard alongside you.

Book writing also carries a heavy responsibility. If a few thousand people spend a few hours each with your book, then the person-hour cost is huge. You owe it to them to have something valuable to say . . . not to mention a justification to explain the loss of trees and use of ink.

In all the discussion of mechanism, let's not forget that writing books lets you play a small part in setting agendas or changing hearts and minds. For me, that's exciting.

Rich Osborne: web designer

Rich Osborne is the Web Innovation Officer for the University of Exeter, and he is interested in how people communicate and interact within virtual spaces. He sees himself as a 'virtual architect', tasked with creating these virtual spaces through the innovative use of Information Technology (IT). He is also a keen blogger and maintains several blogs, including The Sunday Roaster (http://thesundayroaster. blogspot.com/), reflecting his personal interest in cooking.

Thoughts from a web author

Whilst I may have written hundreds of thousands of words over the years, oddly enough I don't really consider myself a writer, merely someone who writes. Writers, to me, are creative, mystical people, wordsmiths who can weave stories from nothing. They are, above all, people who create connections with their readers, new worlds of imagination that can be delved into and explored. I write for the web, and my writing has always been about simple and direct communication, about informing as opposed to connecting. Is this something about me I wonder – or is it perhaps something about the web medium itself?

I've not always been a web writer, of course, as like all adults I pre-date the web. In fact, historically I've been something of a private writer, keeping notebooks and diaries over the years as a method of expressing internal conflict, excitement, loves and losses. These private reflections have been useful ways to steer my thinking, or helpful ways to look back at past events and recast present situations in new ways. Writing for the web has, in its own way, recast again how I write and offered up new possibilities of expression. Most obviously perhaps in the different forms of media I can use, but also – and possibly much more interestingly – in the choices I now have to share my writing.

When it comes to what I write, both professionally and personally, it's generally a product of some real world event. At work this might well be the addition of a new product or service to our portfolio, requiring new content to be written so we can share it with the rest of the world. Personally, it might be the release of a new piece of information technology, something which I'm very keen on, and I'll be inspired to offer my own particular insights or reflections on how it might impact people. More often than not though, it'll be my primary hobby – food – and I'll be writing up a new recipe I've created. I've been a food blogger for many years now, sharing my culinary exploits with fellow foodies from around the world.

I tend to be something of an unplanned writer, inspiration will hit, and I'll have the bare bones of what I want to write pretty much instantly. This does tend to make me undisciplined though, with the result that I have many, many blog posts – my preferred medium – in various stages of completion, most of which will never be finished. When writing about technology, timing is everything, so at least I have something of an excuse when blog posts become old as they become irrelevant, but more often than not I have to admit that it is more to do with waning enthusiasm for the topic in question. Once that candle of inspiration has burned down, it's very hard to get a new one going! That said, I do always try and leave a day or so between edits as a method of quality control; I find reflecting on my writing a day later gives me a fresh perspective on the content. Sometimes, though, a day becomes two days – and then a week – and old writing can be difficult to resurrect.

I always tend to write directly online, using 'cloud services' to store my words directly on the web rather than on the hard drive of my computer. As someone with a passion for technology it's very natural for me to adopt these new possibilities, but I'm actually driven much more by personal need than technological possibility. Being an undisciplined writer, it's important for me to be able to write when the muse strikes, and by storing my words in this virtual cloud I can always access them no matter where I am and continue to work. All I need is a computer and a connection to the web to write, and in a world where a mobile phone can now offer both of those in my pocket I'm rarely disconnected from my potential writing desk. That said though, like many writers I do have my favourite time and place, Sunday morning for preference, in my study at home with a cup of coffee and some peace and quiet.

Of course writing – or should I say creating – for the web isn't just about writing text. Text remains the mainstay of the communication, but it's incredibly rare for me to simply publish a piece without some form of elaboration, and by that I mean the addition of other media or interaction. At its most basic level this might just be hyperlinks within the text, allowing the reader to explore more detailed information about the topic I'm exploring. But hyperlinks like these are not just casually thrown in here, there and everywhere. Like the rest of the text they need to be carefully thought out and blended seamlessly into the main narrative, offering the choice to interact but at the same time keeping distraction to a minimum for those who are uninterested. This requirement for seamless blending often dictates the words themselves, and becomes the primary driver for sentence construction. Imagery is also very important online, providing an eye-catching hook into content that either presents something directly relevant to the text, e.g. a picture of recipe ingredients being prepared, or something that symbolises conceptions within the text, e.g. abstract imagery or diagrammatic forms. I also often use video, especially for my cooking blog, as this form of media gives me the most complete picture so far possible with technology, blending as it does text, imagery and time together.

As to why I tend to include other media and interaction, there is the obvious answer that this is simply possible online in a way that paper simply can't replicate, but there is also the difficulty that in the web world people tend to be much more fickle than in the paper world. The web medium has this wonderful ability to be everywhere, to allow even the most shy and disconnected individual to suddenly be anywhere on the planet. This does, however, have a serious downside, in as much as people can leave your content just as easily as they can arrive at it. In fact, web designers even have a word to describe this, it's known as 'bounce rate', and is a measure of just how many people tend to perform exactly this action – arriving and then leaving again almost immediately. As a writer of web content, this knowledge is constantly with you, so you're very conscious that you need to engage your audience quickly, writing in a special web style that allows for easy digestion. Short paragraphs are the norm, bullet points if possible, lots of headings and at different levels. I've heard it said that if you're moving from the paper world to the web world then you should consider cutting your content down by as much as two-thirds, so you need to be something of a master editor as well! Personally, I feel that this need to cut is now less critical, for as the web has matured so people have become used to richer, longer and deeper content, but it's certainly still true that capturing your audience quickly is still as critical as ever. Experiments have shown that people make up their minds about whether to continue reading a web page they have reached in just milliseconds, so fast in fact that they've often decided subconsciously quicker than they have decided consciously! That's a frightening thought for a web writer.

There is another special factor about writing for the web that I alluded to earlier, which I think is often overlooked, and that is the new sharing choices that are available. Simply put, this might be about being able to publicly share a new recipe, privately share pictures of my new son, or keep totally private some personal thoughts on a new relationship. But alongside this ability to write something and deciding who to share it *with*, is the ability to write something and decide who to share it *as*. The ability to be one thing to one person but something else to another, to cast yourself as separate identities, or perhaps more accurately to be able to reflect different facets of your personality in different ways. As each of us engages more with the web world, so we have a choice as to who we decide to be represented online as, and this choice can directly inform how we write. For most people now this is simply a matter of a work email address or a home email address, what might be considered an artificial split between who you are in the office and who you are at home. But is this an artificial split, or an existing predilection facilitated by the new medium? We're all aware, I think, of the need to remain professional in a web world where statements can easily be misconstrued; you only need to think here of the various Facebook and Twitter stories that have led some people to lose their jobs over inappropriate statements to start to understand the dangers of 'just being yourself' everywhere. Perhaps it's the simple fact that the cues that dictate who we are and how we're perceived in real life – how we dress, how we sound, the physical locales we frequent, etc. – are all missing from our virtual lives, and this gives us an opportunity to use the medium in ways which just aren't possible in reality. Perhaps there are similarities here with how a book author might write different novels as different personas – but in the web world these identities persist continuously, they are not suspended in time by the paper.

Of course I'm only reflecting here on how I write on the web; others will have different experiences. As I said at the beginning of this piece, my writing has always been about utilising the web to inform rather than necessarily connect, but I do wonder just how much this is due to me, and how much is due to the medium. I'm not going to get all McLuhan here, but I do think that in many ways he hit upon something quite fundamental to these emerging mediums. The medium is a critical part of the link between the humans who are communicating, and must in some way effect that communication.

Perhaps the distinction between informing and connecting is a desire by myself to reduce risk – informing is after all unidirectional whereas connecting is bidirectional. But perhaps it is also a product of the medium, in as much as the amount of 'human bandwidth' that is currently possible online is still very limited, naturally restricting the amount of connection that is feasible. Either way the web remains to me a wonderfully interesting place to inhabit, and I look forward to writing – and creating – much more for the web in the future, and will certainly be exploring whatever new opportunities for expression it throws up next.

Commentary

Each of these reflections paints a unique portrait of each writer, underlining the very personal and idiosyncratic nature of writing and being a writer. Taken together, they offer some rich points of convergence and counterpoint, moments where their voices sing in unison, and others where they sing in harmony. Pete Moore begins by recalling the classic romantic image of the writer, struggling alone in a dusty garret – but the way these writers describe their own writing experience is much more about being a writer within a community. Both Julia Eccleshare and Pete Moore note the importance of the professional teams that support their writing, from copy editors to layout designers and printers. And Rich Osborne underlines vividly the virtual space his writing occupies, allowing for sharing writing across time and space boundaries. These are not lone writers.

One theme which emerges in all three reflections is the place of discipline in writing. For both Julia and Pete the need for discipline is imposed externally by deadlines, often short-term deadlines for an article or review, but also the longer-term deadlines required for a book. Meeting deadlines requires the adaptation of working practices to ensure they are met. Julia describes how she invents 'exam conditions' for herself, creating a space for writing which is simultaneously time-limited and high-stakes, while Pete has devised a detailed set of routines that support his writing, involving spreadsheets, preparatory processes, graphic organisers, and a strong self-regulated pattern of writing a certain number of words each day. Julia notes the paradox that although writing can be 'completed' within a tight timeline, writing can also take 'an unlimited amount of time': to an extent no piece of writing is ever finished, although it may be published. Rich Osborne, in contrast, thinks of himself as an undisciplined writer, and he is the only one of the three writers to mention unfinished and incomplete pieces of writing.

The contrast between Rich's 'undisciplined' approach and the more strictly disciplined strategies of Julia and Pete may simply be because the writing deadlines are far more critical and visible for Pete and Julia. However, it may also link with the way they each manage the writing process. Rich describes himself as an unplanned writer, and makes no reference to any planning processes, only to abandoned texts: he writes directly online, exploiting the affordances of technology to be able to write at any time or anywhere, never being 'disconnected' from his virtual 'writing desk'. But both Julia and Pete are planners. Both note that the period before beginning to compose the actual text is the period where they do their thinking – it is 'longer process' for Julia, a 'space in which to reflect' and to research. Equally, for Pete, the preparatory phase, where ideas and structures are developed, is the point 'where the majority of thinking occurs'. Both also refer to the importance of being well researched in terms of the content of a piece, and constructing coherent, well-supported arguments. There may be a distinction here between Pete and Julia, who think before they write, and Rich, who thinks *through* writing.

All, however, mention editing. Rich uses time to give him mental space and create a kind of 'quality control', and neither Rich nor Pete are keen editors. Rich notes his tendency towards waning enthusiasm for a piece, which prevents him from going back to it to refine it, while Pete is explicit about revision and editing being the least favourite part of the writing process. Julia signals there is a discipline in editing – being prepared to cut, taking a robustly self-critical stance, and avoiding self-indulgence. The importance of others in the editing process is significant for both Pete and Julia, from the involvement of Pete's partner in the initial editing process, to the professional support of editors and copy editors who bring a critical eye to the writing.

Common to all is a reference to an impetus to write, something which urges the writer from inside with a desire to communicate. Julia and Pete both refer to adrenaline and the positive impact it has: for Julia it is 'creative', and for Pete 'words flow most fluently' when 'sufficient adrenaline' is coursing through his veins. Rich describes this more figuratively as inspiration and 'when the muse strikes'. But for all three this impetus creates energy and flow in the writing process. Both Julia and Rich are aware of a need for reflecting: Julia sees this as a important interplay between the dynamic flow of writing and the slower, more thoughtful reflective space, which she describes as 'almost two contradictory mind-frames – an energetic one and a dynamic one'.

Perhaps not surprisingly, as all three are professional writers, all are sharply aware of the audience for their writing and of shifting styles to suit different audiences. And all three demonstrate considerable precision in how they describe this. Julia discriminates between her selling style and her reviewing style, noting the typical vocabulary of promotional writing, compared with the greater subtleties of reviewing, where balancing familiar vocabulary phrasing with original and analytical language is more important.

Communicating scientific ideas to diverse audiences also requires very careful management of material, and Pete explicitly consider the reader's knowledge and interest, and the kinds of stories and examples which will support their understanding. Writing for the web shares this need to manage material for the reader, although the ease with which readers can 'bounce' through online material generates its own specific demands. Rich describes both the unique possibilities of web writing, with its multimodal affordances – images, hyperlinks, video – which blend 'text, imagery and time together', and the need for writing choices which allow for 'easy digestion' – short paragraphs, clear headings, and clarity of presentation of information. There are very real links here with writing as design, as described in Chapter 4. Quite apart from the word 'designer' being part of Rich's professional role title, creating web text is very evidently a design activity of making choices from a rich visual and verbal repertoire. But Pete's mapping of structure and argument, and word-banking, and illustrative material is equally a design activity. And Julia likens the process of crafting text to smooth it into a satisfying whole as being akin to the icing of a cake or the shaping of a piece of pottery, both very practical design activities. For all three writers, the creation of a satisfying text is the creation of an artefact, a thing of beauty and pleasure.

The role of technology in writing is evident in all three reflections. Both Rich and Pete explicitly note that they write directly onto a computer screen and Julia implies that she does so too, as she limbers up for writing by 'firing off a handful of emails'. The use of voice-activated software by Pete recalls the use of Dictaphones by authors in the past, but the benefit of voice-activated software is that it allows for oral composition which is simultaneously reproduced on screen: a writer can at once read and hear the written text. For Pete, the software aids text production, but most of the thinking has already taken place. In contrast, Rich uses technology to think and write simultaneously. Blogging provides a medium for exploratory writing, including writing which is never completed or published, and writing which is shared with others. It is interesting, though, that Rich is the only of the three authors who recalls childhood writing – the keeping of diaries and notebooks to express intensely personal feelings – and the only author who suggests that writing for oneself is valuable, a way 'to look back at past events and recast present situations in new ways'. Is blogging simply a technological extension of this natural belief in the value of writing for oneself?

These three reflective portraits offer an intimate snapshot of the writing lives of professional writers. There are moments where their reflections coalesce around common images – the idea of flow and energy, the idea of crafting and designing, the awareness of audience. And there are contrasts, most vividly between the disciplined, carefully planned, thinking-before-writing approach of Julia and Pete, compared with the free-flowing, exploratory, thinking-through-writing approach of Rich. At heart, however, all three share a real commitment to what they are doing: not so much a passion for writing, but a passion for communicating through writing, and the possibility of 'changing hearts and minds'.

I have always loved writing. I remember summer holidays where I would create dens in the back garden to escape into my own world and write. I rather liked the idea of being a Jo March and, having no garret, the back garden seemed a reasonable substitute! The romantic image of 'being a writer' definitely appealed, and the goal of getting myself published was very real. As a teenager, I responded to an advert in the paper for poems for an anthology, and sent my precious poetry to a publisher in Scotland – my initial delight at having them accepted was soon tempered by my hasty introduction to the world of vanity publishing. At school, I enjoyed writing in English, though I never particularly liked writing stories: my real interests were poetry, argument, and a particular kind of overblown purple prose which O-level examiners seemed to like. I do remember being aware that if I wanted to write poetry or purple prose I had to get myself into the right mood or frame of mind, where I was fully absorbed with the images and ideas I wanted to evoke.

Now, perhaps because my research has focused on writing, I have become acutely conscious of my own writing processes and what I do as I write. I know that I approach the composing process very differently for different kinds of writing. If I am writing a poem, it is messy, fragmentary, and very experimental – I will gather on screen, images, half-formed lines or sections of the poem. Multiple versions of the same image, line, word will coexist on the page, and poems can often remain unfinished. For workplace writing, such as policies or reports, I usually create the subheadings first and gather tentatively what will go in those subheadings, then I just write straight onto the screen, and revise and adapt as I go. Academic writing, such as articles or book chapters, are the most intensively planned writing I do. Here I am very aware that an awful lot of the preparation is in my head over quite a period – I mull on what it is I want to say, and what the evidence is for my claim, and much of this advance preparation is trying to tease out for myself just what my argument is, until I feel that my embryonic article is 'ripe' enough for writing. Sometimes I will make myself do some preparatory 'disciplining', where I write the key message of the article in a hundred words or prepare a structured abstract. At this stage, I will often also do some more reading around the principal theoretical ideas that the article will address. Then I move into a written planning stage, where I develop quite a detailed written outline. I use headings and subheadings to create a structure for the article, then gather the material I want to use under these headings, often as bullet points. I spend a lot of time on this, checking that I do have a strong argument and that the evidence to support it is robust, and also checking the coherence of the line of argument from the title, through the introduction, and the various sections, through to the conclusion. This stage is usually the hardest part for me. Once I have the outline and I am happy with it, I can often write the article very quickly. As the article develops, I constantly reread what I have written and revise intensively as I write. This involves lots of local revision as I adjust words, phrases or sentence structures, but also global revision as I reread all that has been written so far and continually refine the line of argument. Whether the final article resembles the original plan is a moot point; I don't regard the plan as a set of instructions for completing the article but a living, working document which helps me organise my thoughts. The process of writing always generates new ideas or nuances on the material but it is rare for me to alter that key argument. If I do, then it is often a real problem and may mean having to undertake a radical revision or restructuring of the whole piece.

Although the 'writer in the garret' identity has long since dissolved, I do still get enormous pleasure from the process of writing and the satisfaction of creating a text which is (I hope!) clearly communicated and fit for purpose.

Debra – author

Conclusion
Synthesising voices

This book has endeavoured to explore and give voice to the rich and varied experiences of writers and to bring to the surface multiple understandings of what it means to be a writer and multiple ways of managing the writing process. The voices we hear in this book range from Summer's emerging voice as a writer, through to the voices of children in both primary and secondary schools, and the voices of teachers and student teachers. We also hear the voices of professional writers, and, of course, our own voices as authors. In this way, we hope to have established *insider perspectives* on the complexity of writing: a kind of multivocal text which hums with the unique and the shared understandings of being a writer.

We commenced with an examination of research into writing, which draws on three rather different academic traditions: cognitive psychology, which seeks to understand the mental processes involved: socio-cultural research, which emphasises writing as social practice and the situated nature of writing; and linguistics, which illuminates the language choices in writing. These three domains of thinking rarely coalesce in research into writing, yet in this book, again and again, their complementarity is evident. Writers describe the routines and practices they develop to create the cognitive space for writing, from keeping scrapbooks of ideas and fragments, or walking with a phone to record embryonic ideas, to collating words and drawing diagrams. Older writers and professional writers, in particular, are very aware of the different phases in the writing process and how they individually manage the planning, the creation of text, and the reviewing of their work. In common with the Flower and Hayes (1981) model of writing, their accounts resonate with an insistence on the fluidity and recursiveness of the process, with ideas emerging both before and during writing, and revision occurring during writing as well as afterwards. The socially situated nature of writing and the ways in which writers' identity is heavily shaped by their social experience is also evident, not least the role that 'schooled' writing, with its emphasis on objectives and outcomes, shapes learners' understanding of what it means to be a writer. But Bianca's reflections on her own writing history point to the influence of the home too: seeing her mother as a writer and being drawn into sharing that process gave her a sense of the value of writing beyond the classroom. And she also had early experiences of writing for authentic purposes – to account for her own behaviour!

Ben too, as a less enthusiastic teenager, locates himself within a community of 'other teenage boys' who don't see the point of writing, beyond a certain funct-ionality in school and the workplace. Ellie also voices the significance of context in commenting that she wants her audience 'to think it is funny' and comments she enjoyed it 'because my teachers and my friends think it is good too'. The crucial role of language, and language choices, is equally visible, often in the agonising that writers record in choosing just the right word, or image, or syntactical rhythm, to achieve exactly what the writer's creative impulse is demanding.

What, then, do these multiple voices tell us about writing and the teaching of writing? Below, we orchestrate these voices to establish some of the bass notes and harmonies of the experience of writing.

Voicing the process

Throughout this book, writers have made visible the process of writing, teasing out, unlayering and revealing the art and the craft of creating text. Perhaps not surprisingly, the professional writers are the most articulate in this respect, providing a window into the secret workings of the imagination. The power of visualisation, living within the creative moment, and letting the writing take you where it will, echo through many of the professional voices; as Philip Gross describes it, 'letting a thought form, holding it a moment, visualised as clearly as I could . . . then dismissing it, clearing the mind like bursting a bubble or wiping a screen'. So too does the amount of preparation for writing which occurs before words begin to appear on the page – it is striking how much the professional writers do before they start. This is planning in the cognitive sense, although much less in the classroom sense – it is not necessarily about creating detailed written plans, although it may involve this; rather it is about getting 'in the zone' and being ready to write. For Pete Moore, this phase is where 'the majority of thinking is done'. The testimonies of both these writers demystify the writing process, and banish romantic notions of artists inspired by a muse. Writing is hard work! As Julia Eccleshare describes it, there are both energetic moments, where the words just flow, and reflective moments of refining and honing, and each have their place.

When teachers engage themselves in being writers, rather than teachers of writing, their insights into this process enable them to understand better how young writers experience writing in their classrooms. Through reflecting on their own writing histories and identities as writers, they can come to reconceptualise writing in the twenty-first century and adopt new positions in the classroom. Writing alongside their students, opening up their own thinking and voicing their own writing processes creates communities of writers who come to know not merely the objectives for writing, but the very essence of what it means to be a writer. As one teacher, Vicky, notes, 'I've always said that talking and reading contribute to children's writing, but I guess I hadn't known it for myself and it's not just that either, it's life experience, looking, listening, thinking creatively, combining ideas and incidents and being determined too.' Through becoming thoughtfully involved, writing about writing, teachers can deepen their subject knowledge and understanding and provide more responsive and informed support for young writers.

The voices of student writers too show that, given the opportunity, they can talk about how they write: building this opportunity to talk about writing processes into the writing curriculum is critically important in developing autonomy in young writers.

Voicing design

An insistent drumbeat pulsing through the voices of the professional writers is the significance of editing and sharpening up written texts, both during and after writing. This is the design element of writing, making the writing pass the author's sense of fitness for purpose. Sometimes this designing occurs concurrently with creating text, a complex interplay of generation and reflection, of spilling out words onto the page, and pausing to reselect and hone: 'trying to convey the complexity of an idea demands such careful phrasing and such a delicate stacking up of words to make the point in exactly the right way' (Julia Eccleshare). At other times, it involves a willingness to be ruthless in editing, to take the designer's knife to precious text and carve what is not necessary to reveal a sharper text within. There is little doubt that the professional writers' mantra is *Cut, Cut, Cut*! For learning writers, this kind of critical evaluation of their own writing is a hard skill to master and one which teaching needs to actively nurture. And evaluation is only ever possible if you have some understanding of what *is* possible. It's important to remember that professional writers have a much more mature and developed palette to draw on: they have more life experiences and world knowledge; they have more reading experience; and they have more experience of writing. They will have a wealth of stored words, images, ideas, and textual encounters, and what Flower and Hayes (1981) called 'stored writing plans'. In the writing classroom, we have to support young writers in acquiring a design palette, through reading as writers, drawing their attention to choices that authors have made and opening up the process of writing as a decision-making activity, helping them become aware of what we have called elsewhere a repertoire of infinite possibilities (Myhill, 2011).

Generative voices

This repertoire also extends to the myriad of ideas which, through reading, thinking, play and interaction, are generated prior to and during writing. As part of the extended process of composition, Linda Newbery for example collects artefacts, books, newspaper articles, poems, pebbles and other unplanned but gradually connected objects to nurture possibilities – 'a gathering of ingredients', as she describes this practice. Other professional writers talk of keeping notebooks – writing journals to retain fleeting ideas and observations – and still others show how they capitalise on opportunities (Vicky's weekend walk), emotions (Sally's fear of writing) or interests (Brandon's passion for skydiving) as resources for writing, although in most cases they explore many other options and possibilities before settling on one. For Sue 'a chance meeting with my A-level English teacher, who I hadn't seen since I left school' triggered a poem of gratitude, although this was written several weeks after their passing encounter. These examples suggest that on the interactive and social journey towards writing, thoughts and feelings, texts and contexts and the activities which surround them are highly influential; the playful exploration of possibilities shapes the emergent intentions of writers. In school, as our earlier work indicates (Grainger et al., 2005; Cremin et al., 2006), the ideational fluency of young writers can be enhanced through verbal, visual and mental play with ideas and options. The time and space to generate and to incubate ideas, through improvisation, exploration and percolation represent an under-recognised part of the writing process: the serious play of composition.

Reflective voices

Being able to talk about how we write and our own writing processes demands metacognitive awareness, and being able to discuss design choices requires metalinguistic knowledge. To give these room to flourish needs reflective space and reflective voices. Our projects with teachers illustrate how being offered space, time and support to engage with writing and share their experiences with others, energises teachers to reflect on their teaching of writing. For many it was a transformative experience, allowing them inside the mind of a writer and gaining a firsthand insight into how young writers might feel and might be positioned in their classrooms. School writing is often preoccupied with 'doing' writing: writing storyboards, plans, spidergrams, drafts, and so on. Even in classrooms which might characterise themselves as process-oriented, they are often remarkably product-oriented and output-driven. This is not simply a consequence of curriculum pressures; it is a rather natural desire on the part of teachers to ensure that children are indeed 'working'. Moreover, the English National Curriculum refers to the writing process as plan-draft-revise-edit, and in practice this has tended to be realised in very linear, chronological terms as a set of rigid procedures, what Czerniewska (1992) calls institutionalised and ritualised procedures. Yet all the testimonies from teachers and professional writers confirm the process as recursive, or messy, switching reflexively between planning, drafting and revising. A very real question is how teachers can create sufficient reflective space and a less rigid management overlay of the writing process to allow for reflection within the constraints of a school day, perhaps particularly in secondary schools where English mostly comes neatly packaged in slots of 50 minutes to an hour. One answer might be to write less and create more space for talking about writing; another might be to ensure that young writers are given opportunities to revisit 'completed' writing at a later stage.

Voicing together

One aspect of writing that has potential for much greater exploration is collaborative writing. This is not simply working together on separate pieces of writing but genuinely sharing in the co-construction of text. The affordances of technology, particularly wikis, gives a real edge to collaborative writing as it enables the easy alteration of text and the holding of several options as simultaneous possibilities. One advantage of collaborative writing is that in order to create text together, writers have to talk about their writing intentions and decisions, making visible the thinking which underpins the creation of text. This can both motivate writers and reduce the cognitive load, as Liam observed: 'It's more fun when we write together, we share ideas and it makes it easier. Casey is good at spelling and I'm good at punctuation and checking'. It's a productive and positive way of sharing the process of writing. In the world of the workplace, the production of texts is an increasingly common practice, as documents are circulated for shared authorship and revisions. In part this has been our experience in writing this book; the original plans were discussed, developed, submitted, reviewed and then reworked though email dialogue and in meetings, before either of us had committed to continuous prose. But it may be less usual to think of collaborating in the writing of a poem, novel or short story. Yet Philip Gross draws our attention to the magic of writing together and the way it builds new, different space for creative engagement: 'How revelatory is it, then, to have an experience in which you find yourself writing something that is both intensely you and also surprising as you each watch it form, semi-independently, in the space between you and someone else'.

Voices and silences

A final theme drawn from the writers' voices in this book is the place of the voice and of silence in the act of writing. Nurturing classroom communities of writers who are reflective, have self-knowledge of themselves as writers, who know how they approach the writing process and can make design choices, demands that we open up fertile possibilities for talking about writing. But beyond that, many of the professional writers and teachers emphasise the importance of hearing their own writing, whether that be literally through reading aloud or through listening to the text read in the head. Voicing your own text creates a dialogic relationship between the writer as author and the writer as reader, and enables writers to do two key things. Firstly, it helps them to hear the cadences and rhythms of their writing and evaluate if it is satisfying their authorial intentions; secondly, it helps them to stand in the shoes of a reader and sense how the text might appear to them. As Anne, a teacher, notes: 're-reading is a vital strategy, not just for drafting, but in order to hear my own voice and reinforce my angle'. Mary Medlicott too describes how this inner voice supports her design choices during the unfolding of a text: 'even as I am composing phrases, getting them down on paper or up on the computer screen, I am sounding them out in my head, my inner voice performing a[s] vital a role in the editing and shaping'. When studying the composing processes of teenage writers, we found a marked difference between able and weaker writers in this respect: the able writers paused a lot more during the writing process, and frequently these pauses were to read back over the text, and hear what they had written. But many young writers do not actively see reading aloud or reading in the head as part of the reviewing phase of the writing process. Classroom activities which foster the development of the ability to 'read aloud in the head' and 'reread at the point of composition' and which generate opportunities for reading aloud with others would help refine young writers' sense of identity as authors.

It is also noticeable how often the professional writers whose voices are woven through the book refer to the privacy of writing and the need to find a mental space for writing. In part, this is about protection from exposure while ideas and texts are forming and developing, a sense of avoiding others' critical comment before the writing has had a chance to crystallise and settle. In part, it is about finding the creative space to become fully absorbed in the writing and detached from other distractions – not just to experience the flow (Csikszentmihalyi, 1999), but also to engage in the battle with words, phrases and ideas. It is a kind of silence, although not all writers need or want complete silence, an external silence or solitude that permits the inner voice, with all its promptings and false starts, to be heard. Writing classrooms can be such busy places that privacy and mental space are sometimes hard to find. So seeking alternative places to write, perhaps alongside professional writers, may help, as can thinking about how the physical organisation of the classroom might be adapted to create literal areas of space for writers to work quietly, or whether the creative use of silence or calm music can create this inner space. In this way, young writers may experience and understand the fertility of solitude.

Finally, in reading this book, we hope that you can hear our distinctive voices as authors. As co-authors, whilst we planned the text together in some detail, we made a conscious decision not to attempt to achieve a consistency of voice, but to let both our voices be heard, sometimes in unison, sometimes in harmony. Each chapter is lead-authored by one of us; we have used 'we' to refer to ourselves as co-authors, but we have also used 'we' to refer to the research teams and teachers we have worked with; we shift between 'we' and 'I' as necessary to signal when we move from the shared authorship to a personal reflection or commentary. Like you, our readers, we belong to multiple communities of writers, each with their own demands and each with their own specific influence on the shaping of our identities as writers. Our hope is that this book presents a new way of thinking about writing, and especially about the teaching of writing: a way of thinking which is neither too dependent on romantic notions of creativity, where writing 'just happens', nor too dependent on a technicist view, where writing is about compliance with accepted norms. Rather, through synthesising the principal arguments from our various research projects on writing, and through giving space for the voices of other writers, we offer a creative challenge for writing pedagogy – to create classroom communities of writers which nurture students' sense of themselves as writers, which develop reflective capacities and design repertoires, and which enable young writers to move with assurance between social and personal spaces.

References

Alamargot, D. and Chanquoy, L. 2001. *Through the Models of Writing*. Dordrecht: Kluwer Academic Publishers.

Allison, P., Beard, R. and Willcocks, J. 2002. Subordination in children's writing. *Language in Education*, 16(2): 97–111.

Almond, D. 2007. *Secret Heart*. London: Hodder.

Almond, D. 2010. *My Name is Mina*. London: Hodder.

Andrews, R. 1989. Beyond 'voice' in poetry. *English in Education*, 23(3): 21–7.

Andrews, R. 2008a. *Shifting Writing Practice in DCSF. Getting Going: generating, shaping and developing ideas in writing*: 4–21. Nottingham: DCSF.

Andrews, R. 2008b. *The Case for a National Writing Project for Teachers*. Reading, England: CfBT.

Armstrong, M. 2006. *Children Writing Stories*. Berkshire and New York: Open University Press.

Atwell, N. 1987. *In the Middle: Writing, Reading, and Learning with Adolescents*. Portsmouth, NH: Heinemann.

Baddeley, A.D. and Hitch, G. 1974. Working memory. In G. H. Bower (ed.), *The Psychology of Learning and Motivation: Advances in Research and Theory*, Vol. 8: 47–89. New York: Academic Press.

Bailey, M. 2002. What does research tell us about how we should be developing written composition. In R. Fisher, G. Brooks and M. Lewis (eds.), *Raising Standards in Literacy*. London: Routledge/Falmer.

Bakhtin, M. 1981. *The Dialogic Imagination* (trans. M. Holquist and C. Emerson, ed. M. Holquist). Austin, TX: University of Texas Press.

Bakhtin, M. 1986. *Speech Genres and Other Late Essays* (trans. V. W. McGee). Austin, TX: University of Texas Press.

Banaji, S. and Burn, A. 2007. *Rhetorics of Creativity: A Review of the Literature*. London: Creative Partnerships and Arts Council England.

Barrs, M. 1988. Maps of play. In M. Meek and C. Mills (eds.), *Language and Literacy in the Primary School*: 101–117. London: Falmer Press.

Barrs, M. and Cork, V. 2001. *The Reader in the Writer: The Influence of Literature upon Writing at KS2*. London: Centre for Literacy in Primary Education.

Beard, R. 2000a. *Developing Writing 3–13*. London: Hodder and Stoughton.

Beard, R. 2000b. Research and the national literacy strategy. *Oxford Review of Education*, 26(3): 421–36.

Bearne, E. 2002. *Making Progress in Writing*. London: Routledge/Falmer.

Bearne, E. 2003. Rethinking literacy: communication, representation and text. *Reading Literacy and Language*, 37(3): 98–103.

Bearne, E. 2009. Multimodality literacy, and texts: developing a discourse. *Journal of Early Childhood Literacy*, 9(2): 156–87.

Bearne, E. and Grainger, T. 2004. Raising boys' achievements in writing. *Literacy*, 38(3): 153–59.

Bearne, E. and Wolstencroft, H. 2007. *Visual Approaches to Teaching Writing*. London: SAGE/UKLA.

Bearne, E., Chamberlain, L., Cremin, T. and Mottram, M. 2011. *Reviewing Writing*. Leicester: UKLA.

Beck, I. 1999. Ian Beck in Carter, J. 1999. *Talking Books: Children's Authors Talk About the Craft, Creativity and Process of Writing*: 40–69. London: Routledge.

Bereiter, C. and Scardamalia, M. 1987. *The Psychology of Written Composition*. Hillsdale, NJ: Lawrence Erlbaum Associates.

Berk, L. E. 1994. Why children talk to themselves. *Scientific American*: 78–83, [online] Available at:<http://www.abacon.com/berk/ica/research.html> [Accessed 23 October 2000].

Berk, L. E. 2003. *Child Development*. Boston, MA: Allyn and Bacon.

Berninger, V.W., Fuller, F. and Whittaker, D. 1996. A process model of writing development across the life span. *Educational Psychology Review*, 8(3): 193–218.

Boler, M. 1999. *Feeling Power: Emotion and Education*. London: Routledge.

Boscolo, P. and Gelati, C. 2007. Best practices in promoting motivation for writing. In S. Graham, C. MacArthur and J. Fitzgerald (eds.), *Best Practices in Writing Instruction*: 202–221. New York: Guilford Press.

Bourne, J. 2002. 'Oh, what will miss say!': Constructing texts and identities in the discursive processes of classroom writing. *Language and Education*, 16(4): 241–59.

Bowler, T. 2002. Write off your plans and go with the flow. *Times Educational Supplement*, [online] Available at: <http://www.tes.co.uk/article.aspx?storycode=367418> [Accessed 10 June 2011].

Bradford, H. and Wyse, D. 2010. Writing in the Early Years. In D. Wyse, R. Andrews and J. Hoffman (eds.), *The Routledge Handbook of English, Language and Literacy Teaching*: 137–45. London: Routledge.

Britton, J. 1982. *Prospect and Retrospect: Selected Essays of James Britton* (G. Pradl, ed.). London: Heinemann.

Britton, J. N. 1970. *Language and Learning*. Coral Gables, FL: University of Miami Press.

Britton, J., Burgess, T., Martin, N., McLeod, A. and Rosen, H. 1975. *The Development of Writing Abilities (11–18)*. London: Macmillan Education.

Brooks, G. W. 2007. Teachers as readers and writers and as teachers of reading and writing. *The Journal of Educational Research*, 100(3): 177–91.

Bruner, J. 1983. *Child's Talk: Learning to Use Language*. Oxford: Oxford University Press.

Bruner, J. 1984. Language, mind and reading. In H. Goelman, A. Oberg and F. Smith (eds.), *Awakening to Literacy*. London: Heinemann.

Bruner, J. S. 1979. *On Knowing: Essays for the Left Hand*. Cambridge, MA: Belknap Press of Harvard University Press.

Buchanan, J., Eidman-Aadahl, E., Friedrich, L., LeMahieu, P.G. and Sterling, R. 2005. *National Writing Project: Local Site Research Initiative Report, Cohort I (2003–2004)*. Berkeley, CA: National Writing Project.

Burnett, C. and Myers, J. 2002. Beyond the frame: Exploring children's literacy practices. *Reading*, 36(2): 56–62.

Burns, M.S., Griffin, P. and Snow, C.E. (eds.) 1999. *Starting Out Right: A Guide to Promoting Children's Reading Success*. Washington, DC: National Academy Press.

Calkins, L. M. 1986. *The Art of Teaching Writing*, Portsmouth, NH: Heinemann.

Camps, A. and Milian, M. (eds.) 1999. *Metalinguistic Activity in Learning to Write*. Amsterdam: Amsterdam University Press.

Carr, M., Kurtz, B. E., Schneider, W., Turner, L. A. and Borkowski, J. G. 1989. Strategy acquisition and transfer among German and American children: Environmental influences on metacognitive development. *Developmental Psychology*, 25: 765–771.

Carter, R.A. (ed.) 2004. *Introducing the Grammar of Talk*. London: Qualifications and Curriculum Authority.

Clark, C. and Dugdale, G. 2009. *Young People's Writing: Attitudes, Behaviour and the Role of Technology*. London: NLT in collaboration with Booktrust.

Cleland, A.A. and Pickering, M.J. (2006) Do Writing and Speaking Employ the same Syntactic Representations? *Journal of Memory and Language*, 54, 185–198.

Cliff Hodges, G. 2002. Learning through collaborative writing. *Reading, Language and Literacy*, 36(1): 4–10.

Coe, M. and Sprackland, J. 2005. *Our Thoughts Are Bees: Writers Working with Schools*. Southport: Wordplay.

Coleridge, S. T. 1817. *Biographia Literaria*.

Commeyras, M., Bisplinhoff, B.S. and Olson, J. 2003. *Teachers as Readers: Perspectives on the Importance of Reading in Teachers' Classrooms and Lives*. Newark, NJ: International Reading Association.

Cope, B. and Kalantzis, M. 2000. *Multiliteracies: Literacy Learning and the Design of Social Futures*. London: Routledge.

Corden, R. 2000. *Literacy and Learning Through Talk: Strategies for the Primary Classroom*. Birmingham: Open University Press.

Corden, R. 2001. Teaching Reading–Writing Links (TRAWL Project). *Reading, Literacy and Language*, 35(1): 37–40.

Corden, R. 2003. Writing is more than 'exciting': Equipping primary children to become reflective writers. *Reading Literacy and Language*, 37(1): 18–26.

Cox, B. 1991. *Cox on Cox: An English Curriculum for the 1990s*. London: Hodder and Stoughton.

Craft, A., Cremin, T. and Burnard, P. 2007. *Creative Learning 3–11 and How We Document It*. Stoke on Trent: Trentham.

Craft, A. R. 2005. *Creativity in Schools: Tensions and Dilemmas*. London: Routledge/Falmer.

Creech, S. 2001. *Love that Dog*. London: Bloomsbury.

Cremin, T. 2006. Creativity, uncertainty and discomfort: Teachers as writers. *Cambridge Journal of Education*, 36(3): 415–33.

Cremin, T. 2010. *Teachers as Writers: Writing Alongside Children*. Research and development project report. London: Newham LA.

Cremin, T. and Baker, S. 2010. Exploring teacher–writer identities in the classroom: Conceptualising the struggle. *English Teaching: Practice and Critique*, 9(3): 8–25.

Cremin, T., Powell, S. and Precey, R. 2007. *Boys and Writing*. Final research report. Maidstone: Kent LA.

Cremin, T., Reedy, D., Sprackland J., and Starling, I. 2010. *Writers in Schools*. Professional development resource pack. Leicester: United Kingdom Literacy Association.

Cremin, T., Goouch, K., Blakemore, L., Goff, E. and Macdonald, R. 2006. Connecting drama and writing: Seizing the moment to write. *Research in Drama in Education*, 11(3): 273–91.

Crowley, T. 2003. *Standard English and the Politics of Language*. London: Palgrave Macmillan.

Crumpler, T. and Schneider, J. 2002. Writing with their whole being: A cross study analysis of children's writing from five classrooms using process drama. *Research in Drama Education*, 7(2): 61–79.

Crystal, D. 1995. *The Cambridge Encyclopedia of the English Language*. Cambridge: Cambridge University Press.

Csikszentmihalyi, M. 1999. Implications of a systems perspective. In Robert J. Sternberg (ed.), *Handbook of Creativity*: 313–38. Cambridge: Cambridge University Press.

Csikszentmihalyi, M. 2002. *Flow: The Classic Work on How to Achieve Happiness*. London: Rider.

Czerniewska, P. 1992. *Learning about Writing*. Oxford: Blackwell.

D'Arcy, P. 1999. *Two Contrasting Paradigms for the Teaching and Assessment of Writing*. Leicester: National Association for the Teaching of English.

Davidson, C. 2007. Independent writing in current approaches to writing instruction: What have we overlooked? *English Teaching: Practice and Critique*, 6(1): 11–24.

Deary, T. 1999. Terry Deary in Carter, J. 1999. *Talking Books: Children's Authors Talk About the Craft, Creativity and Process of Writing*: 88–112. London and New York: Routledge.

Department for Education and Employment (DfEE) 1998. *The National Literacy Strategy Framework for Teaching*. London: DfEE.

Department for Education and Employment (DfEE) 2001. *Literacy Progress Unit: Sentences*. London: DfEE.

Department for Education and Skills (DfES) 2006a. *Primary Framework for Literacy and Mathematics*. Nottingham: DfES Publications.

Department for Education and Skills (DfES) 2006b. *Modelling*, [online] Available at: <http://nationalstrategies.standards.dcsf.gov.uk/node/249323> [Accessed 10 April 2010].

Department of Education and Science (DES) 1975. *A Language for Life* (The Bullock Report). London: HMSO.

Dieman-Yaumann, C., Oppenheimer, D. and Vaughan, E. 2011. Fortune favours the bold (and the italicised). *Cognition*, 118(1): 111–15.

Doherty, B. 1999. Berlie Doherty in J. Carter, J. 1999. *Talking Books: Children's Authors Talk About the Craft, Creativity and Process of Writing*: 145–61. London and New York: Routledge.

Doherty, B. 2001. Recognising yourself in what you read, keynote speech at Just let me think: reflecting on literacy learning. United Kingdom Reading Association International Conference. Canterbury 6–8 July 2001.

Domaille, K. and Edwards, J. 2006. Partnerships for learning: Extending knowledge and understanding of creative writing processes in the ITT year. *English in Education* 40(2): 71–84.

Dowdall, C. 2006. Dissonance between the digitally created words of school and home. *Literacy*, 40(3): 153–63.

Draper, M. C., Barksdale-Ladd, M. A. and Radencich, M. C. 2000. Reading and writing habits of pre-service teachers. *Reading Horizons*, 40(3): 185–203.

Dyson, A. 2003. Popular literacies and the 'all' children: Rethinking literacy development for contemporary childhoods. *Language Arts*, 81: 100–9.

Dyson, A. H. 1993. *Social Worlds of Children Learning to Write in an Urban Primary School*. New York: Teachers College Press.

Dyson, A. H. 1997. *Writing Superheroes: Contemporary Childhood, Popular Culture and Classroom Literacy*. New York: Teachers College Press.

Dyson, A. H. 2001. Where are the childhoods in childhood literacy? An exploration in (outer) space. *Early Childhood Literacy*, 1(1): 9–39.

Dyson, A. H. 2009. Writing childhood worlds. In R. Beard, D. Myhill, J. Riley and Nystrand, M. (eds.), *The SAGE Handbook of Writing Development*: 233–45. London: SAGE.

Earl, J. and Grainger, T. 2007. I love to write at home – there I'm free. Paper presented at the 43rdUKLA International Conference, Thinking Voices, University of Swansea, 6–8 July 2007.

Emig, J. 1971. *The Composing Processes of Twelfth Graders*. Urbana, IL: National Council of Teachers of English.

Feigenbaum, F. 2010. Development of communicative competence through private and inner speech. In A. Winsler, C. Fernyhough and I. Montero (eds.), *Private Speech, Executive Functioning, and the Development of Verbal Self-Regulation*: 105–20. Cambridge: Cambridge University Press.

Ferreiro, E. and Teberosky, A. 1982. *Literacy Before Schooling*. Oxford: Heinemann.

Fisher, R. 1998. Thinking about thinking: Developing metacognition in children. *Early Child Development and Care*, 14(1): 1–15.

Fisher, R. 2006. Whose writing is it anyway? Issues of control in the teaching of writing. *Cambridge Journal of Education*, 36(2): 193–206.

Fisher, R., Jones, S., Larkin, S. and Myhill, D. 2010. *Using Talk to Support Writing*. London: SAGE.

Flavell, J. 1976. Metacognitive aspects of problem-solving. In L. B. Resnick (ed.), *The Nature of Intelligence*: 231–6. Hillsdale, NJ: Erlbaum.

Flavell, J. H. 1979. Metacognition and cognitive monitoring: A new area of cognitive-developmental inquiry. *American Psychologist*, 34: 906–11.

Flavell, J. and Wong, A. 2009. Young children's knowledge about overt and covert speech. In A. Winsler, C. Fernyhough, and I. Montero (eds.), *Private Speech, Executive Functioning, and the Development of Verbal Self-Regulation*: 143–52. Cambridge: Cambridge University Press.

Fleming. M., Merrell, C. and Tymms, P. 2004. The impact of drama on pupils' language, mathematics and attitude in two primary schools. *Research in Drama Education*, 9(2): 177–97.

Flower, L. and Hayes, J. R. 1981. A cognitive process theory of writing. *College Composition and Communication*, 32(4): 365–87.

Fox, C. 1993. Tellings and retellings: educational implications of children's oral stories. *Reading*, 27(1): 14–20.

Fox, G. 2004. *Dear Mr Morpingo: Inside the World of Michael Morpurgo*. Cambridge: Wizard Books.

France, A. 2008. Teaching creative writing: The role of the tutor. *Writing in Education*, 45: 59–64.

Galton, M. 2008. *Creative Practitioners in Schools and Classrooms*. Cambridge: Creative Partnerships/Faculty of Education.

Gamble, N. 2008. *Writers' Secrets: An Insider's Guide to Writing Fiction*. London: Wayland.

Gannon, G. and Davies, C. 2007. For the love of the word: English teaching, affect and writing. *Changing English*, 14(1): 87–98.

Gardner, P. 2010. *Creative English, Creative Curriculum: New Perspectives for Key Stage 2*. London: David Fulton.

Geekie, P., Cambourne, B. and Fitzsimmons, P. 1999. *Understanding Literacy Development*. Stoke on Trent: Trentham.

Gleeson, A. and Prain, V. 1996. Should teachers of writing themselves? An Australian contribution to the debate. *English Journal*, 85: 42–49.

Goouch, K., Cremin, T. and Lambirth, A. 2009. *Writing is Primary*. Final research report. London: Esmée Fairbairn Foundation.

Graham, L. and Johnson, A. 2003. *Children's Writing Journals*. Royston: United Kingdom Literacy Association.

Grainger, T. 2005a. Teachers as writers. In M. Pandis, A. Ward, and S. R. Mathews (eds.), *Reading, Writing and Thinking*: 87–99. Tallin: Estonia.

Grainger, T. 2005b. Teachers as writers: Learning together. *English in Education*, 39(1): 75–87.

Grainger, T. and Goouch, K. 1999. Young children and playful language. In David, T. (ed.), *Teaching Young Children*: 19–29. London: Paul Chapman Publishing.

Grainger, T., Goouch, K. and Lambirth, A. 2002.The voice of the writer. *Reading, Literacy and Language*, 36(3): 135–9.

Grainger, T., Goouch, K. and Lambirth, A. 2003a. *We're Writers: Developing Voice and Verve*. Research report for Tunbridge Wells consortia. Kent: CCCUC.

Grainger, T., Goouch, K. and Lambirth, A. 2003b. Playing the game called writing: Children's views and voices. *English in Education*, 37(2): 4–15.

Grainger, T., Goouch, K. and Lambirth, A. 2005. *Creativity and Writing: Developing Voice and Verve in the Classroom*. London: Routledge.

Grainger, T., Earl, J. and Lambirth, A. 2006.*Creativity and Writing: Engaging Learners Creatively*. Final research report for West Kent consortia. Kent: CCCU.

Graves, D. 1983. *Writing: Teachers and Children at Work*. Portsmouth, NH: Heinemann.

Graves, D. 1994. *A Fresh Look at Writing*. Portsmouth, NH: Heinemann.

Gregory, E. 2001. Sisters and brothers as language and literacy teachers: Synergy between siblings playing and working together. *Journal of Early Childhood Literacy*, 1: 301–22.

Gross, P. 2010a. Writing alongside at the Poetry and Childhood Conference. In M. Styles, L. Joy and D. Whiteley (eds.), *Poetry and Childhood*: 233–9. London: Trentham.

Gross, P. 2010b. Poetry writing workshop at the Poetry and Childhood Conference. British Library, March 2010.

Gross, P., Fulleylove, L. and Gross, Z. 2006. No artform is an island: cross-arts weekends at Northcourt, Isle of Wight. *Writing in Education*, 50(2): 18–26. (Winner of the Liz Cashdan Prize for outstanding contribution to *Writing in Education*.)

Grugeon, E. 2001. We like singing the Spice Girls songs . . . and we like Tig and Stuck in the Mud: Girls' traditional play on two playgrounds. In J. C. Bishop and M. Curtis (eds.), *Play Today in the Primary School Playground: Life, Learning and Creativity*. Buckingham: Open University Press.

Guilford, J. P. 1950. Creativity. *American Psychologist*, 5: 444–54.

Gurevitch, Z. 2000. The serious play of writing. *Qualitative Inquiry*, 6(1): 3–8.

Haddon, M. 2004. *The Curious Incident of the Dog in the Night-time*: 31. London: Vintage.

Hall, C. and Thomson, P. 2005. Creative tensions? Creativity and basics skills in recent educational policy. *English in Education*, 39(3): 5–18.

Halliday, M. 1978. *Language as a Social Semiotic: The Social Interpretation of Language and Meaning*. London: Edward Arnold.

Halliday, M.A. K. 1975. *Learning How to Mean: Explorations in the Development of Language*. London: Edward Arnold.

Hansen, J. 1985. Teachers share their writing. *The Reading Teacher*, 38: 836–40.

Harpin, W. 1976. *The Second R: Writing Development in the Junior School*. London: Unwin.

Hayes, J. R. 1996. A new framework for understanding cognition and affect in writing. In C. M. Levy and S. Ransdell (eds.), *The Science of Writing: Theories, Methods, Individual Differences and Applications*: 1–27. Mahwah, NJ: Lawrence Erlbaum Associates.

Hayes, J. and Flower, L. 1980. Identifying the organisation of writing process. In L. Gregg and E. Steinberg (eds.), *Cognitive Processes in Writing*: 3–30. Hillsdale, NJ: Lawrence Erlbaum Associates.

Heaney, S. 1980. *Preoccupations: Selected Prose 1968–1978*. New York: Faber and Faber.

Heathcote, D. and Bolton, G. 1995. *Drama for Learning: Dorothy Heathcote's Mantle of the Expert Approach to Education*. Portsmouth, NH: Heinemann.

Henderson, S. 2010. *Up from the Blue*. New York: Harper.

Hillocks, J. R. 1979. Another review of 'the development of writing abilities'. *Research in the Teaching of English*, 13(3): 284–8.

Hilton, M. 2001. Writing process and progress: Where do we go from here? *English in Education*, 35(1): 4–12.

Holland, D. and Lave, J. 2001. History in person. In D. Holland and J. Lave (eds.), *Enduring Struggles: Contentious Practice, Intimate Identities*. 1–32. Santa Fe, NM: School of American Research Press.

Horner, S. 2010. *Magic Dust that Lasts: Writers in Schools – Sustaining the Momentum*. London: Arts Council England.

Howson, J. 2011. Jobs market: the verdict. *Times Educational Supplement: New Teacher*, 14 January 2011: 6–8.

Hughes, T. 1967. *Poetry in the Making*, London: Faber and Faber.

Hughes, T. 1976. Myth and education. In G. Fox, G. Hammond, T. Jones, F. Smith and K. Sterck (eds.), *Writers, Critics and Children*. London: Heinemann.

Ing, T. 2009. *Writing is Primary: Action Research on the Teaching of Writing in Primary Schools*. London: Esmée Fairbairn Foundation.

Jacobs, G. M. 2004. A classroom investigation of the growth of metacognitive awareness in kindergarten children through the writing process. *Early Childhood Education Journal*, 32(1): 17–23.

Janks, H. 2009. Writing: a critical literacy perspective. In R. Beard, D. Myhill, J. Riley and M. Nystrand (eds.), *International Handbook of Writing Development*. London: SAGE.

Jeffrey, B. and Woods, P. (2003). *The Creative School: A Framework for Success, Quality and Effectiveness*. London: Routledge/Falmer.

John-Steiner, V. 2000. *Creative Collaboration*. New York: Oxford University Press.

Johnston, J. and Ahtee, M. 2006. Comparing primary teachers' attitudes, subject knowledge and pedagogical content knowledge needs in a physics activity. *Teaching and Teacher Education*, 22: 503–12.

Jones, S. and Myhill D.A. 2004a. Troublesome boys and compliant girls. *British Journal of Sociology of Education*, 25(5): 557–71.

Jones, S. and Myhill, D.A. 2004b. Seeing things differently: Boys as underachievers. *Gender and Education*, 16(4): 531–46.

Kay, J. 2008. The Stincher commentary. In J. Lawson (ed.) *Inside Out: Children's Poets Discuss their Work*. London: Walker.

Kay, J. 2010. Keynote at the Poetry and Childhood Conference. British Library, March 2010.

Kellogg, R. T. 1994. *The Psychology of Writing*. Oxford: Oxford University Press.

Kellogg, R. T. 2008. Training writing skills: A cognitive developmental perspective. *Journal of Writing Research*, 1(1): 1–26.

Koestler, A. 1964. *The Act of Creation*. London: Macmillan.

Kress, G. 1994. *Learning to Write*. London: Routledge.

Kress, G. 1997. *Before Writing: Rethinking the Paths to Literacy*. London: Routledge.

Kress, G. and van Leeuwen, T. 1996. *Reading Images: The Grammar of Visual Design*. London: Routledge.

Kress, G. and Bezemer, J. 2009. Writing in a multimodal world of representation. In R. Beard, D. Myhill, J. Riley and M. Nystrand (eds.), *The SAGE Handbook of Writing Development*: 67–181. London: SAGE.

Lancaster, L. 2007. Representing the ways of the world: How children under three start to use syntax in graphic signs. *Journal of Early Childhood Literacy*, 7: 123–54.

Lenhart, A., Arafeh, S., Smith, A. and Rankin MacGill, A. 2008. *Writing, Technology and Teens*. Washington, DC: Pew Internet.

Lensmire, T. 1994. *When Children Write: Critical Re-visions of the Writing Workshop*. New York: Teachers College Press.

Lin, A. 1997. The child-in-the-world-with-others: Re-visioning Lensmire's critical re-visions of the writing workshop. *Curriculum Inquiry*, 27(4): 387–519.

Loban, W. 1976. *Language development: Kindergarten through grade twelve*. Research Report No. 18. Urbana, IL: National Council of Teachers of English.

Luce-Kapler, R., Chin, J., O'Donnell, E. and Stoch, S. 2001. The design of meaning: Unfolding systems of writing. *Changing English*, 8(2): 43–52.

Mallett, M. 1997. Developing learning: Can you say a little more about that? *Education*, 25: 1.

Marsh, J. 2009. Writing and popular culture. In R. Beard, D. Myhill, J. Riley and M. Nystrand (eds.), *The SAGE Handbook of Writing Development*: 313–24. London: SAGE.

Marsh, J. and Millard, E. 2005. *Popular Literacies, Childhood and Schooling*. London, Routledge/Falmer.

Martin, J. 1985. *Factual Writing*. Geelong,Victoria: Deakin University Press.

Martlew, M. 1983. Problems and difficulties: Cognitive and communicative aspects of writing. In M. Martlew (ed.), *The Psychology of Written Language*. New York: Wiley & Sons.

Maybin, J. 2005. *Children's Voices*. London and New York: Palgrave Macmillan.

McCarthey, S. J. and Moje, E. B. 2002. Identity matters. *Reading Research Quarterly*, 37(2): 228–38.

McClay, J. 1998. Becoming a teacher of writing: Living between and on the lines. *Alberta Journal of Educational Research*, 44: 173–87.

McNaughton, M. J. 1997. Drama and children's writing: A study of the influence of drama on the imaginative writing of primary schoolchildren. *Research in Drama Education*, 2(1): 55–86.

Merchant, G. 2003. E-mail me your thoughts: Digital communication and narrative writing. *Reading, Literacy and Language*, 37(3): 104–10.

Merchant, G. 2007. Writing the future in the digital age. *Literacy*, 41(3), 118–28.

Mitton, T. 2010. Reflecting on writing and performing poetry. Keynote at Hampshire Literacy Conference, 14 March 2010.

Moffett, J. 1968. *Teaching the Universe of Discourse*. Boston, MA: Houghton Mifflin.

Morpurgo, M. 2006. *Singing for Mrs Pettigrew: A Story-maker's Journey*. London: Walker.

Murphy, S. 2002. Literacy assessment and the politics of identities. In J. Soler, J. Wearmouth and G. Reid (eds.), *Contextualising Difficulties in Literacy Development*: 87–101. London: Routledge.

Murray, D. M. 1982. *Learning by Teaching: Selected Articles on Writing and Teaching*. Portsmouth, NH: Boynton/Cook.

Myhill, D. 2001. Crafting and creating. *English in Education*, 35(3): 13–20.

Myhill, D. 2005. Writing creatively. In A. Wilson (ed.), *Creativity in Primary Education*: 58–69. Exeter, Learning Matters.

Myhill, D.A. 2002. Bad Boys and Good Girls? Patterns of interaction and response in whole class teaching. *British Educational Research Journal*, 28(3): 339–52.

Myhill, D. A. 2008. Towards a linguistic model of sentence development in writing. *Language and Education*, 22(5): 271–88.

Myhill, D. A. 2009a. Becoming a designer: Trajectories of linguistic development. In R. Beard, D. Myhill, J. Riley and M. Nystrand (eds.), *The SAGE Handbook of Writing Development*: 402–14. London: SAGE.

Myhill, D. A. 2009b. Children's patterns of composition and their reflections on their composing processes. *British Educational Research Journal*, 35(1): 47–64.

Myhill, D. A. 2009c. From talking to writing: linguistic development in writing. In Teaching and learning writing: Psychological aspects of education – current trends. *British Journal of Educational Psychology Monograph Series II* (6): 27–44. British Psychological Society: Leicester, UK.

Myhill, D. A. 2011. Grammar for designers: How grammar supports the development of writing. In S. Ellis, E. McCartney, and J. Bourne (eds.), *Insight and Impact: Applied Linguistics and the Primary School*. Cambridge: Cambridge University Press.

Myhill, D. A. and Jones S. 2007. More than just error correction: Children's reflections on their revision processes. *Written Communication*, 24(4): 323–43.

Myhill, D.A. and Jones, S. M. 2009. How talk becomes text: Investigating the concept of oral rehearsal in early years' classrooms. *British Journal of Educational Studies*, 57(3): 265–84.

National Advisory Committee on Creative and Cultural Education (NACCCE) 1999. *All Our Futures: Creativity, Culture and Education*. London: DfEE.

National Writing Project (NWP) 1990. *Ways of Looking: Issues from the National Writing Project*. Walton-on-Thames: Nelson.

Negro, I. and Chanquoy, L. 2005. The effect of psycholinguistic research on the teaching of writing. *L1 Educational Studies in Language and Literature*, 5(2): 105–11.

Nelson T., Dunlosky, J., White, D., Steinberg, J., Townes, B. D. and Anderson, D. 1990. Cognition and metacognition at extreme altitudes on Mt. Everest. *Journal of Experimental Psychology*, 119(4): 317–34.

Oakhill, J., Hartt, J. and Samols, D. 2005. Levels of comprehension monitoring and working memory in good and poor comprehenders. *Reading and Writing: An Interdisciplinary Journal*, 18: 657–86.

O'Donnell, R. C. 1974. Syntactic differences between speech and writing. *American Speech*, 49(1/2): 102–10.

Office for Standards in Education (Ofsted) 2002. *The Curriculum in Successful Primary Schools*. HMI 553, October 2002. London: Ofsted.

Ofsted 2006. About creative partnerships, [online] Available at:<http://www.creative-partnerships.com/aboutcp/businessevidence> [Accessed 3 May 2007].

Ofsted 2009. *English at the Crossroads*. London: Ofsted.

Olson, D. 2006. Oral discourse in a world of literacy. *Research in the Teaching of English*, 41(2): 136–43.

Orwell, George. 1946. *Why I Write*. London: Penguin.

Owen, N. and Munden, P. 2010. *Class Writing: A NAWE Research Report into the Writers-in-Schools Ecology*. York: NAWE.

Parr, J. 2009. Building professional knowledge to teach writing: Teacher pedagogical content knowledge and student achievement in writing. Presented at the 45th UKLA Annual Conference, Literacy Today and Tomorrow. University of Greenwich, 10–12 July 2009.

Payne, T. 2011. Inspired by rhymes and a faith in paradise – an interview with Derek Walcott. *Sunday Times Review*, 22 January, pp. 14–15.

Peel, R. 2000. Beliefs about 'English' in England. In R. Peel, A. Patterson and J. Gerlach (eds.), *Questions of English: Ethics, Aesthetics, Rhetoric and the Formation of the Subject in England, Australia and the United States.* 116–88. London: Routledge/Falmer.

Perera, K. 1984.*Children's Writing and Reading: Analysing Classroom Language*. Oxford: Blackwell.

Perera, K. 1986. Grammatical differentiation between speech and writing in children aged 8–12. In A. Wilkinson (ed.), *The Writing of Writing*: 90–108. Milton Keynes:Open University Press.

Piaget, J. 2002. *The Language and Thought of the Child* (trans. by M. and R. Gabain). London: Routledge. Original work published 1923.

Pound, T. 1996. Standard English, standard culture? *Oxford Review of Education*, 22(2): 237–42.

Pritchard, R. 1989. A Fulbright experience with the New Zealand Writing Project. *English in Aotearoa*, 7: 20–3.

Prichard, R. and Marshall, J. 1994. Evaluation of a tiered model for staff development in writing. *Research in the Teaching of English*, 28(2): 259–85.

Prichard, R. and Honeycutt, R.L. 2006a. The process approach to writing instruction: Examining its effectiveness. In C.A. MacArthur, S. Grahamand and J. Fitzgerald (eds), *Handbook of Writing Research*: 275–90. New York: Guilford Press.

Pritchard, R. and Honeycutt, R. L. 2006b. Best practices in implementing a process approach to teaching writing. In C. MacArthur, S. Graham and J. Fitzgerald (eds.), *Best Practices in Writing Instruction*: 28–49. New York: Guilford Press.

Pullman, P. 1999. Philip Pullman in Carter, J. 1999. *Talking Books: Children's Authors Talk About the Craft, Creativity and Process of Writing*: 178–95. London and New York: Routledge.

Pullman, P. 2002. Yes, but . . . . Keynote lecture. United Kingdom Reading Association International Conference, Oxford.

Pullman, P. 2005. Common sense has much to learn from moonshine, *The Guardian*, [online] Available at:<www.guardian.co.uk/comment/story/0,,1396040,00.html> [Accessed6 March 2005].

Qualifications and Curriculum Authority/United Kingdom Literary Association 2004. *More than Words*. London: QCA.

Qualifications and Curriculum Authority/United Kingdom Literacy Association 2005. *More than Words 2: Creating Stories on Page and Screen*. London: QCA/UKLA.

Rees, C. 1999. Celia Rees in Carter, J. 1999. *Talking Books: Children's Authors Talk About the Craft, Creativity and Process of Writing*: 196–217. London and New York: Routledge.

Rees, C. 2010. Submission to UKLA professional development resource *Writers in Schools*. Leicester: UKLA.

Richardson, P. 1991.Language as personal resource and as social construct. *Educational Review*, 43(2): 117–120.

Robbins, B. W. 1996. Teachers as writers: Tensions between theory and practice. *Journal of Teaching Writing*, 15(1): 107–28.

Robinson, K. 2001. *Out of Our Minds*. London: Capstone.

Rooke, J. 2010. Teachers and TAs as writers: A clearer understanding of how teachers learn to teach writing. Paper presented at The Changing Face of Literacy UKLA conference, 9–11 July 2010.

Root, R. L. and Steinberg, M. (eds.) 1996. *Those Who Do, Can: Teachers Writing, Writers Teaching*. Urbana, IL: NCTE.

Rosen, B. 1981. *And None of it Was Nonsense: The Power of Storytelling in School*. London: Bodley Head.

Rosen, M. 1989. *Did I Hear You Write?* London: André Deutsch.

Rowe, D. W. 2003. The nature of young children's authoring. In N. Hall, J. Larson and J. Marsh (eds.), *Handbook of Early Childhood Literacy*: 258–70. London: SAGE.

Rowe, D. W. 2008. The social construction of intentionality: Two-year-olds' and adults' participation at a preschool writing center. *Research in the Teaching of English*, 42(4): 387–434.

Rowe, D. W. and Neitzel, C. 2010.Interest and agency in 2- and 3-year-olds' participation in emergent writing.*Reading Research Quarterly*, 45(2): 169–95.

Samuels, D. 2010. Submission to the UKLA resource *Writers in Schools*. Leicester: UKLA.

Schreiner, S. 1997. A portrait of the student as a young writer: Re-evaluating Emig and the process movement. *College Composition and Communication*, 48: 86–104.

Sharples, M. 1999. *How We Write: Writing as Creative Design*. London: Routledge.

Shayer, M. and Adey, P. (eds.) 2002. *Learning Intelligence*. Milton Keynes: Open University Press.

Shulman, L. S. 1987. Knowledge and teaching: Foundations of the new reform. *Harvard Educational Review*, 57: 1–22.

Smagorinsky, P. 1987. Graves revisited: A look at the methods and conclusions of the New Hampshire study. *Written Communication*, 14(4): 331–42.

Smith, D. C. 2010. Submission to UKLA professional development resource *Writers in Schools*. Leicester: UKLA.

Smith, J. and Elley, W. 1998. *How Children Learn to Write*. London: Longman.

South West News Service. 2000. World Exclusive Interview with J.K. Rowling, 8 July 2000, [online] Available at:<http://www.accio-quote.org/articles/2000/0700-swns-alfie.htm> [Accessed 14 October 2010].

Spiro, J. 2007. Teaching poetry: Writing poetry – teaching as a writer. *English in Education*, 41(3): 78–93.

Sternberg, R. J. 1986. Inside intelligence. *American Scientist*, 74: 137–43.

Sternberg, R. J. 1988. *The Nature of Creativity*. Cambridge: Cambridge University Press.

Stylianidou, F., Ormerod, F. and Ogborn, J. 2002. Analysis of science textbook pictures about 'energy' and pupils' readings of them. *International Journal of Science Education*, 24(3): 257–83.

Susi, G. L. 1984. The teacher/writer: Model, learner, human being. *Languages Arts*, 61(4): 712–16.

Swales, J. 1990. *Genre Analysis*. Cambridge: Cambridge University Press.

Sweller, J. 1988. Cognitive load during problem solving: Effects on learning. *Cognitive Science*, 12(2): 257–85.

Teale, W. and Sulzby, E. (eds.) 1986. *Emergent Literacy: Writing and Reading*. Norwood, NJ: Ablex.

The Guardian. 2010.Ten rules for writing fiction. *The Guardian*, 20 February 2010, [online] Available at: <http://www.guardian.co.uk/books/2010/feb/20/ten-rules-for-writing-fiction-part-one> [Accessed 24 February 2010].

Thomson, P. 2002. *Schooling the Rustbelt Kids: Making the Difference in Changing Times*. London: Trentham Books.

Thomson, P., Hall, C. and Russell, L. 2006. An arts project failed, censored or . . . ? A critical incident approach to artist–school partnerships. *Changing English*, 13(1): 29–44.

Tomasello, M. and Bates, E. 2001. *Language Development: The Essential Readings*. Oxford: Blackwell.

Turvey, A. 2007. Writing and teaching writing. *Changing English*, 14(2): 145–59.

United Kingdom Literary Association/Primary National Strategy 2004. *Raising Boys' Achievements in Writing*. Leicester: UKLA.

Vass, E. 2002. Friendship and collaboration: Creative writing in the primary classroom. *Journal of Computer Assisted Learning*, 18: 102–11.

Vass, E. 2007. Exploring processes of collaborative creativity – The role ofemotions in children's joint creative writing. *Thinking Skills and Creativity*, 2: 107–17.

Vygotsky, L. S. 1978. *Mind in Society*. Cambridge, MA: Harvard University Press.

Walsh, C. S. 2007. Creativity as capital in the literacy classroom: Youth as multimodal designers. *Literacy*, 41(2): 79–85.

Wells, G. and Chang, G. L. 1986. From speech to writing: Some evidence on the relationship between oracy and literacy. In A. Wilkinson (ed.), *The Writing of Writing*: 109–31. Milton Keynes: Open University Press.

Wheeler, R. 2010. From cold shoulder to funded welcome: Lessons from the trenches of dialectically diverse classrooms. In A. Denham and K. Lobeck (eds.), *Linguistics at School: Language Awareness in Primary and Secondary Education*: 129–48. Cambridge, UK: Cambridge University Press.

Whitney, A. 2008. Teacher transformation in the National Writing Project. *Research in the Teaching of English*, 43(2): 144–87.

Whitney, A. 2009. Writer, teacher, person: Tensions between personal and professional writing in a National Writing Project summer institute. *English Education*, 41(3): 235–58.

Wilson, A. C. 2007. Finding a Voice? Do literary forms work creatively in teaching poetry writing? *Cambridge Journal of Education*, 37(3): 441–57.

Wilson, A. C. 2009. Creativity and constraint: Developing as a writer of poetry. In R. Beard, D. Myhill, J. Riley and M. Nystrand (eds.), *The SAGE Handbook of Writing Development*: 387–401. London: SAGE.

Wilson, A. C. Forthcoming.

Wilson, A. and Metcalfe, E. 2010. Mind the Gap: How do invisible children engage with creative writing? Presented at The Changing Face of Literacy UKLA conference, 9–11 July 2010.

Wilson, J. 1999. Jacqueline Wilson in Carter, J. 1999. *Talking Books: Children's Authors Talk About the Craft, Creativity and Process of Writing*: 232–55. London: Routledge.

Wilson, R. 2002. *Strategies for Immediate Impact on Writing Standards*. Wakefield: Andrell Education.

Wood, D. and Lieberman, A. 2000. Teachers as authors: The National Writing Project's approach to professional development. *International Journal of Leadership in Education*, 3(3): 255–73.

Woods, P. 2001. Creative literacy. In A. Craft, B. Jeffrey and M. Liebling (eds.), *Creativity in Education*: 62–79. London: Continuum.

Wray, D. 1993. What do children think about writing? *Educational Review*, 45(1): 67–77.

Wyse, D., Jones, R., Bradford, H. and Wolpert, A. M. 2007. *Teaching English, Language and Literacy*. London: Routledge.

Yeo, M. 2007. New literacies, alternative texts: Teachers' conceptualisations of composition and literacy. *English Teaching: Practice and Critique*, 6(1): 113–31.

Zephaniah, B. 1999. Benjamin Zephaniah in Carter, J. 1999. *Talking Books: Children's Authors Talk About the Craft, Creativity and Process of Writing*: 19–39. London: Routledge.

Index